# Bridging
## *the Mississippi*

**a memoir of racial inequality and missed beads**

# Endorsements

Sandra Baker Baron fully understands her characters because she taught them and worked with them. She captures nuances artfully so that even minor characters become a distinctive memory. Baron is a masterful storyteller whose story shares truth through pain, humor, surprise, and knowing. Sandra's work was not only important then, but it's important now. This struggle continues and Sandra's writing keeps us aware of our history, the present, and focused on moving onward and upward.

—**Everett Bradley,** Grammy Nominated Musician (Bruce Springsteen, Bon Jovi, Quincy Jones)

*Bridging the Mississippi* is the story of children and adults who dared to establish relationships that stretched beyond cultural differences.

—**Johnny Parker,** Author, Leadership Consultant, Executive Coach

When Dr. King was assassinated in 1968, Sandi Baron was a young, White, inexperienced teacher in an all-Black school in New Orleans. She taught her students how to express their anger, fear, and pain through writing. Other teachers may have done that too, but how many retired teachers returned after forty-five years to check in with these same students and return their essays? *Bridging the Mississippi* is an honest telling of a tough time—it's also a story going back to bless and be blessed with even richer rewards. Where might you be inspired to return?

—**Clarice G. James**, *The Least of These*

The author's creative nonfiction takes place in the South during the late '60s, a time not unlike today, where race plays a crucial role in the lives of all Americans.

Questions and assumptions concerning race and ethnicity are raised and must be settled in the reader's heart as to what they truly believe. *Bridging the Mississippi* ends the contemporary search for a book offering hope for the end of a racist world.
—**Reverend Gregory S. Dyson**, Vice President for Intercultural Leadership at Taylor University

My memories of Mrs. Baron are warm, loving, and transformative! She and her husband were our first and only White teachers, yet they didn't just fit right in but stood out! She was a great English teacher but also like a fun aunt. The weekends at her home! Fun! Consequently, racism was never my issue because it's not the color of one's skin but the content of one's heart!
—**Dr. Debra Brown Morton**, Senior Pastor of Greater Saint Stephens Full Gospel Baptist Church, NO, LA, Co-Pastor of Changing A Generation Full Gospel Baptist Church in Atlanta, GA, Author and international speaker

In a delightful way, this is a coming-of-age story about two newly minted and newlywed teachers embarking on their first professional assignment. But *Bridging the Mississippi* defies a label. It's also an adventure tale full of idealism, pain, risk-taking, humor, and romance. Education—in the broadest sense on the word—is at its core as the couple learn about their students, their new community, their profession, each other, and themselves. The story is one of growth and is particularly relevant today as we all adjust to a changing world and struggle to find relevance in it. *Bridging the Mississippi* serves as a model of how cultures can blend rather than clash when participants lean in, learn from each other, and celebrate their uniqueness.
—**Holly Miller,** Senior Editor of *Saturday Evening Post*–*retired*, author of fourteen books

Sandi Baron has penned a vital book for this vital time in history. May this be a bridge builder between hearts and lives today.

—**Pam Farrel**, Bestselling author of 58 books, Co-Director Love-Wise

*Bridging the Mississippi* is a rich and valuable unveiling of how brave Americans crossed the racial divide, despite tensions and tightropes to bridge their cultural differences. With great storytelling savvy, Sandra Baker Baron shows us how to strengthen such diverse relationships, in order to reach vital realms of reconciliation and resolve. How important this book is for our times!

—**Dr. Yolanda Powell**, President & CEO, W.A.I.L. Worldwide Inc.,Washington, DC

# Bridging
## *the Mississippi*

**a memoir of racial inequality and missed beads**

## Sandra Baker Baron

A Christian Company
ElkLakePublishingInc.com

# Copyright Notice

Cover and Interior Design: Kelly Artieri, Derinda Babcock
Editor(s): Carol McClain, Judy Hagey, Deb Haggerty
Author Represented by Write Way Literary Agency

PUBLISHED BY: Elk Lake Publishing, Inc., 35 Dogwood Drive, Plymouth, MA 02360, 2022

---

**Library Cataloging Data**

Names: Baron, Sandra Baker (Sandra Baker Baron)

*Bridging the Mississippi: A Memoir of Racial Inequality and Missed Beads* / Sandra Baker Baron

370 p. 23cm × 15cm (9in × 6 in.)

ISBN-13: 978-1-64949-752-9 (paperback) | 978-1-64949-753-6 (trade hardcover) | 978-1-64949-754-3 (trade paperback) | 978-1-64949-755-0 (e-book)

Key Words: 1960s in the South; conflict between Blacks and Whites; disparities in education between Blacks and White; New Orleans in the 1960s; Mardi Gras; Carter G. Woodson school; Being White in a Black World.

Library of Congress Control Number: 2022947543 Nonfiction

# DEDICATION

Great is His faithfulness; His mercies begin afresh each morning. Lamentations 3:23

Grateful for God's mercy to me in giving me this family.

Dennis Baron, my devoted husband for fifty-five years.

John Foster and Adam Baron, our caring sons.

Christine Baron and Jessie Gritton, priceless daughters-in-law.

Ava Leigh, Ellis Anderson, John Henri, and Luna Belle—our precious and adored grandchildren.

# FOREWORD

I know the courage it takes to be an outsider. Sandi has this courage as an outsider in a Black culture. As a White teacher with kids from the projects, she even refused to let them use the N-word, as it is self-degrading. She helped broaden their self-esteem.

I knew Sandi as a difference maker in my teen years. I witnessed her unconditional love firsthand as she was a babysitter for my younger brother and sister after school. She nurtured them in her home like they were her own. This mindset didn't come overnight. It took a willing spirit which was God-given to be used for his purpose.

When our family moved to Indiana for a better life, we believed a higher economic status would protect us from racist people. My parents were schoolteachers, and I was a star athlete. We lived in a new all-White residential development. Racism stuck out its ugly head immediately when our next-door neighbor refused to speak to us—even after ten years. Our home was vandalized with eggs.

I was blessed to have a father who was not intimidated or deterred by racism. He taught me the importance of maintaining my self-esteem and integrity during a time of crisis to avoid internalizing attacks that could tarnish me for a lifetime. Furthermore, our hope was grounded in the love of Christ.

I know the courage it takes to be an outsider. Regardless of skin color or skill set, all students need hope for future success. Through hard work and love, be a difference maker–what we all need to be.

**—Luther Bradley**
NFL Former defensive back for Detroit Lions

# ACKNOWLEDGMENTS

I could never have written this book without the support of others. My husband outlined our activities and social networking early in our marriage. Because of that outline, I had an accurate record of the events and happenings.

He nudged me through the years to write our story. He researched song titles, timelines, sports articles, slang of 1967, prices of goods in that day, and historical facts. Without him, this book could not have been written. He was willing to let me share our hard times and favorable times from my point of view.

I am grateful to Holly Miller, who volunteered to read and criticize the first half of my rough manuscript. I benefited from her professional and experienced advice.

The Midwest Writers Workshop Committee, especially Director Jama Kehoe Bigger, gave me the knowledge and impetus to continue to learn the craft of writing. I volunteered on the committee for several years, and we helped many new writers develop their writing skills. Because of my constant involvement with the Midwest Writers Workshop, I have been supported and urged to complete this creative nonfiction work.

My sister, Betty Ann Fraley, a writer, listened to me read long distance. I would spend hours on the phone xii | SANDRA BAKER BARON

reading my chapters, and she would critique them from New York. Thank you, Sister.

Our daughter-in-law, Christine, and my son, John, checked details, facts, and the flow of the copy. Our son, Adam, read through the entire first rough manuscript and axed many chapters that did not progress or focus on the true meaning of the story. He was brave to show his mother her weaknesses in writing.

Debra Brown Morgan reminded me to pray, Lily and Millie Garcia taught me how to be grateful, Walter Jones showed me unconditional love, Joan Ellison and Miranda Lee gave me hope. They told their stories, which became my story. Their memories embraced the truth I had held in my heart. To them, I am eternally grateful.

Carter G. Woodson's teachers enlightened my understanding as a beginning teacher and enhanced that understanding years later when I interviewed them for clarity about our 1967-68 experience.

Thank you to Linda Taylor who copyedited the first finished manuscript. Kim Autrey line edited my copy and assisted in formatting my seventh rewrite as well as creating my citation page and answering endless questions. Marcia Smith, a former English teacher who taught with me, volunteered to edit my sixth manuscript during the Covid pandemic. Her constant edits motivated me to continue through my novel with a new passion for rewriting and editing. Amy Grubbs was my first responder. She nursed me through my technology problems and worked beside me when I was frustrated with Word and formatting.

PeggySue Wells encouraged me for ten years in our writers' group. She served as my agent and editor and moved this manuscript into the professional hands of Elk Lake Publishing. Carol McLain was my assigned editor at

Elk Lake. Her suggestions and edits helped me polish and improve my writing.

The Lord gave me an entire team that encouraged me through the last ten years. For this I am grateful.

# LESSON 1

*Perhaps it is only human nature to inflict suffering on anything that will endure suffering, whether by reason of its genuine humility, or indifference, or sheer helplessness.*
—Père Goriot

"Move it, girl, or you be my target!"

The dark-skinned girl stomped across the cement with a determined frown. Her short-sleeved shirt rolled up revealing her massive muscles. Her dark eyes narrowed at the teens playing basketball.

From inside our 1965 blue Malibu, I watched the kids playing at the park across the street from Carter G. Woodson Junior High School. Teenage boys shot baskets at broken hoops. Giggling girls sat on the playground equipment, posing for the boys, and breaking into song every so often.

Would any of these boys and girls be my students? On this auspicious day, my husband and I had reported to our school to meet the staff and prepare our rooms to begin the school year. Since my English department meetings had dismissed early, I headed back to our car to wait for Denny.

*Now here I am, hiding in a car watching this mean-eyed girl.*

The girl turned full-face toward me. I froze. Her penetrating eyes glared at me. *Does she expect me to challenge her? Or is she checking me out?* She turned away and focused on a girl half her size. I scrunched lower into my seat.

Whomp! She smacked the small girl with a powder puff filled with fine white talcum, pasting a white mark on the shiny, dark skin. Wincing from the slam on her cheek, the frail girl cowered.

"Run, Iris, run," the crowd yelled. She turned and darted like a scared bunny behind kids gathered in the back of Shakespeare Park.

I peered out my open car window to see Iris hiding from her attacker. Alone in the hot car, I sympathized with the child seeking to be obscure. I too wanted to hide.

*This coming Monday I can't hole up in a car. I will be alone in my classroom, forced to face every child assigned to me.* I grabbed a tissue to wipe my melting makeup. *Oh my, is it the New Orleans' humidity or fear causing this perspiration?* I scooted forward to see what the bully would do next.

The skinny girl's crooked posture imitated an elderly grandmother. Her body appeared to be a stick figure. In fact, she seemed almost invisible in the crowd to everyone but the provoker. Bullies preyed on the weak and helpless.

One of the boys stepped forward to see more clearly.

"What's you lookin' at, boy?" the stout girl screamed at the onlooker.

Like a hawk she demonstrated her bully control. No one tried to stop her, not even me. I stared, paralyzed. *How can I handle this girl if she ends up in my class on Monday? I want to help Iris, but I am too fearful to try.*

The hawk darted to the back of the park and grabbed her talcum-marked victim. She punched Iris in the face. It sounded like a baseball smacking into an outreached glove. Another punch drew an "ouch" from others on the playground. Bright red blood dripped from Iris's nose. Her small hands covered her face as she tried to flee.

"Let her go, Flossy Mae, let her go." The boy who shouted stepped back a few steps.

Flossy Mae stared at him with a lion's face, ready to grab prey.

She pulled back her shoulders and puffed out her chest like a professional wrestler. She bulked up her arm muscles and planted her hands on her hips. Her fierce stare to the circled onlookers exhibited her fortitude. With bold, giant steps, she strode away stamping her footprints in the minds of the vulnerable spectators.

The victim's nose and mouth bled profusely, and a couple of friends tried to help by dabbing her face with a small handkerchief. As Iris ran toward the housing project, the scene haunted me. Flossy Mae's boiling anger showed all of us what the consequences were when a bully strikes. A sudden silence surrounded me. Calm filled the park, and kids started singing and playing again without the presence of Flossy Mae. I sat up higher in my seat now and tried to still my shaking hands while I wiped sweat from my forehead.

I hated confrontations of any kind. I wanted each day to be smooth and balanced. My older sister and I seldom had squabbles because she protected me from Mama's wrath. When Mama was angry, she smacked us with any nearby object, be it a wooden spoon, wet towel, belt, or brush. Afraid, I would crouch behind my big sister. As children, Betty Ann and I spent hours together on our screened-in porch in Florida—a safe place to play and stay out of Mama's way. I shuddered while watching Flossy Mae beat up the little girl. My wounds merged with Iris's with the memory from my childhood.

The older teenagers returned to shooting baskets, but they continued to glance up to be sure the bully had disappeared. They acted like they knew her. *Maybe she had smacked them with that white powder puff and marked them as a victim too.*

*Will any of these students be in my classes? How could I teach them? If Flossy Mae walked into my room, I might flee and never return.* So far, I only knew two student names, Iris and Flossy Mae. And, from today's first teachers' meeting, I knew three more names—Sylvia, Edna, and Mike. Sylvia and Edna were teachers in the English department, and they had walked me to my classroom. After the meeting, they gave me the same forewarning.

"Don't worry about doin' too much today. Better save your energy for Monday." Edna waved and went to her classroom.

"Honey, straighten your desk and organize your class lists, so you can take attendance and fill out the office cards. You'll be fine." Sylvia's gentle smile and soft voice reassured me. "Now don't stay too long. We can leave when we want today, and I want to leave soon. See you later."

"Thanks." After their advice, I looked around my disappointing room. My shoulders drooped with the heaviness of the day. My stomach tightened. A sense of dread similar to the feeling I have when a roller coaster begins its slow, agonizing uphill climb enveloped me. *What had we gotten ourselves into?*

I did as Sylvia suggested and left early to wait for Denny in the car. Now, my apprehension escalated as I slouched, watching the kids on the playground interact. Emotionally vulnerable, a sense of hopelessness overwhelmed me. I thought back to my classroom. There were so few books for my classes. *How do I prepare for my first day of teaching? What could I teach without books and dictionaries?* I realized we were token teachers. I didn't mind, but I wondered why Mr. Haber, the recruiter, had not mentioned our placement would be in an inner-city, all-Black school.

The only other White teacher had taught in the inner city of Brooklyn. I didn't know her name because she shunned me when I smiled at her. Her experience could help me, but I didn't think our paths would cross—her room was located on the other side of the building. My head ached from the unknowns, and my neck was as tight as if in a noose.

*How can I do this? I am not prepared. Why had no one mentioned this was an inner-city school? How many Flossy Mae's would be in my room? Den and I wanted to come to New Orleans because it would be a romantic city for our first year of marriage. Why hadn't we researched the school system before signing the contract? Oh, please hurry, Denny. I need your broad shoulders.*

With the bully gone, the mood on the playground lightened. The younger children played jacks in one corner while preteens did jump rope tricks with the speed and accuracy of trained gymnasts. The older girls performed dance moves, and their high-pitched laughter attracted guys standing nearby. Typically, teens could find ways to hang out together, and Shakespeare Park worked for them. They looked like normal energetic teens, but I suspected they had hidden layers known only to inner-city kids.

I focused on a small boy. His dark bronzed skin looked like a velvet slipcover, accentuating his handsome features. He rolled his giant brown eyes at his friends. Humming and laughing, he encouraged the others to begin their own antics. Their whistling and street dancing created merriment. Talking their own jive revealed their close relationships.

One boy spun on a single leg and shouted, "Do it."

Another responded, "Got it."

Their laughter echoed into my open window. Their spontaneous glee made my day brighter.

★★★

Denny opened the car door. "Hey, I'm surprised to see you here."

I loved his beautiful grin. "Trying to set up my room today overwhelmed me. All the other English teachers left after our brief department meeting, so I decided to sit in the car and wait on you."

"Well, pretty lady, can I give you a ride to Mary Poppins Drive?"

"You sure can." We laughed about our unique address and kissed.

# LESSON 2

The quest for certainty blocks the search for meaning.
Uncertainty is the condition to impel man to unfold his
powers.—Eric Fromm

Our real estate agent, Mr. Lane, had suggested Harvey
as the perfect fit for us. When we followed his advice and
rented our duplex, we had no idea we would encounter a
traffic jam every morning. We were too excited about our
first apartment to be logical or ask pertinent questions.

The bridge, completed in 1958, was the longest
cantilever bridge in the United States at that time. The
four-lane highway was built to handle eighteen million
vehicles annually traveling to and from Jefferson Parish.
Apparently, the planners of the bridge had not anticipated
the outer-bank growth of New Orleans traffic. Each time
we came to the edge of the bridge to travel into the city,
we sighed at the bumper-to-bumper gridlock of cars
attempting to make the same trek to the Big Easy.

My self-talk began: *Will they dislike us because we're
Yankees? Because we're first-year teachers? Because we're ...?
Why did I let Denny talk me into coming to New Orleans? Why
am I doing this "why" chanting? Breathe, breathe.*

Despite the heat and humidity, I leaned into Denny.
"I'm scared. Really scared. I don't think I can teach at
Carter G. Woodson."

"You're going to be fine. Listen to the radio and watch the barges on the river."

My shoulders stiffened. I hated being told what to do. I scooted away from him. *Too bad our Malibu isn't wider.*

We entered the bridge traffic pattern. I was grateful Denny had interrupted my self-doubt chants, but I disliked his bossiness.

As he flipped on the radio, he hit the brakes. A red truck shot in front of us, not three feet away.

The radio announcer pleaded. "It's nearing the end of the 1967 New Orleans Art Museum campaign, so join today and save 20 percent. The museum's air conditioning is going to feel great when temperatures hit 98. New Orleans needs your support."

From the public service announcement, the commentator went straight to the current news in Memphis, Tennessee. "Their streets are not safe. Race riots keep policemen working overtime. Neighborhoods awaken to vandalism and destruction. The Civil Rights marches are getting out of control."

We listened without comment to the unfamiliar idea of riots. Denny calmed me by rubbing my knee. After the news, the Beatles sang, *All You Need Is Love.* Denny joined in, and his singing delighted my heart chords.

"All we need is love." Denny's joking kept me giggling. I had fallen in love with him because he created laughter wherever he went. When he started singing, I moved back toward him, so I could lean on his thick shoulder. The way he walked with assurance had attracted me to him on our Indiana college campus. His boyish face with pink cheeks prompted me to give him a soft smile.

His unruly, curly hair became kinkier because of the humidity and the breeze wafting through the open window. I ran my fingers through his curls that grazed the back of his starched collar. My heart fluttered when I looked at his flawless skin and gentle brown eyes.

I knew students in his gym classes would notice his broad shoulders and muscular arms. His build would gain him immediate admiration and help manage the classroom behavior.

Since our June 17 wedding, we had shared our lives without discord. We fit well together, but now something new emerged. *Was he aware we were not in agreement? I don't want to stay here. I want a pretty school. Hmm, how should I break this to him that our life is going downhill?*

"Our life is good." He patted my knee again in his affectionate way.

For the rest of the drive, I silently reflected.

★★★

Two weeks earlier, Mr. Lane had helped us find our apartment in Harvey. He recommended this nearby community because the rent would be less, and we could live near other young marrieds, who were choosing to live in duplexes. He asked where we would be teaching. When Denny mentioned Carter G. Woodson Junior High School, Mr. Lane's eyebrows raised. "I'm surprised you and the missus are teaching there."

"Why are you surprised?" I leaned forward to try to be a part of this front-seat dialog.

"Ma'am, it is an all-colored area. You two aren't the right color. You know what I mean?"

Because his question was ridiculous, I drew myself up in a huff and scooted to my back seat corner again. The first time we chatted with Mr. Lane he told us how proud he was to be born and reared in New Orleans. He knew each area well and would be the perfect agent for newcomers to the city. In fact, I hadn't realized crossing the Mississippi took us out of New Orleans' Parish and into the town of Harvey. Mr. Lane did not mention this bridge would be crowded and slow every morning and late afternoon, exactly when Denny and I would be driving to and from work. Confused and geographically disoriented, I felt lost in more ways than one.

Denny and I had arrived in New Orleans early, so we could learn our way around the city and become familiar with our new school. The end of August brought high humidity and extreme heat indexes. One hot afternoon, Denny and I hoped we could see our new school. He stopped to fill our gas tank, and I used a pay phone to call the central office.

"Hello, could I speak with someone about Carter G. Woodson's open hours today?"

The receptionist asked, "Who's calling?"

"Sandra Baron. My husband Dennis and I will be teaching at Carter G. Woodson next week, so we need directions to the school to see and organize our rooms."

"Ma'am, I assure you it is not a good idea. It isn't safe to go into the surrounding area without an escort or other teachers. Please follow my advice and don't report until Friday when the other staff members are present, which is one day before classes officially begin on the following Monday. There will be police on duty in the area during school hours. Have a good day. Goodbye."

*Gosh, I wonder why it wouldn't be safe? Why hadn't Denny and I discussed this more? I guess it's too late now. Mom told me I'm too trusting. I leap into the unknown and then think about my decision later.*

\*\*\*

Pulling myself out of my reverie, I ended my inward chatter as we pulled into the newly paved driveway of our duplex. I listened to the churning of diggers, the tumbling of the cement mixers, and pounding of carpenters. Ongoing construction meant daily noise, dirt, and dust sifting through our two-bedroom apartment.

"You sure were quiet on the drive."

"Thinking about why we located on this side of town and this side of the bridge." I slammed the car door and stomped all the way into our little apartment. Even the new green carpet could not fix my mood.

*Why did we come to New Orleans?*

# LESSON 3

As a young African American boy, I learned a teacher was the one person I could trust. Knowing there would be peace and help each day at school was great comfort when the world around me grew chaotic. My teachers gave me courage, hope, and strength, which sparked my imagination. They helped me think and dream beyond myself and gave me the confidence to know that I could be as good as anyone else in my class.—Reverend Gregory S. Dyson, Vice President for Intercultural Leadership at Taylor University.

The long-awaited Friday morning arrived. Denny and I would meet the school staff and prepare our rooms. Hearing the alarm, I jumped out of bed to beat Denny to our bathroom. I needed time to put myself together. *I don't want to be late for our first day of meetings with the school staff.*

I teased my highlighted hair into a poufy style. I lined my pale blue eyes with dark black eyeliner and applied light pink lipstick. *My makeup needs to be perfect today.* I slipped on my new A-line dress in powder blue and matched my eye shadow with the same blue. I looked at Denny's fine body as he dried off from his shower.

"What a handsome man I married." My breath stopped in my throat.

"No time now, my sweet." He dashed to his closet and located his starched shirt and navy trousers.

"Time to go." He patted my behind on his way to the kitchen.

I followed him with quick careful steps because of my new, slippery heels. We each grabbed our coffee and hurried to the car.

We were so early we got ahead of the Mississippi Bridge traffic. He grinned at me. "Good, we're going to be there in plenty of time today."

On the city streets, our car shook and bounced over decades old pavers, bricks, and Belgian blocks. I sensed the path ahead—the one we had chosen without forethought—held many bumps. "These old pavers are telling us there's a rocky road ahead."

"Oh, no, there you go with your premonition thing." Denny gave me a kiss.

As a child I knew things about the future. At the age of five, I had dreams that came true. I remember when I told Mama my Grandpa Eli would die that night.

She slapped me. "Never say it again."

When Mama got the call from her sister, who was crying because her dad had died, she stared at me with paralyzing, gray eyes. She warned me not to tell anybody I'd had the prophetic dream. I knew I had inherited her gift, and she wanted no one else to know. Dreams and intuitions guided me my whole life, if only I would remember to listen. My dreams about New Orleans were romantic and enticing, yet warned of troubled waters. My current fears blotted out any remnant of those dreams.

Saint Charles's streetcars' clanging bells rang in my ears. I focused on the beauty of this wealthy, White area we passed. The charming antebellum homes with well-maintained grounds reminded me of the old Southern architecture described in novels. I envied their elegant porches and balconies. In my mind's eye, I saw myself entering one of those brick walks and sitting on the wrap-around porch with a tall glass of sweet tea.

*Does Den know I yearn to live in a home like one of those? Could he ever provide me with this fantasy?* I spent my formative years in a sleepy little southern town. My family never lived in a large home, but I knew my mother had wished for a house like one of those we were passing.

On the plush porches, ferns hanging from long iron chains blocked me from seeing inside. The mansions' perfect lawns and flamboyant flowering landscapes spoke prestige. Tall windows disclosed what I imagined to be magical lives. If I could peer past the ferns, I knew I would see waxed mahogany tables with silver tea sets. Maybe having read *Gone with the Wind* three times blurred my reality.

In the few blocks between Saint Charles Street and Woodson, the scenery changed. Within a few blocks of our school, all I could see were small, run-down houses in need of paint. The absence of grass and flowers created a stark landscape. After the Civil War, southern builders created economical shotgun houses. With their limited frontage, they could be erected on small lots nearer to the adjacent houses. Homeowners added rooms in back with no tax penalties. Larger families built longer homes. Since the rooms were directly behind each other with no need for halls, a bullet could go straight from the front to the back. In college, I studied this type of building in my theater classes. Now, I saw them, and I understood their functionality.

As we traveled closer to Carter G. Woodson, each block revealed smaller, more unkempt homes. Children staring at passing traffic sat or stood in their dirt yards. I breathed deeply, trying to quiet my heart palpitations. We neared Carter G. Woodson at 2514 Third Street. This triggered nausea and aching in my stomach.

When I saw the patched-up school flaunting a bright blue tarp draped over portions of the roof, I bit my lip. Windows were boarded shut and others left broken and unrepaired. The boxy structure was meant to be utilitarian, not aesthetic.

I fidgeted with the wrinkles in my skirt as Denny parked by the curb near the school. I checked my nails and laid my interwoven clenched fingers in my lap. In my silence, I held my breath, hoping to smother my fear. I couldn't allow my panic to escalate.

"You look so pretty in your new dress. The staff will fall in love with those big blue eyes like I did."

I cherished Denny's compliments, but right now I wasn't sure my dress or eyes were going to matter. My tongue nervously stuck to the roof of my mouth—I wasn't sure I could speak.

As we walked to the school, a mountain of a man with blue-black skin came toward us. "Hey, you two the Bayronnes?"

At first, I did not recognize our name by the way this man pronounced it. I repeated Bayronne to myself. B-a-y-r-o-n-e. They made the "a" sound long and hard and then made the end rhyme with alone. Bayronne. *Why could they not enunciate Baron? Royals of the world had that name for centuries, but New Orleans' people kept verbalizing BayRone.*

"Yes, we are the Barons," Denny said. "Here for our first visit to our new school. This is my wife, Sandi."

"There is a street named after you here in the city. Baronne Street is right in the central business district." He laughed. "You are already famous. I'm Mike Leonard. Pleased to meet you. Let me show you into the building." He led us through a metal door in the back of the gymnasium. He bounced when he walked and swung his hands, creating a childlike rhythm.

"This is where you and I will teach, Mr. Bayronne. I teach physical education and health. Welcome to our gym team." His full lips opened to a broad smile.

Denny returned Mike's smile. " Glad to be here."

"This is Mr. Foster. He is on our gym team. Welcome to our home away from home." They both laughed.

"Good to meet you both."

I smiled, trying to cover my uneasiness. One by one teachers entered from the back door of the gym to greet each other and catch up on recent news. A distinguished man walked toward us.

"Mr. Bayronne, this is our department head, Henri Todd. Henri is a keeper."

"Good mornin' and welcome to Woodson." Henri Todd had an automatic likeability factor.

"Let's go to the teachers' lounge. I'll introduce you to more of our gang," Mike offered.

We walked on covered sidewalks open to the outdoors, serving as hallways. Each led to a different part of the building. Denny and I looked at each other and then smiled at Mike.

"They are called breezeways. You'll want to teach out here on our hot days. These outside halls are the South's answer to air conditioning."

We all laughed at Mike's comment.

Graffiti on the building and the boarded windows glared in contrast to the well-kept northern school where I had done my student teaching the previous year.

When starting a new job, there's always some uncertainty. But I didn't expect fear. *This place looks like how I imagine New York City ghettos. Now this is my place of employment. I'm going to insist we pack up and go back to Indiana tonight. I want to go home—no matter how much he likes this place. Run back to the car and Denny will follow you. This is your last chance to have happiness. Run, girl, run.*

As we walked through the school, Mike offered some history of Woodson. "Our budget is slim, so the building is in disrepair. We're still workin' on Hurricane Betsy's damage from '65."

*Perhaps this explains the irregular window repair. Well, almost explains. Why would it take two years to repair windows?*

I wondered if my face reflected disappointment and anxiety. Denny and Mom both had mentioned my expressions told them my thoughts. I forced a small grin, hoping to hide my feelings.

*How can I teach here? It looks old and worn. I want a crisp, clean room filled with new furniture and lots of bookshelves.* Swallowing hard, I tried to correct my slumping posture.

We entered another door and walked past a sign labeled Staff Lounge and into a small room with mailboxes on the wall. *It seems tiny for a staff lounge. Perhaps there is another one too. Why call it a lounge? I don't see anything relaxing or comforting about this room.* A giant, old oak table with eight hard chairs around it and stacks of miscellaneous papers filled the outdated room. I did notice a plate of cinnamon rolls at the end of this table. The odor of fresh pecans and sugar tantalized my taste buds.

"This is one example of the homemade treats provided by our cooks," Mike indicated the baked goods. "Help yourself to anything here."

As staff members entered the room, heads turned toward us, and eyes surveyed the two of us. A slim, professional-looking woman extended her hand to Den for a welcoming handshake. She smiled at me. "Hi, I'm Edna. You two in it for the long haul?"

*Why did she say, "long haul"? What a strange question.*
"Lookin' forward to it."

*Are you serious? How can Den be so happy? Is he faking it? I know he lives by the motto what you see is what you get. Gosh, maybe he is happy.*

Edna took me by the elbow. "Let me show you our English wing."

We left Denny as I willingly walked with her out of the small room with so many people.

"How in the world did you two end up at Woodson?"

"Long story short, we're newlyweds and wanted a warm climate and a romantic city like New Orleans for our first year of marriage and teaching."

"You've come to the right city. See you later."

"Thanks, Edna." I repeated her name, hoping I would remember. I knew I would be learning a lot of names today.

The sunlight splashed against the broken and dirty windows that filled two walls of my room. As I reached for the light switch on the block wall, chips of institutional green paint fell into my hand. I looked around and realized the painted walls were shedding. I saw bits of paint along the baseboards. The sunlight magnified the curled, cracked linoleum caked with years of accumulated dirt and dust. Patches of cement showed through the flooring. My toe caught on a piece of the torn linoleum, causing me to stumble and mar my new patent leather heels.

During the last four years, I had visualized how my first teacher's desk would look, when I would decorate my room, and how I would create clever little inviting nooks for my students. My expectations melted like a Salvador Dali distorted clock.

The overused oak desk had been neglected through the years. Splintered wood grabbed at the eyelet sleeves of my dress. Sitting on the wobbly oak chair, I looked across the desktop etched with carved signatures from past students. I read the names: Albert, Mary, Eddie ... The indentations varied from deep gouges to merely scratched-on names.

*Where are these kids now? What kind of students slashed their names into the teacher's desk? God, what have I gotten myself into?* My fingers felt the carvings of the names of kids who had used knives bigger than a pocketknife. *What kind of students would do this?*

Sadness swallowed me as I took stock of the room. No shelves, no bulletin boards, no dictionaries. Only one overworked pencil sharpener dangled on the soiled wall. This neglected room removed the rose color from my glasses. How could I have been so naïve? I realized the inside matched the outside of the building. It silently said no one cared about it or the people inside. *How can I teach here? God, do you really want me here? Have I heard you wrong?*

My nostrils burned. The humidity intensified the putrid odor I could taste on the back of my tongue. I recognized the sour smell. I remembered it from when I was a small child in Ohio and mice had made a way into our basement. Dad found them nesting by the warm coal-bin wall and told me they were speedy reproducers. I now recognized the rancid odor in my nostrils, the smell of mice excretions. I gagged and pinched my nose to block the noxious odor.

"Hey, Mrs. Bayronne." A pretty woman stepped into my doorway.

"Hi, come in." Taking my hands away from my face, I beckoned her to come nearer.

Her almond-shaped eyes smiled at me. Her skin looked golden against her white lace top. A well-fitted, straight black skirt accentuated her curvy figure.

"My name is Sylvia. I'm right next door." She lifted her brows and spoke with lyrical southern tones.

"Good to know you are nearby. I'm sure I'll have lots of questions."

She laughed a deep yet soft laugh. "You'll be fine. First jobs are always the hardest." She winked and broadened her smile.

"Could you find me any bookcases?"

"Maybe there's one extra somewhere. Won't be much, but I'll check for you."

"Where do I find English books for seventh and eighth graders?"

"We should be able to find a few for you." Sylvia's eyes sparkled.

*A few? Will they be a matched set, or a random group left by others? How many can I have?*

Concern wrinkled my brow as I clenched my hands. I assumed my roster would be a considerable number of students because of all the desks in my room. A few books seemed pointless.

"Is there a book room? I need dictionaries too."

"I'll help you. I'll teach you the Woodson way to make do. I'll talk to Joe, our custodian. Don't worry."

*My disappointment must stick out all over me like porcupine quills.*

"Joe will find something for you, honey." Her eyes twinkled, and her dark bob framed her high cheekbones.

"Thanks, I appreciate your help." I liked her and her name. I knew we would be friends.

"I'll check back with you later. I'm going to put my room in order. Jump right over if you need something. Girl, with your big blue eyes, Joe, or anybody else will find what you need. See you later. I'll walk you to our English meeting after lunch."

"I would appreciate it."

"Our English department meeting will be short but look out for our eleven o'clock staff meeting. Our principal likes to talk."

# LESSON 4

The stoical scheme of supplying our wants by lopping off our desires, is like cutting off our feet when we want shoes.—Jonathan Swift

The maintenance man, Joe, appeared at my door with a kind smile and gentle eyes. He brought me one dictionary and ten grammar books. Looking at the worn pages, I recognized the book as the one I had used in seventh grade. Joe managed to find twenty other old literature books with Bible stories written in the King James text. Other pieces included in the anthology were by earlier authors like Walt Whitman and Ben Franklin, who wrote ornate descriptions in problematic language. I did like the poems, even though they were challenging, but one poem by Langston Hughes and another by Lord Byron were promising. I appreciated poetry and hoped to impart some of my enthusiasm to my students.

"Thanks, Joe. Glad you came early so I can organize my classroom after the meetings."

"Sorry, ma'am. Books got damaged during Betsy in '65. The school board never thought they needed replacin'. Some of the teachers think the board needs replacin'."

"You're great. Thanks again."

He reappeared in a few minutes. "Found you a bookshelf and this ol' wooden file cabinet. Don't lock but might help you. Ain't much but will get you started." His low voice expressed his sadness because he could not find more things for me. I liked him right away.

Joe wheeled in the file cabinet and set it beside my antiquated desk then dragged the bookcase to the back of the room. As he wiped the sweat from his head, his gray hair looked like steel wool. His wrinkled forehead above bushy eyebrows reminded me of gathered fabric.

I attempted to find a silver lining in those two worn pieces of furniture. I decided Joe was my silver lining. "You really helped me. Your load lightened my load. Have a good day."

"Yes, ma'am. Every day God creates has some good in it."

As I organized the items he had brought, Joe's blissful eyes remained with me. His insightfulness and experience flowed from him. He knew things I could never know. *Right now, I don't understand much.*

Sylvia stopped by my room to walk me to the auditorium for our first faculty meeting. My eagerness to see Denny and sit beside him in the staff meeting waned when I saw him laughing with Mike and sitting with Mr. Foster and the other physical education teachers.

Denny gave me a quick wave and smile.

"Got your room ready? Did Joe help you?"

"I appreciate your help and thanks for calling him. I had time to put up my happy posters."

"Good, honey. You'll do fine."

Edna motioned us to sit beside her.

"Welcome back, teachers. It is going to be a great year." Mr. Bergeron, our principal, stood tall.

*Man, he is as handsome as a Greek god.* The gaze of his piercing green eyes engaged me. Because of his magnetism, I could not concentrate on his words.

Sylvia leaned over and whispered, "Be ready for his school philosophy."

"Remember, these are the leaders of tomorrow you'll be teaching. They may be rascals, but they will lead someone or something. You must direct them to be giving persons. Teach them the importance of pride in Woodson and community. Let them know you care about the individual."

*Oh, and I worried about books and bookshelves.* The little voice in my head criticized me. *You'll never be able to teach and do all those other things the principal wants.* My condemning voice continued to provoke me as I feigned listening to countless announcements. Lost in my thoughts, I heard my name.

"Mr. and Mrs. Bayronne come to us from the Midwest." He pronounced our name like everyone else in New Orleans. "Would you stand please and tell us a little about yourselves?"

Because Denny did not like speaking in front of crowds, his comments were brief. "We're newly married, new teachers, and new to New Orleans. We're looking forward to our year at Woodson."

"And Mrs. Bayronne, do you have something to add?" asked Mr. Bergeron.

"I'm pleased to be here too. I'm in love with the romance and magic of New Orleans and can't wait to meet my students on Monday. I do know I am going to need help and advice." *Why did I say I was eager to see my students? I told a lie. I am not eager. I am anxious.*

The teachers applauded and nodded at us.

"We'll help you." Mr. LeBlanc dressed professionally and wore a smile that attracted attention. I could tell Denny liked him and his confident ways and goals. I observed when LeBlanc spoke, faculty members showed their respect by volunteering to help him.

"Glad to have you two." Mike Leonard smiled and nodded.

"Welcome to the Big Easy," another teacher added.

Mr. Bergeron introduced the only other new, White teacher, Mrs. Hammock, whose name I'd missed when we met earlier. The music teacher's eyes reflected a permanent passionless stare. Perhaps fighting the traffic and crowds in New York had added to her unpleasant appearance.

The New York teacher stood tall with the posture of a frozen back. "Good morning. I am expecting a lot of learning in my music classes. I am confident this will be a good year." Mrs. Hammock's rhetoric seemed as cold as a steel pipe in winter.

Again, the staff clapped in a polite welcome.

A couple of transfer teachers introduced themselves before Mr. Bergeron introduced the assistant principal.

Mr. Hughes' physical appearance contrasted with Mr. Bergeron's good-looking features and fashionable attire. As he stood, I noticed how his extreme dark skin contrasted with Mr. Bergeron's coffee complexion. Mr. Hughes reminded me of a well-loved stuffed animal which had been carried to many places too often. His sagging suit pants reflected as much wear as his drooping shoulders, and his protruding stomach testified to the richness of New Orleans' cuisine. His experiences may have wearied his body, but when he smiled, his inner joy showed.

Mr. Hughes continued explaining how to fill out student forms and when they were due in the office. The secretaries passed printed papers to the staff. Soon I had a lap full of blue dittos filled with directions. I began reading.

*I don't think I can complete these forty forms. These are overwhelming. This one tells me where to put the trash can. Another form explains how to shut my door. Why do I need an entire piece of paper explaining the obvious?* I pressed my hand to my throat as I thought of the kids arriving tomorrow. *I'm fearful. I'm filled with dread. I'm ...* But my thoughts were interrupted by a loud voice.

One of the teachers in a bright orange dress stood. "I'm working on our social calendar. Trust me. We'll celebrate anything."

Laughter began with comments such as, "Yeah, baby, you got it."

"Let's start now."

"You plan it, and we'll be there." Applause filled the room.

I peeked at Denny laughing and talking with his new friends. He liked being social. I looked at Sylvia and her golden skin glowed. She didn't need makeup to be gorgeous. I suspected my makeup had melted off my cheeks from the gummy humidity.

*Why didn't the recruiter mention to us Carter G. was an inner-city school? I would have done some research on how to reach underprivileged kids.* Panic restricted my breathing. I denied these nauseating feelings the best I knew how. I realized what the term "down in the trenches" meant for the first time in my life.

Our lunch break could not have arrived sooner. The cafeteria ladies had prepared homemade hot dogs and buns, remarkable baked beans, and peach pie. The good food dulled my panic and renewed my energy. After lunch, we returned to our rooms to work on lesson plans for Monday, which did not take long. In my two speech classes, students would give a short introduction of themselves, and the four English classes would introduce themselves on paper, so I could assess their writing skill levels. I wondered if I could use any of my plans with all the forms we needed to complete on the first day.

As I studied these dittos, I recognized Sylvia's soft voice. "You can go now. You'll need energy Monday. Your room looks happy. The kids will like you. Don't be nervous because they'll know it and take advantage of you. See you after the weekend."

"I'll do my best." I waved goodbye.

*My best? What is my best?* I stuffed paper into my new satchel. Right now, it seemed to be the most professional looking thing in my room. I clutched the brown leather to me as I shut the classroom door and rolled my eyes toward heaven. *Please, God, help me do this.*

# LESSON 5

A good heart overrides common sense and sees the goodness through the flaws of misfits and those of questionable character. It merely gives them a chance.
—Everett Bradley, Grammy Nominated Musician (Bruce Springsteen, Bon Jovi, Quincy Jones)

After the long, tangled drive from the school, across the bridge, and back to our apartment, I unlocked the door.

"What's your hurry, babe? Don't you want to look at the building progress on the other duplexes?"

"Nope. I'm starving."

After changing into comfortable clothes, I started our early dinner by emptying a can of green beans into a pan and browning hamburger patties in my single skillet. As I chopped onions, tears tumbled. My eyes blurred and became a flowing fountain.

*Are the onions causing me to cry or is it my fears and my inability to control my situation?* My shaking shoulders and gasping for breath answered my question.

Denny walked into the kitchen, and I turned my back to him, wiping my eyes on the kitchen towel.

"Smells good, wifey."

I needed to dismiss, at least for the moment, my pessimistic feelings. "Well, tell me about your day."

"I knew you'd ask. I think I'm going to like it. The department head is Henri Todd. He's taken me under his wing. He taught me Carter G. and New Orleans's history. He explained how the nearby housing project is where most of our students live. He'll be my mentor. I know it."

"Great."

"Men and women in the department are close. They help each other. We're a team. I like it."

"Sounds like you'll have someone around to help you with discipline. It would be cool to have someone with you all the time." Jealousy crept over me. Denny would have assistance and someone to turn to any hour of the day. He could rely on "his team," as he put it. I stared at him as I pulled my body up into a stiff-backed position. *How can I be alone with all those kids? Can I do it?*

Denny chatted on, but I deliberately did not engage.

"The boys' gym is separated by a folding accordion door from the girls' area. We're all together, all the time. Now, tell me about you."

I began with the surface of my experience. "I decorated my room. Joe, the custodian, brought me a rickety bookcase, a well-worn file cabinet, a few books, and one dictionary."

"Speaking of books, well, this is funny, or maybe sad. Today, we trashed the previous year's health books, *Health and Safety on the Farm*. Yep, those kids used a farm book in the cosmopolitan city."

From my lack of response to his lame joke, Denny looked at me. "Honey, it'll be all right. Don't worry. Supplies aren't everything."

His comment made me flush with anger. *How stupid to say the obvious?*

"At least *you'll* have other teachers around. I wish I did. If the kids succumb to chaos, I'm sure Edna could whip them back in shape." I let out a big sigh. "I guess I should've been a PE teacher."

Denny raised his eyebrows at me.

We looked at each other and laughed out loud.

"With my lack of coordination, I wouldn't have made it through my first physical education class."

The laughter swallowed up my jealousy. I loved this man. His excitement about his team blocked my intentions of telling him I wanted to go back to Indiana.

"Dinner is almost ready." I handed him two paper plates and our only two forks. "Will you put these on the table?"

I could not spit out my practiced words explaining to him why we needed to go back to Indiana. I swallowed them for now but would spew them out at the appropriate time. *I don't care how much I love him. I am telling him I can't do this. I want to go home. Why are we here? Do we have a purpose we don't understand right now?*

Snapping out of my musing, I griped, "Good thing we brought this green table and chairs in the car. God knows it's our only possession." My mom had given us a small, drop leaf table and two ladderback chairs to take with us. Somehow, we had managed to squeeze them into our overstuffed car.

I collapsed on the ladderback, which caused it to teeter, threatening to toss me backwards. *Who wants to be married and cook dinner? Who is tired and works in a rundown school? Who doesn't even notice?* "Let's eat." I poured us both sweet tea and plopped a hamburger on each of our paper plates.

I pushed the green beans toward him so hard they almost slushed out of the tiny pan I had purchased at the Cheap and Good store. We didn't even own a serving bowl. My bitterness gave me indigestion before I ate anything.

Staring coldly at Denny, I choked on the first bite of my greasy hamburger.

"Something wrong, honey?"

I waved my hand in the air, signaling to him it didn't matter. I glared at Denny and picked up my plate and tossed it into the kitchen garbage can. I stomped to the bedroom and slammed the door behind me.

# LESSON 6

What a wee little part of a person's life are his acts and his words! His real life is led in his head and is known to none but himself.—Mark Twain

I had survived Friday's indoctrination day and now welcomed Saturday morning. I lay on top of the blankets—the sleeping pallet we called our bed.

*I'm happy he's jogging right now. I need to think. Think about yesterday's teacher preparation day at Carter G. Woodson. Think about dingy walls, old sliding blackboards. Think about Shakespeare Park, Flossy Mae, kids playing basketball.*

Those images flashed through my mind. The vivid details rubbed my emotions raw. I whispered, "Make do. Make do. Make do."

I licked my lips. My mouth was as dry as the day I pledged my wedding vows. Raking my hands through my stiff morning hair, my inner voice chanted, '*Now this is your life. Your husband wants this. You must commit and at least try to do this for him. Remember, for better or worse.*' *I didn't know the worst in our vows would come so quickly.*

My reverie continued as I sat on my make-do bed, holding my throbbing head. I reflected again on our career interview at Ball State.

\*\*\*

On that winter day, the steady snowfall had formed drifts tall enough to fill the tops of my boots. Denny and I had been cold and nervous as we entered the interview room for that February interview.

"I hope we won't have to put up with this weather much longer. I hate ice and snow." I tugged at my scarf and removed my coat, wet with snow. Denny took our coats and hung them on the rack by the door. I aligned my five-foot-four-inch height to look as tall as possible while I straightened my blue sweater and smoothed my matching A-line skirt over my one-hundred-thirty-pound frame.

"You look cute." He grabbed my hand and squeezed hard.

One placard on the door read, New Orleans City Schools. We walked in synchronized strides into the small office.

"Please, sit and be comfortable." The man we were meeting with wore a dark gray pinstriped suit with a starched shirt and red tie, which was silky with dark stripes. "In New Orleans, we never incur any of this white stuff that keeps falling magically from the sky. I've never seen so much snow."

Then he turned, moved closer. My cheeks became warm instead of cold. He extended his hand and gave us each a firm handshake. Warm and sensual spices oozed from his perfumed aftershave.

"I'm Mr. Haber, the recruiter for the New Orleans School Corporation." His professional persona greeted us like a Southern gentleman. He commended our academic records and commented on my theater and debate team participation. He affirmed Denny's coaching experience.

He gave us a tight-lipped smile. "I'd like to ask a couple of questions."

*Oh no. This is when he'll ask about my educational theory, and I'm not sure I have one.*

"Mr. Baron, are you prejudiced?"

"Sir, I want to be honest with you. I don't know. There weren't any Negroes in my neighborhood or school."

"Miss Baker, are you prejudiced?"

"No, I don't think so." *Should I tell him I was reared in a small town in Florida which wouldn't allow Blacks into our area without a designated purpose? Should I tell him my parents had no Negro friends? Should I tell him I had a Black nanny who cleaned and cooked for us?*

He stared into my eyes. "What did you enjoy most about your major?"

"I loved working in the theater, going to live productions, and reading contemporary novels."

He turned to Denny. "Mr. Baron, do you have a favorite sport?"

"I enjoy playing, watching, and coaching football. I could stay in football all year."

"Sounds like you two picked the perfect majors and are ready to spread your wings." He offered each of us a contract for $5,400. "You two would be a good fit for our system."

He continued. "I have a high school position in driver's education for you, Mr. Baron. Miss Baker, you will be assigned English in junior high."

Denny spoke up immediately, "We have one car, and I'd like to teach physical education and do coaching."

"Well, how about you both teach at Carter G. Woodson Junior High together? Sound better?" His rapid-fire questions caught us by surprise.

I remembered how Denny smiled as he looked at me. I experienced one of my premonition warnings and a tightening in my stomach, but I ignored it.

We signed the contracts. We didn't ask any questions. We didn't talk it over. We didn't read the fine print. It never entered our minds to where the school was located in the city.

Denny shook Mr. Haber's hand and thanked him for coming to Muncie, Indiana, in the midst of a snowstorm. As we left the building, the snow fell faster. Somehow, it didn't matter. We were ready to leave this Midwest weather. After all, we were on our way to the Big Easy in August.

★★★

Denny returned from his run and interrupted my Ball State memory. He sat on the floor beside the pallet still breathing hard from his jog.

"Whatcha thinkin'? Why so quiet?"

"Thinkin' 'bout all the snow the day we interviewed with Mr. Haber."

"What about it? Do you think you'll miss snow?"

"Why'd he ask if we were prejudiced?"

"I think he asked because you looked like the movie star, Suzanne Pleshette, and he couldn't believe you fell in love with a Polack." He winked and made his way to the shower.

I had signed the contract to make Denny happy. He had signed because he wanted a new adventure. We were becoming one. Grandma predicted we would become one when we cared about the other person's happiness more than our own. So, I signed because I am dedicated to the one I love.

Now, I wished I had not signed anything. *I really don't want my grandmother's or my mother's advice. I want out of this place. I am an independent, modern woman. My way is a new way, not his way. I feel it in my bones. I have chosen the wrong path. Big mistake, Sandi, big mistake. I want out of this dreadful situation. Please, God, make a way out of this duplex void of furniture. I need a bed, not a make-do mat.*

Over two weeks had passed, and no word came from our moving company. This confirmed to me we should leave New Orleans. I called the moving company, and they promised our furniture load would be delivered any time.

*I want a pretty place to work each day. I want a cozy apartment. I must tell Denny the truth. We are having a serious talk.*

I practiced in my head. *"I've made a decision. We are going back North and getting better jobs."* I could find no clearer words. Perhaps, I should say it would be best for us to leave right away.

Sunlight poured through our bedroom window, but it didn't alter my mood, which had plummeted downhill fast. I could not believe the condition of my first classroom. *This is not what I expected, yet Carter G. is my new reality— unless we go home.*

In the midst of my pity party, the remembrance of Joe, the custodian, interrupted my thoughts and new plans. He had looked at me with compassion and showed he understood my apprehension.

Besides Joe, I could hear my mother's childhood warnings. "This is what there is. Do not grab at the shadow and miss the meaning of the day or seeing the sunshine within a cloud." Mama had many flaws, but she guided and programmed me to find and expect a life lesson or a secret message. Perhaps Joe was my new encourager.

*What am I not seeing?*

# LESSON 7

How do you know if you are prejudiced if you never experienced interactions with Blacks? "No, I am not prejudiced." It needs to be clarified that prejudice does not equate to racism. Racism relates more to hate, power, and control of Blacks because they are Black.—Dr. Joan Holmes, Special Assistant to the President for Equity and Special Programs at Hillsborough Community College, retired.

As I walked into my classroom Monday morning, I buried my need to talk to Denny about leaving and going back to Indiana. I couldn't think about our opposite views now. My hands shook as I tucked my purse into my desk drawer. The clanging of the bell told me I should have been in my room earlier.

Rumbling in the hall signaled approaching students, bursting open the doors to all my fears and anxieties. *Can I keep their attention? Will they dislike me because I am White? Will they figure out how young I am? Will they take over the classroom and pin me to the wall?*

Faces turned to me. *Oh my, I'm on. Speaketh, dear English teacher.*

"Good morning, class."

"Today is the day," a tall, thin boy shouted as he ran through my classroom.

"Hey, give me my pencil," shouted another student. "It be mine, Jerome."

"Young man, please find a seat."

"Here's one and here's one and here's one." I could see from the look on Jerome's face he thought he was clever.

"Sit in *this* one, *now*." I placed my hands on my hips like my mother did when she wanted me to pay attention to her.

"Good mornin'." A soft-spoken girl took a front seat.

"Man, out of my way." A bold fellow pushed his way into the room.

"Students, please enter quietly and be seated."

"Give me five, man."

"It's all in the name of love, girl," another student sang as he sank into a nearby desk.

"Who threw a spit ball at me?"

"Teacher, your class is out of order," chanted the student the others called Jerome.

I cleared my throat. "Students, please sit in your seats."

"Hey, that's my seat."

"Nope."

"Make Ellis remove herself out of my seat," another student demanded.

Ellis scowled at the boy. "I don't see your name on this seat."

The intercom speaker on the wall popped, cracked, and invaded my room with ear-splitting decibels. I was being attacked from every angle, yet grateful for the interrupting noise because the kids quieted. They grabbed random chairs and sat at last.

Principal Bergeron's voice boomed over the intercom. "Welcome, Carter G. Woodson students. We anticipate a great year and know learning is important to you and us. We're thrilled you're here. Your first assignment is to fill out the student record cards clearly. Thank you for making this a great school year." The intercom squawked and silenced.

"I'm Mrs. Baron, your homeroom teacher, and for some of you, your English teacher next hour."

A thin, long-legged boy leaned back on his chair, nodding as I spoke. Stumbling on a turned-up piece of linoleum, I grabbed the side of my desk for stability. The whole front row grinned at me. They could see my awkwardness, but at this moment they were quiet.

"I'm going to seat you in alphabetical order for the beginning of the year activities. It'll help with my paperwork and for remembering your names."

The long-legged boy's hands swayed in the air like well-tuned windshield wipers.

"What is your name?"

"I be Jerome. Why you come here?" As he asked this question, his long, thin face framed his eyes that focused on mine. He wanted a valid answer.

"Wow, what a great question. I came here because I wanted to live in your famous city of New Orleans. I enjoy the English language and reading. I hope to pass this passion to you."

"Didn't expect your answer." Jerome's large, animated eyes zeroed in on me.

I turned the question to him "Why did you come here?"

"Cause, I'm 'post to. It's the law, you know?"

"Good to know you are a law keeper, Jerome."

The class laughed and clapped in unison.

"I'll read the names for the first row. Please take your designated seat in the order I read your name."

"Man, I hate sittin' like the alphabet. Who came up with this idea anyway?"

"Awwww, I don't like sittin' by him. I want to sit by pretty Lily," another boy chided.

"Please, Ellis Anderson, take this first seat right here." I pointed at the end seat. "Ava Barona, please sit behind Ellis."

Ava took the designated desk. "Will we have to sit this way all year?"

"No, we will keep this seating arrangement until I learn your names."

I continued with my class list, assigning each student a place.

They complained about their new seating pattern but dragged desks across the linoleum to fit into my expected roster.

*Should I have waited until tomorrow? I know the class is out of control. I need to know names, and this is the best way I know. Difficulties today will help me have order tomorrow.*

"Jerome, how will you be my favorite if you don't sit in the front?"

He grabbed the front seat. "I ain't ever been a favorite. I didn't know sittin' in the front would do it." His bugged eyes and raised eyebrows kept a constant look of surprise on his face.

"Arthur, please sit in the third seat in the third row. It will be easy for you to remember."

Those around him laughed, but he did take the suggested spot. "Yes, ma'am."

I sighed and continued. "Joan, will you sit here, please?"

She nodded, tucked her purse under her arm, and sat where I asked with no backtalk.

How could it be this difficult to assign seats? At last, I had all thirty-four students seated. It had taken half the hour, but I had accomplished something on my first day of teaching. Of course, this was only the first hour. It gave structure to the day. Turning toward the door, I saw a young, well-groomed student standing there with her hands on her hips.

"May I help you?"

"I need today's attendance."

I assumed she was the office helper. "Could you come back? I'm not quite ready."

A boy in the second row scanned me with dark and focused eyes. "Mmmm, you a good-lookin' White woman. You have the longest eyelashes, and those blue eyes shine at us. Kinda scary."

My cheeks felt warm, and I knew I turned red when complimented. I hated my light Celtic skin.

"Look at our teacher. She be all pink. James, you stop makin' Mizz Bayronne blush."

I looked up and another office helper stood in the doorway. "Can I have the alphabetized student office cards?"

"What office cards?"

"You're to have your students complete them the first day. We need them now." Her stern voice indicated she meant business.

"How about if I bring them to the office later?"

"Mizz Bay–rone don't have her assignment done," Jerome's chanting ignited the conversations of others. Loud talk and laughter escalated, and I clenched my jaw so hard my teeth ached. I wondered if I had cracked a molar. *Dear Lord, what should I do?*

I looked for the third time at the door, seeing another presence. Mike, the gym teacher who had shown us around school the first day, filled the doorframe with his six-foot-four stature and muscular body. "Sit and be quiet. I don't want to hear one word."

Thirty-four students sat at attention as if they were in boot camp. I wished for Mike's magical powers. He earned their reverence with his voice, his large presence, and his reputation as a hard paddler. I had none of those qualities, nor could I paddle anyone. I needed and appreciated his help. *How could I ever manage these classes on my own?*

"Fill out your student cards now. Use a pen. Say nothing unless you would like to go to the gym office with me."

Mike turned, gave me a quick wink, and bellowed, "Please send me any student's name who does not cooperate." He turned in a sharp military style as he left the room.

I was embarrassed someone had to help with my class, but I was grateful he had stopped the chaos.

All eyes were on me. *Perform, girl. Perform. Be quick and don't lose the order created by Mike.*

I labored as I explained what went on each area of their cards. "On the first line print your full name. On the second space, please write your address."

Staying focused created a challenge for them and me, but with coaching they completed the office forms. At the sound of the bell, they got up and headed to the door, throwing their finished product across my desk.

*I have a blurry worry. I am worried about many things and cannot focus clearly on one thing, not one, not any. The staff appears ready, but I am not. I'm not sure I have chosen the right profession. I loved being a teenager and thought it would be fun to teach them. Now, I am thinking I've made a big mistake.*

As each of my new classes came in my room, I continued to assign seats, mispronounce names, and labor over completing the student office forms. At long last, the day ended. I held my head in my hands as I sat at my desk. I wondered if the other teachers who had sat at this desk had experienced days like this. My sigh echoed off the walls.

I revised tomorrow's lesson plans. Because of my seating charts, I would be able to call students by their names and keep control. *I declare tomorrow is going to be a better day. I'm still not brave enough to tell Denny I want to leave New Orleans and return to the Midwest. I must do my best until I find the perfect time to confront him. God, hope you heard this declaration as a prayer request.*

*I think I can. I think I can.* I want my English classes excited about literature and writing. *Maybe, I can make a difference in one or two of my students' lives.*

# LESSON 8

In learning you will teach and teaching you will learn.
—Phil Collins

On my second day of teaching, I arrived early, straightened desks, and looked over my lesson plans one more time. I put the charts in order and in a wire basket, so I would know right where they were. I took a deep breath and silently prayed, asking God to help me.

As soon as the students entered, I welcomed some of them by name. Others, I looked into their eyes and motioned them to their chairs. I stumbled over the Creole pronunciation of some of their names and called them by their first names. I checked for empty seats and wrote those names on the attendance paper. If they changed seats, I worried my attendance would be wrong. But I was determined I would manage my students better than yesterday.

"On the board are ten words from a story I'm going to read to you today. Please write those ten words while I fill out the attendance slip."

Arthur, excited to perform his first assignment well, smiled the biggest smile. "Yes, ma'am."

I grinned at his enthusiasm.

"I ain't got any paper or pencil."

"There is a stack of paper on the corner of my desk and a few extra pencils. Put your hand up if you need paper or pencil." *Thank you, Lord, for giving me the insight to buy extra.*

I gave out the needed supplies, and they started writing. They worked hard at copying the words. Several students had to check the words on the blackboard two or three times. I suspected some had problems reading and writing.

Ready for the feisty office girl today, I clipped the attendance slip on the hanger outside my door. *Hey, maybe I can do this. Today is so much better than yesterday.*

Debra Brown finished her assignment before the others. A yellow ribbon in her hair created a giant bow on top of her head. She wore a black checked dress starched and ironed to perfection. Wide-set eyes gave her face a trustful look. Her eagerness and quick interactions with me indicated someone had helped her become confident. Her ease with communicating with an adult verified she had support at home.

Joan, who sat near me, copied the words, and rechecked her paper carefully. I watched as she checked the spelling of each word. With her gentle countenance, Joan appeared mature for a junior high girl. She wore her hair pulled straight back behind her ears, which accentuated her strong determined jawline. Her military posture and intentionality revealed that she came ready to learn.

Lily, a petite girl, had lacy lashes like fans around her brown eyes. As soon as she caught my eye, she turned her head as if embarrassed that I caught her looking at me.

When the class finished writing their vocabulary words, I read from the beginning of *Huckleberry Finn*. I had purchased five new copies, so I could use them in groups and kept my one used copy. As a college assignment, I read this novel and discovered compassion for the Black man's struggles and daily obstacles and an understanding of man's inhumanity to man. I thought we all could relate to this story. I believed they would enjoy the humor as well as the idea of a boy their age, learning and growing. I hoped through this study my students would understand all Whites are not prejudiced. I began to read:

> At first, I hated the school, but by and by I got so I could stand it. Whenever I got uncommon tired, I played hooky, and the hiding I got next day done me good and cheered me up. So the longer I went to school the easier it got to be. I was getting sort of used to the widow's ways, too, and they warn't so raspy on me.[1]

After reading to the students, I asked them to write definitions for the words they had copied from the board. Because they had listened to these words in the story, I thought they would be able to write their definitions. They used the few dictionaries we had and shared their work in groups of five.

By the end of the day, my breath could not push out one more reading from *Huck Finn*. My dry, cotton mouth demonstrated I needed to change my future lesson plans or bring some water with me.

The next day I worked on grammar. We had smelly, dog-eared grammar books. The fact we only had used books irked me. I suspected the White schools had purchased new books and passed the used ones to the inner-city schools.

I remembered as a student how I loved the smell of new books. I even enjoyed the paper sticking together because I knew I was the first to see each shiny, new page filled with colorful illustrations and perfectly printed words. I took secret sniffs of the book. The aroma of ink would linger in my nostrils for a few minutes. These old grammar books reeked of a nauseating sour smell. The odors repulsed me. *How will a student be excited about a disgustingly dirty grammar book? Why do they have to share books? Doesn't anyone care at the central office?*

Softness fell over my students' faces as I read how Huck became Jim's friend. They giggled as I read how Miss Watson attempted to teach Huck to pray, without much success. Intrigued with this idea of two ladies trying to reform this boy, the class listened closely. Their breathing became shallow, and some leaned on propped hands. I could captivate them with the story instead of fighting for order like my first day. Reading brought privileges to them and me.

*Can I read every day, every hour? I must find another way to help them read. Right now, I am treading water, which is exhausting, but I am afloat.*

# LESSON 9

What you're supposed to do when you don't like a thing is change it. If you can't change it, change the way you think about it. —Maya Angelou

As I walked to my room, I saw a boy I did not know run out of my doorway.

"Hey, what are you doin' in there?"

He ran so fast I could not identify him. I remembered Sylvia's words: "Girl, never leave your purse in the room and keep your back against the wall. These kids will steal, and they carry blades."

*Sheesh, so far in my first week I've broken both of those rules. How can I keep my back to the wall when I move from group to group?* As I walked into my room, my eyes stared at the partially opened drawer where I kept my purse. The sticking desk drawer had slowed the boy from reaching his goal, my purse. My heels clicking on the linoleum must have alerted him I was near, and he darted out, not to be caught.

I plopped in my chair, wiped the beads of sweat from my brow, and breathed a deep sigh of relief. My eyes focused on my purse in the drawer. I caught a break this time, but I needed to be more careful.

*Thank you, Lord for protecting my purse today. I haven't spent much time with you lately. Denny doesn't believe in*

*you, and I've been busy. When I ask him to go to church
with me, he always says no. Sorry, Jesus.*

"Hey, how you doin'?" Sylvia's sexy voice and her
politeness had glued our friendship and soothed my
anxieties.

"Hangin' on. Can you tell me about these green office
cards?"

"Honey, don't be frettin'. Don't let those office girls
push you around. Have the students check their addresses
and birth dates on the cards. It's the same info yearly. Let
one of your smart girls alphabetize them and take them
to the office. Be done. Those are the last of the required
cards for this week."

"Sounds so easy when you say it." I grinned. "What do
I do with this memo from Mr. Hughes? He wants homeroom
teachers to make Thursday into Tuesday. Has he the power
to change the calendar?"

"You are so funny, baby. Put those blue memos in
a folder and worry about them later. Keep calm. Stay
peaceful."

"Peace? Peace? Have you been in my room lately? I
can't manage my kids or keep them focused." I looked
into her kind eyes as she smiled at me.

"Yes'm, I hear you. Quiet doesn't mean they are
learnin'. Try to reach the listeners. They want to engage.
The others? Oh well.'" She patted my hand as she leaned
on my desk. "Smile, baby. Smile. It's almost Friday."

I took my purse out of the drawer and walked to the
teachers' lounge to check my mail. More blurred mimeo
memos. One paper disclosed a whole column of missing
students. *Missing? Missing? Where have they gone? Maybe
they moved. Seems like a mystery to me. How could I know
where they are? The next memo: homeroom goals.*

I read the homeroom memo in disbelief.

> Keep children quiet and make the time meaningful. This is not a paper grading time. Help your students complete any assignments they bring ... math, science, even writing. Make this a time to relate to the students. You can build relationships and show you care. You will have these same young people all year, so you can shape them and make a difference in their choices.

*I need more hours in my day. I cannot do all these things. I want to go back home. These memos, this school, these new people are weaving my life into a strange pattern. I don't know what to expect from hour to hour. I am vulnerable and unprepared. Oh, my, gosh, what is happening to me?*

Henri Todd entered the staff room. "Ms. Bayronne, how are you doin' today? We are enjoyin' your husband in the PE department. He's a fine man, as you already know. We're so happy you two are here and a part of our Woodson family."

Sylvia told me Henri, a soft-spoken and seasoned teacher, had gained respect from the other staff members because of his contributions to the causes of the Black community. He mentored Denny like Sylvia coached me. A likeable guy, Henri knew much about how the Woodson system worked, and we both were grateful for his outreach. I liked seeing his nose wrinkle and his freckled cheeks move toward his nose when he smiled. Even with his childlike freckles, his countenance took on a sophisticated look.

Another teacher entered the room. "Have you met Mr. Gritton?" Henri asked. "He's in the social studies department and teaches history. He's wise and Woodson's greatest cheerleader and historian."

Henri's description would help me remember him. "Good to meet you, Mr. Gritton."

"Nice to meet you too." He reached for a cinnamon roll. "Have a good day." He waved goodbye.

Sylvia suddenly appeared, hooked her arm in mine, and whispered in my ear. "Do what you can with what you got. Then, go on. We just make do. Come on, let's make do together." We walked arm in arm to our rooms.

I gave myself another inner talk as Sylvia walked me to my room. *Breathe. Breathe. Breathe. Relax. You are making do.*

On Wednesday morning, Sylvia declared we were nearing the weekend. *Wishing away the days and wanting Friday to come? I don't want a coping device like hers. I want joy and discovery each day.* I had so many things flying through my head and knocking on my conscience. I wanted more in my life than wishing away every week. I hoped to make an impact on my students' lives and futures, but first I needed to earn their appreciation.

During my preparation period, I finished grading the introductory assignment. I had stacks of papers to grade, but I wanted to take time to write positive notes on their papers by finding something they did well. *Can my affirmations improve their attitudes about learning English? Maybe.*

In Jerome's introduction, he emphasized he loved coffee. He wanted me to remember this fact about him, and he did help me understand chicory. The coffee I enjoyed in Louisiana came from a root, not a bean. New Orleans caught me by surprise most every day. The Midwest simple life contrasted dramatically to this intricate, multi-layered southern city. I smiled to myself because Jerome had finished his assignment. *Was I making progress?*

Jerome's behavior proved to be a nightmare the first few days, but then I recognized his sense of humor. He came into class dancing and doing smooth moves.

Jerome's body, lanky and lean, moved quickly around the classroom. He could make me laugh even when I did not want to smile.

As I thought about Jerome, I heard a new bell and noises I had never heard before. I looked out my open window and stared at the two girls who were fighting like boys. They weren't slapping. They were throwing hard punches.

"You, bitch! Hit me again, and I'll knock your teeth out." The stout girl seemed big for a junior high student.

"Your mama don't have no teeth. You hit her too?" This shout-it-out was from the lips of a tall, thin girl. I did not know either of them.

The same paralyzed feeling I experienced the first day I saw Flossy Mae hurting the little girl in Shakespeare Park flooded back.

"Hit her hard. She can't talk about your mama."

"Push her, girl."

One girl hit the other and the sound caromed from their cheeks to my ears through my window. Deep grunts and loud breathing continued as they punched each other. They swirled around and hit each other again with jaws clenched as tightly as their fists. The fighting girls were a hurricane of anger, cheered on by the crowd that had gathered. The thick atmosphere swirled like a whirlpool sucking everyone into frenzy.

Frozen in fear, I could only stare, unable to move. I had never witnessed such fury.

I couldn't stop the fight or understand why these two girls were hostile so early, even before third period. Coach Mike came running, and Mr. Foster pulled the two tigers apart. The gym teachers created human handcuffs by holding the girls' arms behind their backs. Robbed of their punching arms, the girls spit in each other's faces.

"Settle, girl. Stop now and don't make this worse than it is," Mike told the girl he was confining.

Mr. Foster dragged his victim through the hall, threatening her with suspension.

The fight happened so fast and ended the same. Mr. Foster and Mike Leonard stopped them like I would mop up a spilled glass of water. Thwarting anger and conflict seemed but a rudimentary drill to them. This familiar routine had been repeated many times, and they seemed not to be affected. Their calmness in calamity contrasted with my fast breathing and shaking hands let me know I had a long climb ahead of me.

Mr. Hughes ordered the crowd to go to their classes. The high-energy students and their sweaty bodies entered my classroom. *Oh, great, this is going to be an impossible hour. How can I settle them? They are pumped for action, but not the kind I want.*

Mr. Hughes stuck his head into my room. "Sit now. Shut your mouths." He intuitively knew I would need help after the brawl. I gratefully accepted his assistance.

I wasted no time, took attendance, and opened *Huckleberry Finn.* I decided to read a little to calm them. I introduced the scene and began reading.

> The Widow Douglas she took me for her son, and allowed she would sivilize me; but it was rough living in the house all the time, considering how dismal regular and decent the widow was in all her ways; and so when I couldn't stand it no longer I lit out. I got into my old rags and my sugar-hogshead again, and was free and satisfied.[1]

To my surprise the students listened as I read. Despite the violent beginning of the hour, they were enthralled with this runaway kid finding his way in the world. I suspected somewhere deep within, they yearned to be free like Huck. I must win their regard but in my own way.

I could not scream like Mr. Hughes, nor was I strong like the gym teachers.

Even as I read, I wondered why those two girls were so angry. I wondered if any of my third-period students had such pent-up anger. *Will I ever relate with their world and poverty? Can* Huckleberry Finn *help me give these kids a new look at life? Can Mark Twain bring me a new understanding on truth telling as he did in Huck Finn? Can my storytelling reach them like Twain's tale? I don't want to be like the old widow, living in my world, trying to make them look and act like me.*

# LESSON 10

Sometimes racial prejudice is like a hair across your cheek. You can't see it, you can't find it with your fingers, but you keep brushing at it because the feel of it is irritating.—Marian Anderson

I despised this bridge traffic. Our commute stole two hours of every day. We did, however, learn a lot about each other as we sat in traffic and talked.

"I'm jealous of you," I confessed. "You're so muscular, and girls look at you. You're too cute."

Den laughed. "Well, I have muscles, but I'm jealous of your gift of conversation. You ask so many questions. All of a sudden, people are sharing their inner thoughts with you. I can't converse. I think too long about what I will say."

"Maybe we're on the same path to help each other."

"I'm glad we are." He rubbed my knee in his affectionate way.

I leafed through my lesson plans for the day, confused about what to teach. Most of my students had minimal reading and writing skills. If they could trade some of their street smarts with me, and I could give them some of my English skills, we would all be ahead in the game of life.

Mr. Todd explained few of our students had ever been over the Mississippi bridge we traveled daily because we lived in a predominantly White area. He explained most

Blacks were not comfortable there, and my students were afraid to come near the area.

"Listen to what Walter shared yesterday."

"Listening."

"He said, 'We never be over that bridge. Mama neither. Black folks don't leave out of here. Never be over the bridge. Never will.' Walter is excited when he tells me things."

"You are lovin' these kids, aren't you?"

"I am working on teaching better use of the 'be' verb, but it's so difficult for them to understand. This is their cultural way of saying everything. Who am I to change it?"

"I'm not sure."

"Not sure of what?"

"Not sure of Walter's bridge theory. Maybe Walter is more sheltered."

I got quiet and thought how much Walter helped me. When I presented lessons and asked the class questions, he offered answers. Always respectful, he never overstepped his bounds. "I like him. He enjoys explaining life in New Orleans to me, and I love his warm personality."

Walter helped me understand his borders were uptown and the Magnolia Housing Project. The inner city was their home, and they liked it because they had built-in friends and a mama who gave them food.

"Their project is their prison, holding them there by poverty, prejudice, and self-identity. Those streets hold their music. Their babies. Their secrets. I'll never understand their culture. Should I quit trying? How am I going to help them leave the project and go on to something better? I guess it's better for them to be content where they are than to be like me, unsettled and wanting to leave."

"Are you talking to me? You are fading."

"Nope, talking to myself."

At the edge of the city, the aroma of fresh-cooked grits and sweet ham filled the air. The scent of chicory coffee replaced exhaust fumes. My growling stomach cued me in on my hunger. I knew when we arrived at the teachers' lounge there would be crisp, French baguettes and hot chicory coffee. School cooks baked pies, cakes, and most everything else from scratch. This city was a cooking heaven. Denny and I could not find a bad restaurant. My twenty-seven-inch waistline bulged, but I'd found it impossible to say no to this tasty cuisine in the three weeks we'd lived here.

I especially liked Mondays. Every diner, house, and cafeteria simmered a pot of red beans, sending aromas of garlic and Andouille sausage throughout the city. I could not wait until next Monday to eat the cafeteria's red beans. Since next Monday would be our first parent-teacher meeting, I expected it would be more stressful than the guilt I felt now from eating too many of those perfectly seasoned beans and buttered French bread. My clothes were beginning to have a snug fit. Sylvia called it my New Orleans' waistline.

Every day was celebrated with food. Who could resist Friday night's all-you-can-eat shrimp at the McLaughlin Cafeteria? Crisp crust with its special seasoning kept us craving more, getting refills, and dipping those delicate tasting, but colossal shrimp into a sweet tartar sauce with traces of dill pickle. We ate until we felt like ticks ready to burst and left holding hands and laughing about how much we ate. We were not only making memories but gaining pounds together in this constantly celebrating city.

A jolt in and out of a pothole jarred me back to the moment. *Is it hard to repair brick streets? Oh, why can't he drive smoother?*

"Can't you miss a few potholes?"

He ignored my comment and kept singing along to the song on the radio. He used music to cope with all the potholes we were certain to hit at school. After Denny parked, we kissed goodbye and went to our separate wings of the building. Now those sweet smells of Cajun food and fresh bread made me hungry. I stopped by the cafeteria to grab a baguette and coffee. Sylvia did the same, and we walked to my room.

"I heard it through the grapevine," Sylvia sang. Her early dancing in her sleek scarlet dress and matching fancy footwear helped me face the day. "Honey, I heard it through the grapevine."

"What did you hear?"

Sylvia sang made-up words to Martha and the Vandellas' melody, "Dancing in the Street." She jived and clapped her hands to the beat. "Will be a big crowd tonight, and dancing in the street. They're dancing in the street."

"Why? Stop it. What big crowd?"

"Come on, girl. They like you because you are different. The mamas are comin' to check you out at the first teacher-parent meeting." She continued in song. "Everyone comin' to Woodson. They'll be dancing in the street. Mamas and papas comin' to meet. Sandi and Denny so sweet. They'll be dancing, yes, dancing."

I loved Sylvia. She accepted me regardless of my color and naïveté. Sylvia's gentle ways reflected her healthy soul, and her song and dance embraced the music she lived by.

"Like I am checking you out," I returned. "You're so scrumptious in your ruby red dress. It accentuates your positives, you know?"

Sylvia grinned. "I sure need something positive in this school, and you're it."

Henri, Mike, LeBlanc, Edna, and others had volunteered to help us. They taught us to *make do*, the Woodson Way. They taught a dynamic lesson of how upbeat thinking could keep my days brighter. The staff did not expect new desks and books because they did not rely on equipment. Instead, they intentionally added laughter to their day. They found this through positive conversation and storytelling. They lived to the beat of the music playing in their hearts.

Henri Todd's professional ways rubbed off on Denny, and his soft voice and encouragement changed me and brightened my days.

Henri met me as I picked up my mail. "Mornin', Mrs. Bayronne. You are lookin' poppin' pretty today. The mamas are going to love you."

"You're so kind. I hope the parents are as gracious as you."

He grinned his special smile with the freckles on his cheeks moving together. I could understand why Denny enjoyed working with him.

Laughing, Edna popped into the room. "How's the star of our program tonight?"

"You hush." I waved her away. "We're not important to this neighborhood. It's going to be a normal night."

"You keep dreamin', girl." Her mischievous grin spoke loudly.

The warm welcome of our new friends during this first week had made our transition much easier. Yet, all these comments about the parent-teacher meeting tonight were giving me the jitters.

Immediately after the last class, we raced back across the bridge. I took a twenty-minute nap, Denny jogged and showered, and we ate a lunchmeat sandwich for dinner. It had taken me forever to decide to wear my black linen skirt and crisp, baby blue blouse.

"Do you think I look professional?"

"You look perfect. I hope those black, shiny shoes can help you walk fast since we are running a little late."

I wanted to look mature and attractive. *Why am I so nervous about a parent-teacher meeting?*

Den grabbed the keys, and we hurried out the door.

At the school, Denny dropped me at the front door, so I could find us a seat in the auditorium. Cars were parked fender-to-fender all around Third Street and Shakespeare Park. A large crowd filled the nearby parking places, so he went searching for a new location to leave the Malibu.

*Breathe. Breathe. It is going to be over in no time. You can do this. Breathe and walk.* I took a deep breath and entered the auditorium door.

# LESSON 11

The intensity of the moment when one becomes painfully aware of our own "otherness." Adding to the weight is the majority in the room who also recognize my otherness. To act accordingly implies a duty to know your place, assess and follow social cues and mores, and by no means openly challenge any of it. Fit in as seamlessly as possible, quickly, and don't upset the tone of the room in the process.—Angel Dixon, CEO, Crossing Color Lines

I searched the auditorium, looking for two empty seats. I scanned the room filled with people of all shades of color. I had never been in a room with all African Americans.

I tried to blot out the harsh stories I had been told by my southern relatives. I feared I would unintentionally say something offensive. My hot skin reminded me how pink-cheeked and greasy I must look. I was sweating. I hated being on display because I was White. Sylvia teased me about it, and I knew she was correct. She understood being judged by color, instead of credentials. Because my color differed, I became unsure and self-conscious.

Clutching my quilted purse under my arm, I silently chastised myself. *Why am I late for my first parent-teacher meeting? Denny asked me to start getting ready sooner. Why am I always late?*

I spotted two empty seats in the middle of the row. I beamed at the staring parents. With hands shaking,

I asked, "May I please pass in front of you to reach the vacant seats?"

"Sure, baby, let me tuck in my feet," one lady offered.

The rows didn't have much space between them, and I practiced tightrope-walking skills I didn't know I had. "Oops, oh my, please forgive me," I hated my high-pitched, little girl's voice.

As I tried to smooth my hair behind my ears to calm myself, I realized the sauna-like heat had zapped my hair into a ball of frizz. I tugged at my skirt sticking to my behind. With all the warm bodies, the heat index must have been at least a hundred. Perspiration dripped into my eyes. Stinging eyes told me my mascara would streak my cheeks. The humid September day had succeeded in wrinkling my clothes and gluing them to me. I inched my way tentatively through the narrow aisles on my high heels.

"Excuse me, pardon me," I muttered as I continued toward my destination. New arrivals kept bubbling in. They tipped a hat or offered a cheerful greeting and nodded and smiled at one another.

"Yuze the new teacher from the North?"

"Yes, I'm new."

While wiggling past another large woman, she stood and got right in my face and looked hard at me. "Why, yuze a chile yourself. You be a little crazy if you think you can teach these youngin's. They don't want no learnin'. They need lovin'."

I moved in front of her without any contact. The vacant chairs were three people away.

"Uh-huh, honey. This be the biggest parent-teacher meeting Carter G. Woodson ever have. Everyone want to see yuze new White teachers." Her comment turned me away from my focused balancing act, and my size six shiny patent heels intertwined with the feet of a tall, thin man. I tripped and plopped into the lap of an obese woman sitting next to the tall man. I became klutzy Lucy from an *I Love Lucy* episode.

"You look too young to be a teacher. Too pretty too." When I crawled from her lap, I noticed she wore a long-sleeved, polka-dotted polyester dress. *How could she stand such confining clothing in this humidity?*

"Oh, I'm so sorry, ma'am ... mercy me ... oops."

I knew all eyes were on me now. I rose to my feet again, and my heart pounded so hard I thought it would burst the buttons off my blouse. My hands were as clammy as my armpits. The beanstalk man, whose feet I'd stepped on, said, "Aw, baby, I didn't mind."

At last, I reached the empty seats. I collapsed and took a deep breath. Grateful to be sitting, I looked up. Curious eyes stared at me. Broad smiles and polite nods surrounded me.

'*Maybe you are afraid to be here tonight. Maybe you shouldn't have agreed to come to New Orleans. Your mama didn't like the idea. Was she right? Maybe you shouldn't have gotten married.*' *Stop it!* I shouted silently to the voice whispering all those "maybe" accusations.

Denny stood in a nearby doorway, glancing around as if searching for an answer. He caught my eyes and recognized I was frantic. Winking, he gave one of those *I understand* gazes. He shuffled through the row to sit beside me.

"I love you," he whispered and patted my hand. "It will be fine."

*I never expected this big a crowd. The auditorium is packed. I thought I'd be talking to a few parents, but with this crowd, we might be here all night.* My mind kept going around in circles—jumping from one thought to another.

*I'm so hot. When will this be over? What should I say to these parents?* I closed my eyes and drew a deep breath.

"Attention, attention. Can I have your attention?" Mr. Bergeron quieted the auditorium. The antiquated sound system screeched the crowd to silence. "We have a delightful turnout tonight. I wonder why?"

The crowd roared with laughter. Responses of uh-huh, and yes, sir, echoed around us.

"He knows. He knows." The woman next to me elbowed me and laughed deep in her belly.

Mr. Bergeron continued. "We are anticipating a year of successes. Our students at Carter G. Woodson will learn because we have a faculty ready to teach. As you know, we have five new teachers. Now, you folks stand up when I call your name."

I remembered the first time I met Mr. Bergeron. His eyes had attracted me. Part of his charisma came from his unusual light eyes against his warm tobacco-colored skin and inviting smile. Mr. Bergeron's tapered body and height created a fashionable look in his beige linen suit and copper-striped tie. He carried the handsome Creole traits of high cheekbones and a pouty-shaped mouth.

I tried to show no expression when he spoke. His melodious tones lulled me into a place of admiration. I didn't want to seem starstruck by his choice of words, but I liked him. Listening to him was like wearing my best slippers.

"All right, Mr. and Mrs. Bayronne," he spoke in his Southern drawl, "will you stand?"

I still struggled to recognize my name with this strange pronunciation. Denny tugged on my arm, and we stood. Scanning the crowd, we smiled broadly. Loud thunderclaps burst through the room.

Parents around me called, "Good choice."

"Glad to have you."

"Why you two here?"

Surprised by spontaneous and vocal greetings, we both reacted to the audience with affirmative nods and frozen smiles. Sweat rolled between my thighs, so I pulled my skirt daintily, hoping the adjustment would hide the skirt cupping under my derriere. When we sat, I felt lightheaded and wanted to end this experience. *Dear God, I thought my introduction would never be over.*

Mr. Bergeron continued. "This young couple comes from the Midwest to teach our students. Mr. Bayronne is teaching physical education and will coach track, and Mrs. Bayronne is teaching English and speech. They come well recommended. Now, let's give them a warm Woodson welcome."

*Everything in this room is warm.* I listened to loud applause and whistles and tapped my foot to an inaudible rhythm. My jaw muscles ached from clenching my teeth. *Why had Denny made this stupid decision to come to New Orleans?*

The principal continued, "We have an experienced music teacher who comes to us from New York City. She has taught in inner city schools, so she will be beneficial to our students and staff. Let's give a southern welcome to Mrs. Hammock."

Mrs. Hammock stood. "I am pleased to be here, and I will teach your children classical music. They will be exposed to new challenges." She sat stiffly with her chin jutting forward.

"Two teachers are being transferred from a school across the city. Welcome Mr. Winston and Miss Avery." They waved hello because most of the crowd seemed to already know them. Again, the crowd applauded and chatted among themselves.

Being one of three White faces in this auditorium crumpled my confidence. Feeling alone, yet surrounded by a crowd of people, I wanted to run. When the color of my skin did not match those around me, I became anxious. My head felt foggy, and the swirling lights created more anxiety. I was waiting to become more comfortable. It didn't happen. Neither did the visitors' stares and frowns stop targeting me. This audience not only looked different from me, but their loud laughter and noisy chatter increased my nervousness.

Later in the year, our closest friends told us we three White teachers from the North were not expected to make it in this tough neighborhood. Henri Todd explained we were hired so New Orleans could meet federal standards of integration. We had no idea there had been an ongoing turbulent battle trying to integrate schools within New Orleans. We later learned the school board had tried transferring a few local White teachers to a couple of Black schools and the program had failed miserably, so they sent Mr. Haber north to interview prospects.

For the last five months, Denny and my conversations had been laced with anticipation and excitement, looking forward to living in this famous and charming city. We assumed our new school would be a typical mix of students in a picturesque place in the city. I looked around at the somber faces staring at me or heard others laughing. *No, this is not what I expected.*

One woman announced to another mother, "I bettin' on the New Yorker teacher. She know how to treat these kids. She experienced."

I pretended I didn't hear but wondered if she was right. In fact, I questioned if I could accept this lifestyle, this task of teaching in a run-down, overcrowded school, and if I could meet these challenges to please my beloved husband. Denny's competitive nature enjoyed a challenge, and he could not stop talking about the great city of

New Orleans. He did not understand the inner and outer struggles eating at me. My reason and self-doubt battled my passion to please my husband. Right now, I wanted out of this hot, sticky room. It smelled like overworked bodies. *Hold on, Sandi. Hold on. It's almost over. Stay calm.*

Finally, Mr. Bergeron introduced the assistant principal, Mr. Hughes, who was dressed in a striped shiny suit with saggy trousers.

"I'm delighted to be back." Mr. Hughes lisped through a missing tooth. "Welcome to all of you, and we hope to see you at our next parent-teacher conferences."

Later in the year, I realized Mr. Hughes knew this large number of parents would not return. They had only come to see the new White teachers.

# LESSON 12

What has once happened will invariably happen again,
when the same circumstances which combined to produce
it, shall again combine in the same way.
—Abraham Lincoln

My restless night's sleep was too short. Mondays were difficult and the parent meeting weighed heavy on me. I moved at a slow pace to my closet trying to decide what to wear. My deep thoughts were interrupted by Denny's loud voice. I mindlessly dressed and grabbed my makeup bag, so I could finish grooming in the car.

"If we'd left ten minutes earlier, we wouldn't be in this mess." His taut knuckles gripped the steering wheel as he spoke with exaggerated pronunciation, "I would like to leave for school on time."

Cognizant of the traffic gridlock, I glared hard at him, and the heat of my anger flushed through my body on this sultry morning. I was tired of Denny always being right. I had been way too slow this morning. I could not decide what to wear, so I chose my new gray plaid dress to make me feel pretty. As I blotted my melting makeup, I observed my hair looked like an alien with a pointed head because of my restless night and caked hair spray. My mood added a negative to my morning, and now, another fight about being late increased my anger.

My words shot out like bullets. "You are impossible."

As I slurped my coffee, I tried to ignore him, but we were sitting three feet apart in our car. Five mornings a week, this lineup of grappling drivers attempting to cross the Mississippi River confined us. This morning's traffic clog and my lateness darkened our mood and tolerance for each other. We were both mad before the school day even started.

In the angry silence between us, my mind drifted to the small shotgun houses and stark cement projects where my students lived, or stayed, as they described it. Quarreling at home and rumbles at school had become my lifestyle. I never imagined my first year of marriage would be filled with so many arguments and petty issues. Our marriage had begun with honey in his words and actions—now replaced by vinegar and tart remarks. We were enduring each other's imperfections but not in a kind way. I had a sharp tongue and closed body language when he did not agree with me. How had we fallen into this trap of endless struggles?

Denny slammed on the brakes, and the abrupt movement sloshed coffee onto my linen dress.

"Oh great. Now, my new dress is ruined." I blotted frantically at the spill.

"It's your fault! Why can't you be on time?"

"Excuse me? Why is the man changing lanes my fault?"

The radio announcer interrupted my words. "Goin' to be a hot one, folks. Look for temperatures in the high 90s with humidity. It's 7:30. Have a good one."

Our postures stiffened when we heard the time. Tension was as thick as the humidity because we needed to be ready for the 8:15 bell. I hoped this argument and spilled coffee were not an indication of my whole day. I wasn't prepared for my English classes and wished again

I had textbooks for my junior high students. I planned to have students write a paragraph on the place they enjoyed most.

After the first few days, I realized my students lacked opportunities I took for granted. Many endured daily struggles. I knew Jerome came to school hungry because when he popped into Henri's office, he was encouraged to sample an orange or apple. Drake always looked angry and wore dirty, wrinkled clothes. He smelled of cigarette smoke and body odor. Timid Lily could not talk without her twin Millie acting as her spokesperson.

Many of my students knew hardships I would never experience. Their tough outer shells reflected a wall built to shield them from more disappointments. Especially Drake. His body language screamed, "Don't bother me."

I needed to destroy those walls, but I didn't know how.

Denny dodged another car and another pothole as he drove onto St. Charles Street. Potholes were everywhere throughout this part of the city, and my body shook each time we bumped over one. Despite my pent-up frustration, I calmed myself as I peeked into these fine homes, trying to glimpse at their original art works. I admired their well-chosen antiques and rich royal colors. The neighborhood was filled with pillared, prestigious homes. Gardeners kept bushes trimmed into pleasing manicured shapes. Porches, verandas, and balconies provided multiple sitting areas to view purple salvia and hydrangea blooms. Iron fences with decorative shapes on top—like stalks of corn or wheat—framed the properties. Irish green grass spotlighted original-designed sculptures and fountains.

And yet, a few blocks away from St. Charles Street, overcrowded government projects stood tall and bleak with no landscaping. Bare dirt replaced grass. New Orleans, Louisiana (referred to as NOLA), insightfully applied for federal monies to build projects. I learned from Mr. Gritton, the history teacher, the Magnolia Project had once been a prestigious place. Black professionals chose to live there because the apartments were nicer than they could buy or rent in Black housing districts in other parts of town. Magnolia advertisements boasted the project included a theater, fine playgrounds, and new landscaping.

By 1967, the facility had suffered much abuse and neglect. In the beginning, inspections ensured renters kept their apartments clean and in good repair. As the buildings aged, however, and regular inspections became less frequent, lower-income, single parent families moved in. The professionals moved out. The Magnolia Project, where most of my students lived, became more and more dilapidated.

Many of my students had been born on a treadmill. No matter how fast they ran, the track never changed, never went anywhere. I wished to give them the same freedom Huck found on his journey. *I will read them Huckleberry Finn as often as I can fit it into our curriculum. I know Twain's words will be beneficial. I want my students to find their own raft and travel the Mississippi away from a dead-end treadmill.*

NOLA was a place of extremes in tight juxtaposition. The heavy, sweet odor of magnolias on St. Charles clashed with the sour garbage smell seeping in the window of my classroom. Rotted garbage brewed in the sun. Pinching my nose shut, I tried to shield myself from this putrid smell of decay. My action was as efficient as the government's negligent approach to service of the urban school areas. The school board's prejudice showed its neglectful hand when it came to providing equal or adequate repairs and supplies. Mr. LeBlanc told me White government businessmen had no experience or desire to understand and evaluate the inner-city's real needs.

Two separate worlds crowded into this one city. As we traveled between our apartment and Woodson, the narrow streets cried out poverty. *How could women live in such meager dwellings?* I could not comprehend waking every day to dirt and degenerating conditions. *How could Den and I fit into this community?* I did not belong here anymore than I did to the pillared neighborhood we passed through on St. Charles.

Denny turned into a parking place and shut off the engine. Ignoring me, he climbed out of the car and gave Mike Leonard a warm smile as he waved to him. Denny told me last weekend how much he admired Mike and his teaching strategies. Mike taught Denny how to live the Woodson way and what rules would profit his profession. Mike modeled how to conduct gym class and keep order. Denny and Mike loved football, and since the New Orleans Saints were forming a team this year, it created another bond.

I admired how Den could easily fit in with the teaching staff. His easy social ways had attracted me at Ball State. He had a captivating, beaming smile, and I could feel his warmth across the room. I desired his charisma today.

As we locked our midnight-blue convertible, Mike asked, "How are the Barons?"

"Made it over the bridge in one piece," Den answered, trying to be a jokester. Today his humor left me cold.

He hurried to the gym area to organize his equipment for class. I knew he did this because of his obsession about keeping things in exact order. I hated his lecture on order: "Put things back where they belong, and you won't be searching half the day for them." I never understood how he could be so neat. And I abhorred when he treated me like a child.

Even though I was still mad at him, I waved goodbye because Mike was watching. I took deliberate long steps, trying to hurry in my high heels. Their click on the cement followed me to my classroom. The pain from my new high heels caused me to stub my toe and turn my ankle on the gnarly flooring. Parts of the linoleum had worn away, and those missing pieces reminded me of this exasperating lifestyle Denny had chosen. Denny seemed different here than when we were in college. Plus, my noisy and disrespectful students were not what I had expected. Gaining weight added to my defeat and lack of self-worth. I sensed I was drowning in a tidal wave.

As I put my purse into my desk drawer, I spied the large furry spider that decided my drawer would be her home, even though I had removed her several times. I had no time to worry about spiders now. A cacophony of voices and the clanging bell reminded me students were coming into the room. As they entered, I wanted to exit. They were a weight, pushing me through those torn tiles.

Walter slid into a front seat and grinned, showing his broad, white teeth. Other students sauntered to their desks at their own pace.

"Students, please be quiet."

"Hey, you think you funny? Fart over there," Jerome shouted.

"You look groovy girl," Debra encouraged her friend Miranda.

"I want to go back to bed." Ava yawned and stretched her arms high into the air to make her point.

"Hey, man, this is my chair," Lily's soft voice sounded forceful.

"Please sit in your assigned seat." *Boy, not effective.* Their voices and laughter grew louder. "Please be quiet." I raised my voice to overcome theirs.

Since no one listened or cared what I said, I went to my desk drawer and pulled out the tropical spider. I held up the furry creature in my hand and walked to the front of the surprised and gawking students.

"Suzy lives in my desk drawer and is my pet. If you want anything from inside my desk, you must ask Suzy." With this little demonstration, I put Suzy beside my leather purse.

I closed the drawer, smirked, and faced a now quiet class. Who knew spending my childhood in Florida and living with spiders would help me with classroom management?

"She be a witch. Be quiet," whispered Jerome. "Bet no one try to swipe *her* purse."

"Yeah, the music teacher should have been a witch like Mizz Bayronne," said Walter.

"I don't think a spider could keep kids from settin' her room on fire." Joan straightened her school items and posture signifying her need for order.

This was news to me. "What are you all talking about?"

"Haven't you heard about the music teacher? She came in this mornin' and someone had set her room on fire. Burned her papers, her grade book, and wrote all over, 'Go home, Yankee,' and other things you won't let us say out loud," answered Jerome.

"Looks like you and Mr. Bayronne be the only White folks at Woodson now."

"What do you mean, Walter?"

"She be gone. Walked out. Went back home to New York."

"Now, how do you know that?"

"I heard her screamin' at Mr. Bergeron this mornin'. Said she was goin' home today."

"Oh my, I'm sad to hear she left."

"We ain't. She a mean old White lady. She didn't tell us stories or be kind like you do, Mizz Bayronne."

"Thanks, Walter. I think we should stop talking and move on to our assignment."

I passed out paper and pencils to each student who eagerly felt the smooth unsharpened end. They appreciated the simple yellow No. 2 writing instrument.

"Today your assignment is to write a paragraph describing a favorite place. Use at least five complete sentences, and please pay careful attention to punctuation."

I stopped and realized they were all listening. The quiet surprised me.

"For example, maybe you like spending an afternoon with a friend at the park. Tell me why that's fun and why you enjoy this place. Perhaps, your favorite room is in the kitchen, learning to cook or eating your mama's pecan pie, or you like watching the sun setting at the end of the day."

They looked at me with blank stares, sitting as still I rarely saw them.

"I can't write a whole paragraph on making a muffuletta in my kitchen," Jerome's shrug lifted his shoulders to his ears.

"Look at those handouts I gave you last week."

Lily lowered her head so she wouldn't have eye contact with me.

Jerome showed me a wadded piece of paper. "I can't find mine. Do you have any more?"

Disturbed my writing tips and handouts were lost or purposely thrown away, I wondered how this could be so hard for eighth graders.

"No matter where we are in life, we need to find a positive image and hold onto our memory of that experience. I remember as a child I loved the feeling of warm sand sifting under my feet at the beach. The soft sand warmed my heart and my feet. Now, when I am discouraged, I pretend I'm walking on the beach and my mood improves."

Joan and Debra smiled. Those two smiles affirmed they were listening. I could see others were engaged because of their head nods. They held their pencils in writing positions.

"Go ahead, start your paragraph with the phrase, 'One place I enjoy is ...' I will write one as well. My mood could use improvement. When I write, it fills an empty place. I will show you my paragraph in a few minutes."

All of them, to my surprise, were writing. One part of me wanted to show the same excitement as a child opening Cracker Jacks and finding the prize, yet another part of me insisted I remain reserved and proper as a southern lady. Mama had always discouraged loud praise or excitement because it wasn't ladylike.

I breathed deeply and wrote about the seashore, the sun, and the sand. Oh, how I wished I could be walking in warm sand, listening to the soothing rhythm of waves on the shore.

I read my paragraph aloud and asked who would like to share theirs. Walter waved his hand.

"Great. Share your best place."

He read, "My favorite place is my mama's kitchen. She loves to cook, and I love to eat. She makes the best red beans and rice in the city. Her bread pudding should win a prize. She makes all these things in our kitchen, so that's my favorite place."

"You did great and whet our appetites too."

Miranda volunteered next. "My favorite place is on the field marching and twirling. I love hearing the marching band behind me and seeing fans ahead of me. Being a majorette has brought me friends and happiness. It gives me exercise and makes me proud. So, my favorite place is marching on the field."

"Good job sharing your passion. Your five sentences gave us a peek at what you enjoy and why."

Others volunteered, but the bell rang too soon. For the first time, I wished this class would last longer. Their writings gave me wings of inspiration.

"Goodbye, ma'am. I'll try to read tomorrow." Lily's timidity made it difficult for me to know her well.

I tried to look at her world through her questions, which were few. I watched as she batted her eyelashes at the boys, so she could move through the door. Her braids lined up in rows across her tiny, dark head. When she wrote, her small hands held the pencil painstakingly, trying to create perfect cursive. I'd encouraged her to be brave and volunteer to read a passage of *Huck Finn* next time. When she read her paragraph, she lifted her eyes, and I saw how they glittered as if her accomplishment sparked contentment. I looked forward to seeing Lily and hearing her read tomorrow.

# LESSON 13

Growing up, my sister and I were labeled latchkey kids. I have mainly fond memories of our time building relationships by being in homework groups, playing inside with board games or outside on the playground. Nestled in the fond memories is the catalytic moment that opened my eyes to how other people saw me as well as how people in our world sometimes saw one another. I asked our latchkey coordinator, "Miss P, can I sign up to be a part of the science club?"

She looked at me with gentleness, "It would take a lot for a little latchkey boy like you."

The response shocked me. In fact, it wrecked me. It took my childlike innocence away. It stripped me of my dignity. It categorized me, it segregated me, it ostracized me. How does a child respond to that? I'm not sure. I remember taking what she said and simply walking away, answering with a childlike "okay." But then, having a new sense of understanding—I wasn't just a child, a little boy—I was a little Black boy, separated, different, not the same as the other boys.—Geoffrey L. King, Author, Pastor at Fellowship Missionary in Fort Wayne, Indiana

The heat and humidity turned my room into a sauna. I relished any breeze that came through my open windows. My most difficult class met during the hottest part of the day.

I cringed at the clanging bells. The banging of the metal lockers and high-energy voices resonated in the hallway. Tromping sneakers signaled the building momentum of energy headed toward my classroom. By sixth hour, the teenage bodies were ready for action, but their minds were disengaged. The temperature and my morning argument with Denny left me drained. With my sixth-hour students, teaching was an uphill battle, and I wasn't winning.

"Hey, teach."

"Aww, English again."

"Here I be. I know you waitin' for me," chanted Denise.

"Move your booty, girl. Make it dance," a boy jested.

"Mizz, I don't have no pencil."

"Help me help you today." I pushed back frizzy hair from my eyes and smiled at the class. "First, we need to correct yesterday's verb assignments then do our vocabulary study."

"We already did those verbs. Why you axing us again?"

"Correcting your errors will help you remember the correct verb forms," I reminded them.

"Wish it was true. Ain't gonna happen."

Then, Drake sauntered in, slowly dragging his size twelve shoes. His blue-black skin glistened in the humidity. He stared at me with his eyes of coal that showed no life, no soul, no understanding. He collapsed into his desk, folded his arms, and laid his head down, exposing the top of a disheveled Afro. He wore the same torn black shirt to class every day. My stomach knotted as I thought about asking him to sit up.

When he looked at me, I tried to make eye contact, but he always looked away. I wondered if he knew I was afraid of him.

He pulled his brows into the scowl of a seasoned boxer. He was a foot taller than me, and his defined arms had muscles larger than Denny's. Puffed up veins lined his humongous hands. He looked like a man rather than a young teen. Later, when I checked his school records, I discovered he had been detained several times because of absences and suspensions.

Drake raised his head revealing his stern facial expression. He refused to attempt any assignment and would wad up his paper and leave it on his desk. Sylvia told me he had never learned to read or write. He had fallen through the gaps in the system. There were no special classes and no budget for aides. Teachers chose to spend their time nurturing the learners, not those who slept or rebelled. I understood he had a problem, but so did I. I feared Drake. I could not engage him in class activities, and I certainly never confronted him.

When I smiled at him, he flared his nostrils and dismissed me. His outer shell remained distant and unaffected by his surroundings. The other students knew Drake's reputation and left him alone in his harsh world. Two deep scars on his jaw and forehead disfigured his face. I could not estimate the scars he carried within.

"He is streetwise and book dumb." Mike warned me not to push Drake because he held a lot of rage and a police record to go with it. I needed to be careful.

Disregarding Drake, I counted the number of students present. A few sat on top of the desks and others leaned against the wall. All were present, so I pinned my attendance on the appointed office clip by my door.

"Students, please sit in a chair. Guys on the wall, sit at your desks. Ladies, please continue your conversations later. Harrison, sit." I needed to yell my loudest primal scream. And I longed to stop sweating. I wished I could make this class disappear. I suspected they knew and continued to squander the time.

"Look. She be gettin' mad. She turnin' red. White folks turn red when they be mad," Felix remarked.

"Thank you for noticing, Felix. Now shut up." I seldom used shut up unless I was losing control, like now. This late in the day, I reacted rather than thinking about my words and actions.

"Attention all students," the static speaker blared. "Young ladies and gentlemen, it has been brought to my attention students are moving too slowly in the halls and are perpetually late. This must cease today. We expect you to be in your seats when the beginning bell rings. No exceptions. Offenders will be taken to the gym office immediately."

"Ooooh, baby, butts are gonna be skinned." Felix put his arms behind his head and forced his head to methodically move left and right as if trying to stretch his stiff neck.

Miraculously, the announcement lured my students into their chairs. Thank God, I did not have to confront Drake.

Four boys shouted to each other and laughed as loud as they could.

"Gentlemen, please complete these corrections for me." I handed them their assignments, and they spoke louder and chuckled as I moved past.

When I looked back at the four noisy boys, they were making paper airplanes and flying them to others.

"Put those airplanes away." I let my morning arguments with Denny and the rudeness of my students create a volcano within me. I knew I would erupt any minute.

Paper pelts bombarded me from the corners of the room. A few had f-you written on them, others suggested I "Go home." I noticed the misspellings of their intended words on the planes that landed on my desk.

Deep within, I felt anger rising as fierce as Drake's.

*Good Lord, what am I going to do now?* I attempted to look calm, but my face was burning. I gathered the airplanes and bellowed. "I have had it with your lack of cooperation. When the dismissal bell rings today, the entire class will remain in this room to learn respect and review classroom rules."

"What you say?" Felix asked.

"You know what I said. Now, correct your papers. When you finish, I will collect them." I spoke with a new authority, which startled even me. "If I can't acquire cooperation in school, then I can teach you cooperation *after* school."

When the bell rang, I spoke with the force of a tornado. "Stay in your seats." I was more surprised than the students when they remained at their desks. As I passed out clean sheets of paper, I sensed eyes watching me. I looked toward the doorway to see Mike Leonard standing there. "Title your paper, Respect, and follow the directions I write on the board."

Passersby gawked in the windows at the detained students. I knew mass punishment was not recommended classroom management. But when I had shouted at them minutes before, I couldn't take back what had spilled out of my mouth. I did not dare go back on my iron-fisted words, or I would appear weak.

Experiencing remorse because of those unrelenting words, I met Mike at the door.

"Please don't do this," he spoke softly. "This is dangerous. It is hard to control thirty cornered kids."

"I have to gain control of this class. They give me fits every day. Today, they will see me make a line in the sand, and they will not cross it. Today, they will understand I can and will lead them away from small mindedness into being bridges for tomorrow."

"Be careful. A couple of us gym teachers are going to be near in case a fight breaks out." Mike stuck his head in the room and said, "Detention has begun. No trouble, you understand?"

They stared ahead and copied my three rules off the blackboard as I wrote them:

1. Be in your seat when the bell rings. Be quiet and ready to start our day's assignments.
2. Show respect by following directions, listening, and caring.
3. Complete assignments to show your progress.

The halls had cleared. An eerie quietness prevailed. Only the scratchy sound of pencils writing on paper could be heard.

"Please complete this assignment by writing three ways you can help create an educational environment in our room. Number your items and write in complete sentences."

I knew if this punishment was to be effective, I needed to keep the activity short and release these kids as soon as possible.

Drake stood up, slammed, and overturned his desk on the cement floor. I jumped at the deafening crash. The students watched big eyed, silent.

I stared at him but did not move.

"They be thirty of us and one of her. I ain't stayin'. We can walk over you."

I stood in my doorway like a bulldog protecting her pups. "Over my dead body." *Oh, God why did I use those words?*

Drake got right in my face. His breath was hot. His nose touched mine.

A sudden wrath surged within me. I imitated the anger my mother had used on me. Her verbal abuse had often made me frightened for my life. I copied her tone, and my temper grew to a point I could not control. It grew larger. I grew madder. I screamed.

"Drake, do your assignment, and then you can leave."

"I ain't doin' no damn assignment after school."

He turned with stiff and abrupt body language, went to the back of the room, and crawled out the window. I could not believe my eyes. He moved those large shoulders through the window like a baby laboring through a birth canal.

I looked at the class. Their rounded eyes were big with expectation. Because they were afraid of Drake, they did not follow him out the window.

Composed now, I said, "All right, let's complete our assignments, so we can all go home. Let's try exiting out the door."

They looked at me and showed their submission with a giggle or a nod. I was dumbfounded. *Vincere diem*. I had won the day. I had earned their awe because I stood up to Drake. My knees shook, but my years in theater helped me fake strength and composure. One by one the students finished their contributions.

"Thank you all for finishing your work. I appreciate your commitment. When you have completed your lists, put them in the wooden tray, and you may leave."

My pounding head triggered exhaustion.

Joe came in to empty my wastebasket after all students were dismissed. "Mizz Bayronne, please be careful. These kids have tough backgrounds and a lot of stories. Don't push them too much."

His eyes held compassion, and he watched out for me. "These kids need more breaks and more food and more caring people like you. Their attitudes reflect their environment. Forgive them but be mindful."

Joe left, and Denny and Mike rushed into my room.

Mike again warned, "Don't push Drake."

Denny kissed me on the forehead, and the three of us walked to the parking lot.

On the ride home, I didn't notice the grandeur of the houses on St. Charles Street, and the potholes didn't annoy me. Amidst the traffic jam on Interstate 90, I poured out my pent-up feelings to Den. "Oh, I was so scared, but I don't think the kids realized it. I could hardly speak because my tongue kept sticking to the top of my mouth."

"What were you thinking? Why did you tell them they had to stay after school? You could've been hurt."

My hands trembled. A new reality came to me. My life was not simple anymore. My tongue could not only entangle me, but it could also misguide others. "I am feeling growing pains."

"What's that mean?" He slammed on his brakes to keep from hitting an intruding car.

"Every word I say makes a kid react." I tucked my hair behind my ears and moved closer to Den.

"Of course, that's life, act and react." He reached for my knee to assure me he was by my side.

"But here I have to guard my words." I held my head trying to lighten the pain.

"Do you realize you put all those students in danger? What if a fight broke out? What if Drake had decided to stab you or them? You have to protect yourself and them. Don't try to be a hero."

I realized my students were vulnerable, and I needed wisdom to guard them. Despite this morning's priority to look cute, coffee and perspiration stains had soiled my clothes. A ruined dress was the least of my worries on this frazzled day. I was overwhelmed. "Let's go back north. I'm so scared. I can't endure these kinds of days. I can't do this one more day."

I wept, dripping tears on my soiled dress. I had screamed at Denny this morning, and now, I sought his comfort.

He patted my knee and suggested we have dinner out and go to bed early. "Next week will be better."

I laid my head on his shoulder. "I sure hope so."

# LESSON 14

Life is like riding a bicycle. To keep your balance, you must keep moving.—Albert Einstein

I focused on recovering from my Friday detention trauma.

Denny jogged his usual Friday and Saturday loop. He encouraged me to run a short way. So, after sleeping in late, I decided to be a faithful wife, put on my shoes, and attempt to become Den's jogging companion.

"Hey, Larry and Man of La Mancha," I greeted our landlord and his dog.

Larry and his wife, Helen, had purchased our duplex and lived in the adjoining side. They were near our age and newlywed. They were great landlords and our only friends outside of school. We teased about who had the loudest newlywed arguments.

"What? Are you jogging?" Larry ran beside me with hands in the air in disbelief. "Going to struggle again?" He laughed as he passed me in my new attempts.

I picked up one foot after the other and landed with a thud each time. My rubber soles slapped on the pavement. Not a flowing slap, but an offbeat rhythm. I pressed on, but my arms felt heavy and in the way. I swung them, which seemed awkward, yet it felt burdensome to keep them stiff. My shoulders were tense and heavy.

Suffering a runner's low instead of a high, I wanted this ordeal to be over. Nothing about a jog was euphoric. Perspiration stung my eyes and soaked my hair. My sticky skin reminded me of kindergarten when I had white glue all over my hands and arms. Reared as a true Southerner, I had not been allowed to run. Mom called sweating "unladylike." *I detest running. My shins are stinging.* I continued to put one foot in front of the other, gasping for each breath, and trying to ease the pain. Plus, I loathed the heat, the humidity, and the ten extra pounds I had added to my figure. Saying no to New Orleans–style shrimp and dirty rice had to be easier than this torture.

*Keep going, girl. You know you never say can't.* I curved homeward on the loop around our neighborhood. Gasping, wiping the salty drips from my forehead, I could not take one more step and slowed to a walk. I began pondering yesterday's nightmare. I wondered where Drake went after he climbed out the window. I worried what would happen when I faced him again. I agreed with Denny and Mike. I shouldn't have called a detention. I had put my students and myself at risk, but I really didn't know how to fix the sixth-hour class. They were impossible, and this type of class behavior was never addressed in my college classroom management class.

*Well, if I think jogging is hard, what about facing Drake again? Am I really moving forward in my class discipline? Am I touching any one kid's life? Do I know how to teach? Can I make it all year? Can I make it to next Friday?*

All these questions rambled through my mind as I walked into our driveway. The sting in my shins created even more negative voices in my head. Why hadn't the moving van delivered our furniture? We had been sleeping on a floor pallet for six weeks. The frustration with the unfurnished apartment, compounded with the heat and the classroom discipline, wearied me. I needed a shower followed by shopping therapy to push me out of this downward spiral.

I limped to the door of our bathroom, turned on the shower, and let the hot water beat off the accumulated sweat. The steaming water loosened my aching calves and washed away my unrest about teaching.

*A shopping marathon or jogging? The answer was obvious.*

I needed space from Denny, and I had a perfect plan. I wanted to look at pretty things for our apartment. I needed to buy fun earrings, makeup, and an outfit to wear to the Saints' football game. I would spray perfume from the samplers in the cosmetic department.

As I finished dressing, Denny returned. "Who smells good? Did you enjoy your jog and the fresh air?"

"Well, *enjoy* wouldn't be my word."

"I feel great now. Nothing like jogging to pick up my day."

"Shopping picks up my day."

"Where you goin'?"

"Shopping at a department store and those nearby shops."

"Well, go easy. Money is tight. I'm taking Monday off to be here with a cashier's check for the moving van."

"What? Our furniture is here?"

"They called while you were still asleep."

"At last. We can sleep in a bed again. Please could you call today and check on the easy chair we ordered? Maybe the furniture store could deliver while you are home."

"Want me to go shopping with you?"

"Not really." I did a polka turn and hopped away.

"Have fun." He waved from the window.

Driving away, my stomach had butterflies. Thinking about shopping made me so excited. As I pulled into the strip mall, my rapid heartbeat told of my expectations.

Inside the store, I wasted no time by first choosing three yellow pillows to spiff up our used couch. A plush green velvet pillow attracted me and would be perfect with our new chair. I reached for olive-green linen napkins and a matching table runner. I was on a shopping high when a painful step reminded me how tight my calves were.

I found four wooden napkin holders for the olive napkins, which would complement our yellow pottery dishes. I couldn't wait for them to be delivered. I charged the household items and decided to make a trip to the car to deposit my overflowing shopping bags.

Back inside the store, I made my way to the women's department. I looked at several blouses to wear to the Saints' game on Sunday and decided on a bright gold top and black pedal pushers to match the team's colors. Charging felt a lot like opening gifts at Christmas. I continued to pick out things I liked, one after another. Each item created happiness and lightheartedness in me. Not once did I think about my awful sixth-period experience on Friday.

Seeing the big sale banner in the shoe department, I perused the styles.

"May I help you find a certain shoe?"

The clerk brought my size in a black and white high heel and two other styles. Placing my feet into the shoes, I flinched from my burning shins. Not to be defeated, I persevered with the challenge until they were found—the perfect shoe and fit.

"Yes, ma'am," I answered the clerk. "This will be on my charge."

Watching her ring up my purchases, conviction covered me—I had not even thought to total my items from one department to the next. *Maybe I should go home now. I admit it. Shopping fuels my excitement, but I probably need to stop now.*

Spending gave me an escape and a vision. I thought of how our front room would look classy with the tailored pillows. *Besides, seeing Denny's eyes light up when he sees me in my new clothes will take away the guilt of overspending.*

On the drive home, I owned up to the fact I needed to be a bit more forgiving of my husband's lack of kind words. I expected surprise gifts, but they hadn't arrived either. After all, I fell in love with Denny because he was such a good listener. He let me talk and never interrupted, all the while looking at me adoringly. While we were dating, I loved it. But now I wanted him to respond and share his thoughts.

I determined right then to tell him I was sorry for my harsh words on our way to school. *I am going to have to do more than apologize tonight to make up for all my purchases.*

# LESSON 15

It's not whether you get knocked down, it's whether you get up.—Vince Lombardi

On Sunday, we went to our first Saints' game at Tulane University.

Denny had explained a professional team did not usually play on a college football field, but the Saints' first year would be played in a borrowed stadium. They had not built one yet. Denny purchased expensive season tickets and incorporated them into our three-thousand-dollar bank loan. We had little money when we arrived in the city and had to wait four more weeks before we received our first paycheck.

Our banker encouraged him to buy Saints' tickets with part of the loan. Denny got his highs from the Saints—I got mine from shopping. Both were expensive.

We woke early for a Sunday, went out for breakfast, and drove to a shopping center to park. We loaded onto a Saints' bus filled with noisy, excited fans shuttling to the game. Everyone was decked out in an array of black and gold. *I fit right in with my new outfit.*

The fans shouted, laughed, and stuffed their mouths with Cajun chips and peanuts, drowned by gin and tonic or a scotch and water. *I've never experienced such excitement on a bus. Or experienced liberal drinking privileges like today.* In New Orleans, folks could carry a drink while they walked Bourbon Street or enjoy endless choices of wine and liquor in the grocery store. People drank everywhere, and this fan bus was no exception. Those on the bus were merry and celebrating before they arrived at the stadium.

Den acted like a child on his birthday. His energy spilled out in loud conversation, and he rubbed my arm as if I were his lucky charm. He hugged me every few minutes, ending with a wet kiss. His instant enthusiasm and prediction of a win drew me into his arena. Even though I was not much of a football fan, I was excited to support a new team in the Crescent City. I joined Denny's enthusiasm as we did a New Orleans' shuffle with the crowd to the stadium. We swayed then took synchronized steps forward and backward while waving our handkerchiefs in the air. Methodical steps and hand clapping brought us into the stadium. With 81,000 fans, we sang, *When the Saints Go Marching In.* The cheers were deafening, and the thrilled fans roared when the team came onto the field in their black and gold uniforms.

Denny had read in the *Times Picayune* the Saints' expansion team had drafted Paul Hornung from the Green Bay Packers. He was chosen with the expectation he would bring in fans. The projection was accurate because there were 80,879 tickets sold for this first game. The Saints acquired another all-American from LSU named Jim Taylor. He and Paul were known as "thunder and lightning" when they played for Green Bay. But the dynasty would not continue. Hornung was forced to retire because of a neck injury in training camp.

In the first play of the game, John Gilliam executed a ninety-four-yard kickoff return for a touchdown. Whenever I learned of a Black role model, I took time to share with my students how he was living his dream. I wanted them to know their dreams could come true.

The expectant atmosphere delivered a high-octane game. *I really don't understand one thing that's happening, but Denny's in rare form—even coaching plays from the bleachers as if the players can hear him.* Unfortunately, the Saints lost thirteen to twenty-seven to the LA Rams. Den called this a learning day, and said wins would come. The fans filed out with comments about plays and players. We boarded the bus back to our car. I enjoyed my first professional game because I was with my husband—we were like babies, seeing things for the first time.

I reached for his hand, and we said together, "There's no place I'd rather be." *We are becoming a team, much like the Saints. I love this man. I really do.*

We returned home with a steaming pizza. I squealed, "I can't wait to see our house tomorrow. All our furniture and wedding gifts will be here, at last."

Denny grinned and explained he had called Mike Leonard to confirm the procedure for taking a personal day, so he could stay home to pay the movers.

*I guess I'll be crossing the Mississippi alone tomorrow. I'd need to review my lesson plans, finish my comments on my sixth-hour detention assignments, and go to bed early.* Balancing all these new things and trying to find clarity in how to teach these kids was about as clear as a muddy creek. I laid my head on my pillow and cuddled into Den's arms.

"Tomorrow, we will have furniture and dishes. Our little home will feel complete." With these words he kissed me on the shoulder, and I fell asleep listening to his soft snores.

# LESSON 16

Education is the passport to the future, for tomorrow belongs to those who prepare for it today.—Malcolm X

"Hurry up. You're going to be late. Traffic is bad on Mondays."

"I *am* hurrying. Oh, I hate mornings, curly hair, streaking makeup, and a screaming husband." Den and I had developed a pattern of shouting at each other, especially in the mornings.

I took off another outfit. Nothing looked right. *Choose. Choose. This sleeveless blouse and seersucker skirt will have to do.* I moaned when I tried to put on my new shoes. My shins were splintered and hot. *Why do I keep trying to jog?*

"Where are my keys?" I asked.

"If you'd put them back where they belong, you wouldn't have this problem."

"Shut up." I frantically moved magazines and turned drawers inside out. Nothing. *"I'm going to be late, really late."*

Denny dangled the keys in front of me. I grabbed them from him, gathered my school bag and purse, and ran out the door.

"Hey, my kiss?" I heard him say as I jumped into the car. I backed out of the driveway and screeched my tires as I turned sharply.

What a morning, I thought as I eased into the lane to cross the bridge. *Now, this is what I need. A wreck in my lane. I'm going to be obviously late, and I wonder what will happen? Why am I always tardy?*

Bells rang as I parked. I was soaking wet from sweating while trying to negotiate the bridge traffic. I ran from the car, cringing at the pain in my shins as I hurried to my room. The attendance girl stood in the doorway blocking my entry.

"Excuse me." I tried to enter my classroom. She reluctantly moved aside.

The kids were clustered in corners, against the windows, and sitting on desks. Although close together, they shouted as if they were at a party with loud music.

"Could I have your attendance, please?" The office girl stared at me.

"No, come back." I turned my attention to my class. "Students, sit in your seats."

"Mizz Bayronne, why you laggin'?" Walter asked. "What's wrong, ma'am?"

"We be gettin' a paddlin' if we be tardy," added one of the boys.

"I know. I'm a bit slow today. Now, please help me by sitting at your desks. Lily, see if you can tell me who is absent."

"Everybody be here." She spoke softly.

"Thanks." I wrote all present and put the attendance form on my door clip.

"You got new shoes, Mizz Bayronne?" Debra looked at my feet. "You walkin' funny."

"Yes. But that's not why I'm walking funny."

"Yeah, tell us more." Jerome teased, and the class laughed.

"I've started jogging, and my shins and calves are so tight they are killin' me."

I didn't think any of this conversation was amusing. But one by one, they found their seat. They seemed to want to help me.

"Head your dictionary papers and teach me five new words this morning. Put them in a sentence, so I am sure to understand them." We had been doing this assignment since the beginning of school to enable me to learn cultural terms and facts about New Orleans. They liked teaching their teacher, so they enjoyed this assignment. The practice created a teeter-totter effect. I would teach them a new concept and then it was their turn to balance the teeterboard. They would teach me a fact about the city or their life.

"No, Jerome, no off-color words." I spoke before he asked.

"Yes, Joan, they can be food related."

"Yes, Lily, I'm going to read more *Huckleberry Finn* as soon as the entire class finishes their assignments."

"Mizz Bayronne be a mind reader. She answers those questions before we even ask them." Jerome stretched out his arms and then pointed at me.

"He think he be funny." Joan turned to Jerome. "Pointing isn't kind."

"Be sure to do a good job on your sentences. I need to include them in your six-weeks' report. Some of you need a little lift in your grades."

"Yuze can lift my grade all you want." Jerome smiled and did his bobblehead doll imitation.

All but a few students had completed their sentences and were awaiting the Huck reading. I glanced at Lily and Walter. "Who needs more time?"

Three students raised their hands. I suggested they finish them at home and bring them tomorrow.

We picked up on Chapter Five as I read:

And looky here—you drop that school, you hear? I'll learn people to bring up a boy to put on airs over his own father and let on to be better'n what *he* is. You lemme catch you fooling around that school again, you hear? Your mother couldn't read, and she couldn't write, nuther, before she died. None of the family couldn't before *they* died. I can't; and here you're a-swelling yourself up like this. I ain't the man to stand it—you hear? Say, lemme hear you read.[1]

I stopped reading. "What doors are opened for Huck because he could read?"

Hands went up across the room. These kids related to Huck. I knew I was making progress with their thinking and reading.

"Choose me, Mizz Bayronne, choose me." Jerome waved his hand as fast as a windshield wiper in the pouring rain.

"Yes, Jerome."

"He can read directions to places and legal documents now."

"He can learn his friend Jim to read." Lily's glistening eyes told me she was ready to apply her new life lesson.

"He can know new things his daddy won't never know," Walter said.

"He can keep goin' to school and not be held back no more." Joseph seldom responded, and his shyness kept me from knowing him well. I smiled within knowing he expressed hope through his comment.

Each answer left its fingerprint on my heart. I had gone through my years of study and never appreciated I could read anything, anytime, anywhere. These kids were shaping me as much as I shaped them. They were showing me how much they valued an education.

I tried to spend a little time each day with those students who had difficulty reading. They needed a full-time reading teacher. When I asked Mr. Bergeron, he explained the limited budget at Carter G. but promised to look into it. *Like I don't know about this limited budget, duh.*

I started buying supplies and anything else I wanted them to have. I loved watching them feel their slick, shiny red folders in which they added their corrected dictionary papers. They smelled the wood of the new pencils. They rolled the ballpoint pens in their fingers and looked at them like they were treasures. They understood living a grateful life. I did not.

The bell rang, and as they said goodbye, Walter asked, "Ma'am, read more *Huckleberry Finn* tomorrow, please?"

*I experienced a new way to get blessed. Walter was asking for more reading. He was responding to my planning and my prayers. Thank you, Lord for Walter—and his enthusiasm.*

During my second-hour prep time, I took a breath and tried to understand my entire extra task. For forty minutes, I followed the blue ditto instructions for filling out forms to report our attendance, academic progress, and evaluations. The forms asked the same things over and over. Perhaps, repetition established truth.

*If I didn't have to spend so much of my prep filling out forms, maybe I could meet more of my students' needs.* I wanted to give them my best, so they could share as much learning as I could cram into a class hour.

# LESSON 17

One learns people through the heart, not the eyes or intellect.—Mark Twain

The third-hour bell signaled time for speech class. Teaching the students to make presentations and do impromptu speaking came naturally. I could encourage them to think on their feet. As I listened to them share about their lives and goals, they inspired and encouraged me. In their speeches, students shared their fears like people laughing at them or forgetting their words. Delivering presentations helped them develop and gave me greater insight into their culture.

Petite Debra was a natural speaker. She bounced when she walked. Her friendly eyes twinkled when she spoke, and her innate ability to connect with her classmates pushed life into her messages. During one of her presentations, she approached our makeshift podium. She pulled herself to a strong and straight posture. She stretched her four-foot-seven-inch frame to make herself taller. A narrow patent-leather belt accentuated her tiny waist. Debra's full, black-checked skirt and crisp white blouse created a well-fashioned image.

"My grandmother is the person I esteem most. She has goals and writes them on paper. She shows me how she will reach the challenge by doing one little step at a time.

She always has a plan. I am going to persuade you today to have a plan and teach you how to do a little each day to make it happen. My grandmother taught me none of these things could happen without prayer."

Debra's loud voice and broad gestures mastered the persuasion speech assignments one step at a time. Her grandmother's influence came out in most of her speeches. Debra had continual energy, yet she knew when to stop. She took nothing for granted but willingly tried new things.

One day when I was demonstrating how to do an informative speech, she raised her hand.

"Yes."

"Love your red high heels."

"Thank you." She taught me gratitude even if her timing was a little off.

Walter excelled on impromptu speeches. He could think on his feet and hold the class's attention. He was one of the reasons I enjoyed Woodson. In one of Walter's speeches about Mardi Gras, he revealed a few places outside of the projects to watch Mardi Gras parades. He explained about "understood boundaries," and that his people were not permitted to watch parades in some locations.

I wanted to touch his life and make a difference in his destiny. Each day he leaked a little more of his hopes and his private experiences, and that knowledge oiled my teacher machinery.

Joan and Debra told me stories of their elementary days. The treatment they received as Blacks was different than the White kids got. Their stories of these social injustices forced me to look through my "this-isn't-fair glasses."

After school, when Joan straightened my desk and helped me organize the room, she talked the whole time.

She explained memories of being taught to lower her eyes as she walked through the White neighborhood and only being allowed to walk on one side of the street.

"That is not fair. You look me or anyone else in the eye. You are bright and gifted."

"Mizz Bayronne, don't let our customs upset you."

"These understood rules are outdated and no longer legal."

As Joan erased the boards, she started giggling.

"Why are you laughing at me?"

"You remind me of my elementary teacher. She was always plantin' seeds in my brain. 'If you want more, you have to make good grades and have good behavior as part of your program.' You be planting seeds through those stories you tell us. Right?"

"I'm trying. I'm trying."

"You don't seem to notice Woodson has lots of kids not following the good-behavior program."

We both bent over laughing.

"You don't even see the craziness."

"Sometimes, true. Many things bother me and yet don't bother you."

"Like what?" She looked at me with questioning eyes.

"Like you havin' to walk on the Black side of Washington Avenue and never talk to the Whites."

"We know our boundaries Livin' in the Irish Channel neighborhood taught me lots of things early. I accept them. You should, too."

Joan Ellison, smart and mature, and responsible for her age. From the first week of school, she helped me and rolled her eyes when the guys smarted off to me. She laughed with me and sometimes at me when I dropped things or and stumbled in a pair of new high heels.

Her ability to organize anything convinced me she would go far. On Woodson dress-up day, she wore her

Sunday dress and best anklets and beamed with pride as she entered the classroom.

"Mornin'. You lookin' good on dress-up day."

"You're lookin' snazzy yourself, Miss Joan."

By the light in her eyes, I knew I lifted her day.

Joan made me comfortable speaking truths about our lives that came to the surface that usually stuck in my throat. We spit right out the injustices and blessings of living in a housing project. She shared it was hard not to have a mom. More mature than many of my college friends, she focused on having a purpose. *I hope to impact Joan and help her visualize her goals. If I can help her see her value, she will be ready to fly. Joan tethers me to my career. We have a symbiotic relationship. I need her, and I hope she needs me.*

Debra, Joan, and Walter were ready to learn and be all they could be. We had a common goal. I understood high winds were going to blow my hair and rustle my comfort zone. Yet, I would adjust my sail to guide me where I needed to be. Prayers helped me make that corrected adjustment. I wasn't as afraid of the storms anymore.

## LESSON 18

To most people I seem like the easy-going guy who just happens to be Black. My upbringing was not that rosy as I grew up in the only Black family in a White neighborhood. I was only five, but I remember the hate towards our family: eggs and tomatoes thrown at our house, skid marks driven through our lawn, and signs left in our yard that said, "Get out, niggers."

I had "the talk" with my dad. He taught me how to cope with being Black in a White world. He explained how to respond to that ugly behavior, how to respond and talk to the police, how to handle disrespectful people at school, and if I was touched, how to physically defend myself. In high school, I worked for a moving company. The guys called me nigger and made me move heavy things by myself, and then laughed at me. Those dark memories and feelings keep me guarded.

Today, I realize it doesn't matter how much money I make or how happy I make other people feel when I tour and perform my music. I am still being treated with discrimination—just for the color of my skin—even twenty years into the 21st century.—Everett Bradley, *Grammy Nominated Musician* (Bruce Springsteen, Bon Jovi, Quincy Jones)

While teaching third-hour speech, I heard a commotion in the hall. I expected another fight.

I yelped in surprise at the sight of four boys shouting and pulling Albert out of a locker. "What in the world?

Class, stay in your seats. I don't want you to gawk or get involved."

"You be careful, Mizz Bayronne," Debra shouted. "Those are bad boys out there."

I found Albert, one of my favorite students, curled in a fetal position on the ground, completely naked.

One of the larger guy's heehaws echoed through the halls. "Hey, little guy, what you doin' in the locker?"

In a brief moment of lunacy, the boys spewed hatred and aggression.

Albert gulped to a point of choking. His words were lost in this moment of terror. Then another guy slapped Albert's butt and kicked him. Albert cried louder and louder like a small child taking a beating for the first time. Nearby doors flew open as Albert's shrill scream pierced the hallway.

"Get up, little light boy," the bullies yelled.

As usual, I didn't know what to do.

"Baby, what is happening? Why that boy naked?" Sylvia called from the room next to mine.

"Not sure. I opened my door when I heard the teasing and cries." My heart ached at the sight of such misery.

Mr. Hughes's bellowing voice matched his loud clunking footsteps. "Go back to your classes now," he shouted at the ornery boys abusing Albert.

They continued to tease and torment their victim until Mr. Foster and Mr. Leonard grabbed two of them and locked their hands behind them like shackles. The men pushed them both toward the gymnasium office. The two other boys disappeared.

Mr. Hughes wrapped his sports coat around Albert and told him to go straight to the office. Dwarfed in the principal's tent of a coat, Albert raced to assistant principal's office.

I returned to my class rattled and sad. This speech class was well behaved. I could not hide my tears.

"Now, don't be sad," Joan counseled. "You'll get used to these Woodson fights. Don't mean much except to the one being beat up. The rest of us learn to stay out of the way."

Debra added, "And we keep our clothes on." The class giggled.

My love for them washed over me as I looked at these precious children. They knew love when they saw it.

"Come on now. Teach us by telling one of those Florida stories. This is your impromptu assignment." The class responded like they would in church.

"Yes, ma'am, teach us."

"Go on, now."

For the moment, I put aside the terrible incident outside my door and grasped the silver lining inside my classroom. "When I was eight years old, we moved to Ohio because my daddy needed a better job." The bell rang and the students filed out.

"Remember," Joan said on her way out. "You must finish your story tomorrow."

"All right, I will. Thank you for your help today." As she passed by me, I gave her a pat on her shoulder.

As the kids entered my last class on what seemed the longest Monday in my life, I swayed back and forth on my feet. I wanted time to fly because I couldn't wait to go home and see how our furniture looked in our little, green-carpeted apartment. I wrestled with my conscience overtime because I knew how blessed I had been my entire life.

What had happened to Albert? Were those boys paddled and expelled? Many of my students had no soft place to sit, no bright colored pillows, nor enough dinner to fill their bellies. Yet, they continued their lives and acted happy. I needed to learn from them that a sweet orange or a relaxed greeting could make a day complete. They had learned to hold suffering in one hand and joy in the other. *Thank you, Lord, for these kids who teach me so much.*

Thankfully, Drake was not in class this day, and the other students filed into their seats like little toy soldiers. *Maybe Friday's detention created a new mindset in them. Maybe I am looking at them in a different light today.* Regardless, they hurried and wrote their definitions, so I could read *Huckleberry Finn* to them.

As I finished the reading during the end of sixth hour, Mike Leonard came to my door and beckoned me into the hall.

"What now? Am I being asked to be a witness to what happened outside my room this morning?"

"Looks like things are going pretty well." Mike didn't say Bayronne anymore. He must have learned from Denny how to pronounce our name. "Hey, I know Mr. Baron called about being absent today and trying to obtain your furniture. The faculty took up a little donation for you."

In his large, outstretched hands, he held a fist full of bills and tried to hand them to me.

"What's this for?" I asked.

"Baby, we have all known hard times here at Woodson. At times life gets crooked, and you need help to straighten it out. This is the faculty helpin' you straighten."

"I can't take this."

"Now, we all have pride. I know it's hard," he insisted as he nudged the bills into my hands.

"I am overwhelmed. You really care about us."

"Of course, we do."

"The problem is with the moving company. We have the money, but we couldn't persuade the moving company to transport our few things to New Orleans. They said they needed a larger load to add to our small amount of furniture to make the trip cost effective."

"Sounds like our school system. They say 'maybe tomorrow,'" he quipped.

"I am so grateful. But we can't take this money."

"Yes, you can."

"The staff's outreach means more than the money." I stopped because my voice quivered, which meant I would cry any minute.

"We collected this for the Barons."

"Please, keep the money in a fund for others or return it to the owners. We are grateful." Warm tears rolled from my eyes as I tucked the money back in his hands. I lowered my head and wiped my tears on my sleeve.

Before me, I saw the gentlest man I had ever known. His giant frame could not contain all his kindness and love. It tumbled out with each word and smile.

"Thank you, thank you," I said.

"You sure now?" He flashed his wonderful Mike Leonard grin, which swallowed his whole jaw line.

I had almost forgotten my class. I turned around and looked at them sheepishly.

"You cryin'?" asked a student. "Why you sad?"

"Did something happen to Mr. Bayronne?"

"We be good. Don't cry," one of my sweet girls offered.

My sixth-hour class was showing me compassion and tenderness. I looked at them in a fresh way. I received their gift the only way I knew how—with tears overflowing. My tears magnified their hearts. I knew they needed me as much as I needed them.

The faculty's outreach and those students' concern ended my day with an exclamation point. Woodson was contouring our lives. The bell rang and the students hurried out, but most took time to say goodbye. A couple of the girls gave me a hug before they left.

Days like this affirmed why I chose teaching as my career.

I hurried out the door and ran to our Malibu. I couldn't wait to tell Denny about the best Monday of my life. Woodson's love came in the form of dollars today. Being wrapped in the arms of the staff felt wonderful, and the trip across the Mississippi Bridge was effortless. Before I knew it, I turned onto West Mary Poppins Drive.

I burst into our duplex energized and my voice boomed, "At last, this looks like a real house. Oh, this is my cream of the crop day." I embraced Denny with the vigor and love given to me an hour earlier. A current of love flowed between us.

"Man, I didn't think you'd be this excited about the furniture." Den embraced me and continued to admire our new look. "Do you like our new chair?"

"It looks wonderful. I have to tell you about this incredible day. Astonishing. So amazing," I walked into our bedroom. "Man, that bed looks inviting."

"What? I can't believe furniture is so important." As he spoke, I folded myself into his arms.

I sobbed, releasing all my hurts and disappointments over our move to New Orleans. I let go of the fear of my sixth-hour class and the problems in our marriage. I poured out my soul into his strong arms. I recognized Woodson loved us no matter what our skin color. Woodson staff and students had reached out and perfected my understanding of unconditional love. When I finally stopped crying, I told Denny of Mike's visit and the faculty's generous donation.

"They collected a pile of money to give to us?"

"Yes."

"Most of the coaches work an extra job after school. They've formed a little cleaning company, and they mop and wax businesses and apartments at night. They need money yet gave it to us."

"Do you know what this means? Woodson accepts us as we are." He rubbed his head and nodded his head. "I've suspected all along. Their gift is evidence they care about us."

"I've got to tell you another strange happening. While teaching sixth-period English, I heard a commotion outside my door. One of my favorite students, Albert, was lying naked on the floor after some bad boys pulled him out of his locker while he was trying to put on his gym clothes. He is so small he fit into the locker and was using it for a changing room."

"What in the world are you talking about? This makes no sense..He's one of my favorite students too. Never causes problems. In fact, Henri Todd and I bought him new gym clothes last Friday."

"Big boys were laughing and shouting at him. They pulled him out of the locker and kicked him."

"Why was he in the locker?"

"I'm going to find out more. I'm going to Mr. Hughes's office and ask what happened when I go to school tomorrow." I grinned at him. "Nothing but surprises at Woodson."

He grabbed me and gave me a hug. "Never a dull day." We both chuckled before our warm kiss.

# LESSON 19

I am a person who is unhappy with things as they stand. We cannot accept the world as it is. Each day we should wake up foaming at the mouth because of the injustice of things.—Hugo Claus

Monday had created a lot of opportunities for me to appreciate our marriage and the people we worked with at Carter G. Woodson. My despairing circumstances had turned around since the first week, and I enjoyed New Orleans as much as Denny.

As soon as my first hour and homeroom were over, I went to see Mr. Hughes.

"He's talking to a student right now, but as soon as he finishes, I will tell him you are here," Miriam, Mr. Hughes's secretary said in her soft, southern drawl.

The doorknob turned on Mr. Hughes's door, and he stepped out with a wilted young man beside him. "All right, son, I don't want to see you here again. Understand?"

"Yes, sir." The wide-eyed student left the office.

"Mr. Hughes, Mrs. Bayronne wishes to speak with you," Miriam said.

"What can I do for you today?"

"Would you explain why Albert was naked in the lockers by my room?"

"This incident seemed unusual even for Woodson." He invited me into his office where I took a seat. "Albert had received a new set of gym clothes from your husband and Mr. Todd. Since the boy doesn't receive many new clothes, he wanted to dress early for his gym class. Being proud of his gym shorts and shirt, he snuck out of Mrs. Mabry's class and slipped his small body into a nearby locker to change into his gym uniform. Albert didn't want to be late, so his 'toes would be on the line' when Mr. Baron blew his gym whistle."

"My husband's threats forced him to do it?"

"Mrs. Baron, it's not a threat. Mr. Baron wants all his students to understand his requirements for class and not be tardy."

I tried not to let my emotions show, but my hot, red cheeks showed my anger. *How could Denny make such rigid demands of his students? Albert had those beautiful eyelashes and velvety skin and sported cuteness. He didn't have a lot going for him ... poverty, slight frame, and bullies picking on him. What was Denny thinking?*

I curled my shaking hands in my lap. My voice cracked, and I squeaked, "I am so sad for Albert. The big kids treated him awful."

"That's how it is here at Woodson. There's a pecking order, like in nature."

His answer repulsed me. I couldn't decide whether I was angrier at Mr. Hughes's pecking order analogy or my husband's demands on his students. I needed to leave before my rage spilled out at my superior. "Thank you." I stood and hurried out his door.

He followed me. "What's wrong, Mrs. Bayronne?"

"Nothing, I'm fine."

Struggling to force my tight and strained legs to move one after the other, I returned to my room with my heart pounding in my ears and thumping in my tightened chest. Tears spilled onto my cheeks. *Who am I crying for? Albert or me?* I lowered my head and dripped my frustrations onto the old oak desk. How many tears could it hold?

By the end of my prep time, I'd composed myself. Those long, hard cries made me breathe more deeply. I listened to my soul while washing my emotions.

I knew Denny and Henri loved little Albert enough to buy him new gym clothes. I knew Denny followed the patterns of the rest of his team and set his rules in place to match theirs. My heart told me not to be mad, but my mind was stuck on Mr. Hughes's comments about pecking order. The bell buzzed, and my focus moved to my third-hour class.

# LESSON 20

Blacks, from the 1960s to the present, find happiness among their own family, their own children and friends. This is the essence of their survival under overt racism, glaring disparities, and humiliating treatment. In the 1960s, the White dominant world was the education system which included smelly books, used furniture, second-class citizen schools, and discriminating events where Black children in New Orleans collected the missed beads from Mardi Gras parades.

The Black culture needs more White people willing to take this evolving journey from Black prejudice to White privilege to White guilt to White fragility. If White people were willing to engage to learn about another culture other than their own, and become advocates for those underserved, they would truly become anti-racist.
—Dr. Joan Holmes, Special Assistant to the President for Equity and Special Programs at Hillsborough Community College, retired

My third-hour class settled by listening to announcements. I asked if anyone knew why Josie had been absent for over a week.

"She have sickle cell," answered Luna Belle.

"Is she at home?" I asked.

"No, she in the Charity Hospital. She be real sick."

"Why?"

"We inherit the disease. White folks don't. We can die of it," Luna Belle's eyes saddened and looked down. She seldom shared in class but clearly understood the danger of the disease. Later Joan told me Luna Belle's baby sister died from sickle cell.

I realized I knew nothing about this African-American disease. At lunch, I went to the library and checked out a book on sickle cell anemia. I learned the sickle-shaped cells couldn't absorb the protein needed to nourish the body and organs. Children go into crisis and must be hospitalized to keep it under control. Many of the Woodson kids didn't have the means to obtain proper medication and care. Charity Hospital was a lifeline. If neglected, this disease can kill. There is no cure, and the victims have severe pain and weakness when suffering a sickle-cell anemia attack. Luna Belle's report and experience lined up with the research I found.

I read more information, and my rueful acceptance of this terrible disease brought my thoughts back to Josie. *Would she die? Is she in a lot of pain? Why little Josie? She is sweet and loves to read. She doesn't have an aggressive bone in her body. She is as delicate as an apple blossom. Why did she have to suffer?*

Many of my students lived with the minimum of essentials. They ate their best meal at school. Friends and teachers created what they perceived as safety from their harsh world. Education created their future. It hit me. I, too, had become a significant support person to these students. Teaching meant taking time to care and encourage the individual. I had a new identity and needed more training and experience. My education never taught me how to teach the *whole* student.

Most days I experienced defeat, not because of my students, but because of the unjust system. I needed teaching strategies on how to reach slower learners. I needed more supplies. I bought as many teaching supplies as I could. I gave willingly, but my $5,400-a-year salary limited how much I could buy. Even more undeserved, the plague of the sickle cell trait upon my students' lives added an unknown factor to their future. After walking through the doors of Carter G. Woodson, I realized how unfair and unequal their lives were. These children had won my heart. They were drowning in overpowering circumstances. *Could I make a difference in discrimination—in any way? How would I comfort them? Be a stable force in their lives?*

I decided to start with Josie. I made a small package of supplies for her and stuck them in my purse.

Den was waiting in the car.

"Hi, husband. Could we go to the Charity Hospital and visit my student, Josie?"

"Sure. Get in and give me the scoop."

"That answer makes me love you more."

It took us some time to unravel the streets and find the Charity Hospital. The outside was barren of landscaping and in need of paint. As my anxiety rose, I couldn't catch my breath. We entered and asked for the room of Josie Bishon.

The White clerk looked at me from her cluttered desk. "She's in the colored part of the hospital. You'll have to climb the stairs to the third floor." She pointed us to the door that led to the upstairs entrance.

We followed one steep step at a time up the dark and gloomy staircase until we came to a door labeled Colored Ward. Those words whirred in my head. I hated labeling people by color as if they still wore shackles. In 1967, the color of one's skin dictated the places a person could get medical care. Biases and losses were daily parts of my students' lives. Nevertheless, I did not expect to see this extreme discrimination in the hospital.

As we walked down the hall, we saw the patients lined up military style in jam-packed rooms. I reached out to hold Denny's hand while we looked for Josie. As many beds as could fit into one corridor were lined together. Patients could almost touch each other and had no privacy. As they lay alone, moaning and dying, they were exposed to communicable diseases like tuberculosis. I swallowed hard and held my breath, trying to deny the smell of dysentery. My near exploding lungs forced me to gasp for air. Dirty bedpans and overflowing vomit pans were left unattended. The stench rose and triggered my stomach to tighten and turn. There weren't enough nurses to care for the sick. Patients waited their turn.

Vomit pooled in my throat. Grateful I hadn't eaten lunch, I swallowed back my urge to heave.

Denny and I had no one to ask directions, so we kept walking, looking into the overcrowded rooms.

"Look, I think I see Josie." I spotted a tiny golden-skinned child, her tiny body curled into a ball. Josie faced the door, and I recognized her large, sorrowful eyes.

"Josie. Josie."

I pulled Denny into the room, looking into his face for the first time since we entered the building. His skin had a greenish cast. He said nothing. His eyes looked like the patients who were drugged and focusing far away. I had not known Denny long enough to realize he did not handle hospital scenes well. He, too, was doing all he could not to heave or run back to the car.

"Josie? Josie Bishon?"

"Yes, ma'am. Whatcha doin' here?" Her weak voice was more of a squeak than words.

"We're here to see how you're doing."

"Awww, you shouldn't be here. White folks don't come in this ward."

The painful whine of the person next to her sent more awareness of suffering.

"I was worried about you."

"I be all right."

Whines turned to screams from the nearby patient. I could barely hear Josie. I bent to reach the fragile child and hugged her. As I held her to me, I could finger every bone in her tiny back. When I wrapped my arms around her, the hollowness reminded me of a dying tree. "Oh, Josie, I want you to be well and come back to school. I will pray for you."

"You be sweet, Mizz Bayronne."

"I know how you like to write and sketch. I brought you paper, a pencil, and some crayons, so you can color your drawings." *Will she get to color and draw? Is she dying? Please, Lord Jesus, touch this child with your healing hand. I know you love Josie even more than I.*

"You be sweet. Thank you, ma'am."

I closed my eyes trying to contain my tears. I kissed her on the cheek, and whispered, "Be better soon. Jesus loves you and so do I.

We left her room and rushed to the exit. As we made our way out of the building, I hurried yet held my breath. I could taste the terrible smells of sickness on my tongue. Once again, vomit filled my mouth and throat. I swallowed hard and breathed in fresh air as we exited the building.

When we reached our car, Denny spoke. "I had no idea it would be so bad."

"Me either." The tears began to flow. I could no longer hold them back. Little Josie deserved so much more than this. She was precious to me, and sickle cell had tied her into a knot I could not untie. I blinked my eyes to bring me back to the safe place next to Denny.

Silent on our drive home, my mind tried to sort social truths I had never considered until we moved to New Orleans. My White skin allowed me opportunity and privilege. For the first time in my life, I was ashamed and agonized over being a part of this racist elitism. Amid my crown of gloom, I visualized Joe, the custodian, whose caring eyes brought a familiar feeling of love and understanding. His voice reminded me of the tender sound that nudged me to hear God's words and obey. Denny's warm arms wrapped around me, enhanced our partnership, and redirected my stress and melancholy.

# LESSON 21

I remember past moments. Catalytic events in my life, happened when I least expected them, often in my younger years. Those prejudiced words and situations caused me, as a Black child, to know that stereotyping, partiality, and the sin of racism was real, nearer to me than I had thought or realized. Those racist events impacted me and shaped me into the way I now engage with others, respond to situations, and see the world.—Geoffrey L. King, Author, Pastor at Fellowship Missionary in Fort Wayne, Indiana

"Mizz Bayronne, come back to us. Whatcha thinkin'?" The voice of one of my students broke through my thoughts.

"Ma'am, your attendance is not posted on the door. The office needs it now, please." The administrative helper's insistence snapped me out of the indelible imagery of the dire hospital situation

"Oh, I'm sorry. Students, anyone else absent beside Josie?"

"No, ma'am, we all be here but her," answered Miranda. Debra and Miranda reached out to their peers daily, welcoming them into their fortified happy place. I learned from Debra how to bring others closer. When I didn't understand how to communicate or was clumsy in understanding cultural differences, I watched her. She did it naturally.

While I filled out the attendance slip, I listened to Mr. Todd's announcement. "Due to inclement weather, there will be no physical education outside today."

Daily, Woodson's staff adapted to unexpected hardships. Even though the Woodson way was difficult, the staff and kids were not only teaching me how to accept the unforeseen but to persevere through adverse circumstances. *Was this colorblind education a lack of the school board's support? Or did the students draw a short straw of life?*

"Today, let's try to understand Jim's plight of finding freedom." The students quieted, and I began reading *Huckleberry Finn.*

"Mizz Bayronne," Miranda raised her hand, "why don't you read what is written? He say nigger, right?"

"Yes, but I can't say the N-word. It doesn't give you honor."

"Hey, it's what the author wanted to say. You have to write your own book if you want to leave it out." Miranda spoke literary truth, and I knew she was correct. I had no right to change Mark Twain's dialogue.

"You're right, Miranda, but I can't speak the N-word."

"Guess you'll have to write Mark Twain and tell him."

The class laughed in soft harmony. They had learned to cooperate by softening their former boisterous laughter. My smaller third hour class was easier to handle and enjoyable.

Since my first week of teaching, my attitude had changed in so many ways, especially concerning my students. Walter's kindness and readiness to serve me pulled at my heart. I needed Lily's sweetness as well as Debra's boldness and wisdom. Jerome's humor and stating of the obvious lifted my mood each day. While teaching me unconditional acceptance, my kids, especially those who could not read, were molding me—their college-educated teacher—into a stronger, wiser educator. Deep in my heart, I thought they knew I loved them too. Maybe that is how love works—feeling blessed and being blessed. Whatever was happening, this student-teacher reciprocation was working. My passion to help more was traded for my students' eagerness to learn more.

My life at Woodson was a perpetual card game. When I was dealt aces, I rejoiced in my understanding or ability to reach out. Other days, I didn't know how to play my hand. Woodson played by hard, ruthless rules. I would have been thrown out of the game if it weren't for Walter being my bridge to his culture and the New Orleans' way, and Debra insisting I have a plan and a prayer. Mike's consistent charismatic love and Henri Todd's wisdom and kindness lifted my spirit when I most needed hope.

Because of the students, teachers, and administrators—I learned to play my hand smarter and faster. Some obstacles could beat me—disrespectful students with street-smart experience, the unconcerned, shrewd school board, and the heartless, discriminating practices of the South. Apathy would always be an obstacle. I was determined to play the best I could each day.

# LESSON 22

To live without feeling or exciting sympathy, to be fortunate without adding to the felicity of others, or afflicted without tasting the balm of pity, is a state more gloomy than solitude; it is not retreat, but exclusion from mankind. Marriage has many pains, but celibacy has no pleasures.— Samuel Johnson

"Thanks for helping me clean our apartment. You're the best." I wanted Denny's help, and he had offered to clean the bathroom and to vacuum without me asking.

"Best what?" Denny asked.

"Best husband, best lover, best friend," and before I could finish my sentence, his soft kiss warmed me. He continued stroking my back.

"I'm so nervous. I want our dinner to be perfect for the LeBlancs."

"It will be perfect. You're cooking it." This time I kissed him long and hard.

I finished arranging the fresh flowers in my centerpiece as the doorbell rang.

Denny opened the door for Mr. and Mrs. LeBlanc. "Welcome. Pleased you found us."

I motioned toward the sitting area. "Please have a seat."

Our guests sat close together on the couch. The LeBlancs were respected for their community support of addressing equality of the races. He was a great guy who taught me day by day a little more about the Cajun and Creole cultures.

"Your home is so cozy." Mrs. LeBlanc's elegant southern dialect and soft toned voice settled us all.

I asked about her family, and she shared their children's names and interests. "Would you excuse me a minute? Need to check our bread."

"Something good is happening in the kitchen. I can smell it," added LeBlanc.

Seeing the French baguettes were a delicate brown, I announced dinner. "You all come to the kitchen."

Denny pulled out the chair for Mrs. LeBlanc. We had not hosted anyone from New Orleans. Because we enjoyed company, we wanted our hospitality to be welcoming.

After serving herself, Mrs. LeBlanc waited until we all had helped ourselves. She took one bite of squash. "Your yellow-squash casserole melts in my mouth."

LeBlanc agreed, nodding, his mouth too full to speak.

"Would you share your recipe with me? And please, call me Susan."

"I'd be honored."

"This chicken is crisp like we Southerners like it. Denny, you are a fortunate man."

I returned Ray's affirmation with a sheepish smile. The legs and thighs were overly browned and the meat a little dry.

Denny's eyes sparkled as he smiled at me. The LeBlancs' encouragement gave me new confidence in my hospitality skills.

"Sandi likes to give us all heart failure." Ray winked.

"What do you mean?" Susan glanced at me.

"About three weeks ago, she decided to detain her students after school. We all were concerned for her. She might look and act sweet, but she has a tiger in her."

"Ray, be polite."

"No, it's a compliment from anyone who works at Woodson. The detained class included a real bad apple, Drake, a seventeen-year-old with a record. Our little tiger, Sandi, stood in her doorframe and would not let anyone pass, including Drake. Thank the Lord, he decided to crawl out the window instead of barreling right through her. And the rest of her students sat frozen in place when they saw her stand up to Drake."

"Oh, my, you must be careful. A few of those students are positively dangerous." Susan wiped her mouth on her napkin. "All they've known is violence all their lives."

"I'd say Drake's a lost cause. The word on the street is he's back in jail for allegedly killing a woman. Supposed to have happened on the same Friday you detained him."

I swallowed hard and stared at LeBlanc. "I had no idea."

"We kept it from you, so you wouldn't have more fears, or perhaps even leave Woodson. We don't want to lose you two."

I let out a long slow breath.

"Don't feel like you are in any way responsible," volunteered Ray. "Drake chose the wrong road long before you two got here. But you need to keep your eyes open and not take risks. Drake is bad to the core. Most of us are relieved he's gone. You gave him a chance to do right, but he could have easily turned on you. A couple of us silently hung around until all the kids were out of the building."

"Thanks for telling me. My heart goes out to those kids. But rest assured, we aren't going anywhere. Woodson is our home now." Looking at the seriousness in my eyes, Denny popped out of his chair. "Hey, let's lighten up this conversation. How about a piece of pecan pie? I spent hours making it today."

We finished our dessert and chicory coffee and moaned in satisfaction. My pie did not compare to Mama's, but even with brown on the edges of the crust, it was tasty. We shared more about our adjustment to Woodson and living in the Big Easy.

Over an after-dinner drink, LeBlanc reminded us he had planned a traditional celebration with lots of drinking and dancing. "You are going to love the principal's birthday party next weekend."

We walked them to their car and thanked them for coming over the bridge for dinner. We headed back arm-in-arm into our little duplex, loving each other and our evening with the LeBlancs.

A week after the LeBlancs' visit, I meandered into the school lounge surprised to see so many people. The sweet odor of cinnamon, sugar, and yeast filled the air. The Woodson cafeteria ladies had baked a giant, iced cinnamon roll to celebrate Mr. Bergeron's birthday. Chicory coffee and a hunk of one of those gooey rolls began our day with joy.

"Hey, you coming to the party after school?" Edna cupped her hand around her ear as if she needed to hear our answer.

"Of course, but we have no idea where to go. We'll need some directions."

LeBlanc piped up. "We got it all taken care of, baby. Dennis can follow Henri Todd. We're leaving right after school. So, no detentions today. You hear?"

I saluted him and promised to leave right after the sixth-hour bell.

LeBlanc became a guiding star in his community because of his wisdom and smart choices. I enjoyed his stories with vivid descriptions of New Orleans. I learned his natural gravitas and storytelling transferred well to local politics, and he was sought after as a public speaker. The light color of his skin opened opportunities to him other dark-skinned men were denied. Henri Todd once told Denny if a Black man resembled the color of a grocery sack or lighter, he would be more apt to be accepted by Whites and Blacks. LeBlanc's beige skin with freckles on his cheeks gave him a boy-like appearance. His laugh generated smiles in those around him. When his glasses slipped onto the bridge of his nose, and he peered over them, he reminded me of a watchful professor.

Even within the Black community, skin color mattered. This paradox surprised me. The lighter-skinned Creoles advanced more easily and received more praise. Staff often remarked about a light-skinned child being brighter or more handsome than his black-skinned peers. Mr. LeBlanc had been accepted as a token in his political positions in the city government. The staff put him on a pedestal and saw him as a future leader of New Orleans.

I looked at the cinnamon roll in my hand. Denny and I both kept gaining weight. When I went through the lunch line, one of the cooks always looked at me and smiled. "You lookin' pale today. Here's an extra helpin'." Denny merited the same extras, and we both noticed our clothes were uncomfortable especially at our waistlines. We continued dining on rich food and talked about dieting tomorrow.

Because I had included group work and summaries of the week's lessons in each class, my day vanished quickly. I gathered my things after the sixth-hour bell. Sixth-hour's class had demonstrated respect and improved in attention since I'd enforced the detention. Nonetheless, I felt a cold shiver whenever I walked past Drake's vacant desk.

I stopped at the bathroom to freshen up and hurried out to the car.

"Why didn't you come right out? Denny asked. "We have to hurry. We are following Henri to the Zulu Club."

"I did hurry."

"Shut the door and let's go." He waved at Henri.

We followed Henri down back alleys and on streets we didn't know existed. We crept past dilapidated shotgun houses and elegant mansions surrounded by ornate iron gates.

"Where are we going for this party? Why didn't they have cake and punch in the faculty room?"

"Because, Henri says, this is a big deal," Denny answered.

At last, Henri pulled in behind a building and parked. We did the same. I slid my hand into Denny's when we were out of the car. "I love being married to you."

"I love you too, sweet pea."

Henri gave three knocks and then two quick knocks on the door. The social studies teacher, Mr. Gritton, opened the door. "Welcome, Barons," he said as we stepped into a large, dimly lit room complete with a dance floor. Mr. Gritton's gray hair and curved back reflected his senior status. His eyes mirrored his gentleness. "This place is one more of Woodson's accomplishments." His deep laugh reminded us how much he loved his workplace. He encouraged the Woodson spirit in all the kids and staff.

As we entered, we were welcomed by a little jazz quartet playing New Orleans R&B, warming up for the party.

"Let me snag you a drink, Sandi," Ray LeBlanc offered. "Do you want scotch or Jack Daniels?"

"Scotch and water would be fine." I looked at Denny with big eyes. "I'm sure this is not quite the punch and cake principal parties we have in the North."

"Another reason to love New Orleans."

With drinks in hand, we hung close together until the rest of the staff came. Mr. Bergeron presented his charismatic self—smiling, hugging, and dancing with his staff. This amazing birthday bash wowed us. There were no presents. Instead, they celebrated with laughter, food, and drink.

Layers of boiled crawfish were served on one of the tables. Friends called them crawdads, and others called them mud bugs. Because of my Florida roots, I knew they were a fresh-water crustacean and a staple of Cajun cooking. Folks were sucking out the heads and smacking their lips, applauding the crawfish freshness.

"You eatin' crawfish?" Henri gave me a hug.

"Going to try."

"You, Denny?"

"Naw, I'm sticking with my muffuletta." He held up a half-eaten ham and salami sandwich oozing Swiss and provolone cheeses from the giant bun. He clinked whiskey glasses with Henri, and they grinned at each other like long-lost brothers.

I waved at Sylvia across the dance floor standing next to Edna. They beckoned me over. "Denny, I'm going over to see my friends."

"Come find me when you finish your drink with Henri." I crossed the floor greeting many of my colleagues as I made my way to Sylvia and Edna. It looked like most of the faculty was here.

"Girl, this is what New Orleans is all about." Sylvia gave me a hug. "Now, let's boogie."

Edna had the beat and joined several of the staff in moving to the music with a smooth rhythm. She became the music as she joined the circle of dancers—in a Cajun zone of moving what mattered.

In contrast, I was self-consciously conservative and stiff. Once again, when in a spotlight, I became uncomfortable.

Denny joined in the dancing circle and showed off royally. He used all his moves, and the ladies loved his energy. His sexy dancing had attracted me to him when we dated.

"Nice moves," Edna said, and took Denny's hand. They moved to the middle of the circle.

"Come on, Edna, give us a turn with Yankee boy." Other women teachers were vying for their turn. "Dennis, you are quite the dancin' man. Okay, ladies, your turn." Edna winked at him on her way to find another partner.

Denny, on the other hand, relished the spotlight. He smirked at his partner, wiggled his butt and strutted his stuff.

As I looked on from the sidelines, anger and jealousy gnawed at me. *Why is he showing off like this? We have only been married a few months, and he is flirting with other women. I thought Edna was my friend, and now she is going after my man.*

I watched Denny out of the corner of my eye as he continued his seductive dance moves with other teachers. I pasted on a fake smile and danced with Mike, Henri, and other staff members. My wifely duty told me to appear to have fun, but I was seething. Then Mr. Bergeron said he wanted a birthday dance with me. I let him lead because he was holding me so close. I was uncomfortable but tried to follow his sways and turns.

At last, I managed to dance with Denny and asked him to slow his drinking since we had a long drive home across the Mississippi.

He kissed me on the cheek and pulled me tight to him. "Come on, baby, loosen up. We'll be fine."

I pulled away at his reckless, carefree response, but we continued our moves to our 1960 jitterbug bop. I wanted to enjoy our dancing, but my internal tension built until I thought I would explode.

The revelry continued until long after midnight when, at last, Denny's intoxicated, animated behavior was subdued. He ate only to counter his high alcohol content. I knew I drank over my limit as well because of my dizziness.

"Oh, Dennis, she's a movin' and a swayin'. You gettin' lucky tonight, man." LeBlanc continued his mantra of coaxing and encouraging Denny.

"Yeah, we're headin' out now," Denny answered with a broad smile.

"Thanks, Mr. Bergeron. We enjoyed your celebration," I lied.

Mr. Bergeron gave me a warm hug and thanked us for coming. I don't remember much. We were weaving as we drove, following unfamiliar alleys and back ways. Trying to find our way to St. Charles Street was more difficult inebriated.

At last, finding St. Charles, Den turned onto the busy street and drove our usual route to the bridge and home. "Hey, the best principal's birthday party ever. They know how to party."

"I'm really mad at you. You ruined my night."

"What are you talkin' about?" His innocent tone really irritated me.

"You doin' all those dance moves with my friends. How dare you trespass."

"Aww, honey, we were just havin' fun."

"I didn't like watching you flirt and come on to Edna. She is sexy. You like her thin body better than my widening waistline."

"We were movin' and feelin' the music, not flirting. Get off your high horse."

I began to cry. The alcohol and my attitude launched a dramatic, eardrum-shattering tantrum until Den pulled into our driveway. I jumped out of the car, unlocked the front door, ran into the bedroom, and slammed the door. I didn't want anything to do with Denny Baron.

The next morning, I realized Denny had not slept in our bed. I remembered our fight and how mad I had been the night before.

Stumbling to the bathroom, I washed my face with cold water. My stomach tightened. Waves of nausea swept over me. I held my head trying to stop the dizziness and restore balance in my spinning brain. A pair of sad eyes, underlined with dark circles, stared back at me from the mirror. I saw a wretched image of a woman who had not only consumed too much liquor but had also let envy consume her. Jealousy had controlled my feelings last night.

I cracked open the door and slipped out to see Denny, still asleep on the couch, with no covers or a comfortable pillow. *He deserves it. Maybe at the next party he will dance only with me.*

I brewed a pot of coffee. I sat eating my dry toast alone, feeling sorry for myself. Then Denny placed a soft kiss on my neck. "Honey, I hated sleeping without you."

"Yeah, you probably wished you were sleeping with Edna," I snapped.

"Come on. I didn't do anything so bad."

"You hurt me. You didn't care you weren't dancing with me."

"I think you hurt yourself."

I threw my toast across the table. Hot coffee sloshed over the table and me. I stormed to the bedroom and slammed the door.

I flopped onto the bed and cried. When Denny didn't follow, I cried louder and beat on the pillow, kicked my feet, and squalled like a four-year-old having a tantrum. Still no response. *What do I need to do to gain his attention? Is he sitting in there scared, or is he laughing at me?* I got up, opened the door, and shouted, "I don't want to be married to you."

Silence.

I stepped out of the bedroom to see our back door open, revealing the closed screen door.

*Why, he's not even home. Did he go jogging—in the middle of our argument? Men are morons. I hate how stupid they act. Why can't they be sensitive and reasonable like we women?*

I took a long, hot shower to cleanse my tarnished spirit. My thoughts about our argument laid my existence as bare as my body. Tired of fighting at school and at home. *I am lonely. I want out.* Even though I had limited logic at this time, I understood I reacted as I had seen my mother react. *How had this happened? She always ran when she couldn't live life as she wanted. I want to run, too.*

Exhausted, went back to bed and drifted off into a deep sleep. I never heard Denny return and shower.

I woke to him patting and rubbing my shoulder. "Let's not fight again. I'm sorry if I hurt you. I didn't mean to."

The very words I needed to hear.

We made up with passion equal to the fury we had fought with a few hours earlier. Marriage was proving to be much more difficult than I could have ever known. Giving and sharing forced me to become someone new. Sharp knives stabbed me daily, making me aware of pain and suffering in the Black community. Briars poked me when Den and I clashed. Scrapes and bruises from weakness and mistakes exhausted me. Being carved by humanity and marriage were sculpting me into a new woman.

# LESSON 23

The barricade closes the street but opens the way.
—Graffiti during French student revolt, 1968

Sylvia slipped through my door and watched me grading. "Hello, sweet friend. What's on your agenda today?"

Her eyes sparkled and smiled. She told me the traditions of Mardi Gras had become rules written on a holy tablet. Her New Orleans' soft vocal tones were as harmonious as the street musicians on their old-time banjos. She never hurried to tell her story as opposed to when I excitedly told her of a classroom calamity in a fast-clipped pattern. I looked forward to her coming into my room and offering professional advice. I cherished our relationship and understood she held me close to her heart.

Instead of the typical expected dialogue of two English teachers, Sylvia brought me unexpected news. "Could you come over to Mama's Saturday? She'll teach you to cook Cajun."

"Really? Your mama would be willing to teach me to make shrimp gumbo and red beans? She won't mind me being in the middle of her kitchen?"

"Naw, she really likes you. The last time you and Denny came to dinner, you told her over and over how you couldn't stop eating her amazing dinner."

"I've never tasted shrimp creole so delicious. I would be honored if you would ask your mama if I can study Cajun cooking by her masterful hands."

"Masterful hands?" She laughed out loud at my choice of words. "Come on over for po' boys at lunch. We'll work together later on cookin' Cajun for dinner—with Mama's masterful hands."

"We'll be there about noon." I smiled and waved goodbye to Sylvia. We were both exhausted from our tough week at school.

I straightened my desk, packed essays into my bookbag, closed my door, and walked to meet Denny.

"Hey, how's your day?"

He looked at the steering wheel, making no eye contact. No answer to my question.

"What happened?" He shrugged and started the car for our trip over the bridge. "I hurt for these kids. Really hurt."

"Me too."

"Today, I had outside lunch duty. I watched the kids shooting at the disintegrated basketball hoop. One of them had an orange—a fresh one from the vendor in the alley." Denny began to repeat the conversation he had overheard.

"Man, shore looks good."

"Sure is."

"Where'd you git it?" A young fellow eyed the fruit as if it were a queen's treasure.

"Here, have a piece," offered the kid holding the juicy treat.

Denny continued, "So, five guys circled around the kid with the orange. He gave them each a section. They savored it like a twenty-ounce steak."

"Then what happened?"

"Don't you see? They have so little yet share so willingly. I know they were all hungry. The kid who bought the orange probably used his only dime. These kids know a lot more about life than we know at twenty-two and twenty-four."

I scrunched by his side, laid my head on his shoulder, and we sang with the radio, "All you need is love, all you need is love."

Denny and I knew about passionate love, but we were witnessing and learning sacrificial love at Woodson each day. Even though those kids had trials and troubles, they knew how to make do. One shared orange could bring a slice of sweetness to many.

The traffic crawled. Friday workers were eager to return home and hung onto the bumper in front of them. The boats on the Mississippi had a much better system. They moved and passed each other with ease. The bridge became our marital incubator. It was our time to patch things up and listen to each other's heart when we were not fighting.

"Have you forgiven me for my temper tantrum after the principal's party?"

"I guess so."

"I love you so much. I am jealous. I admit it," I said. "You are mine, all mine."

"I forgive you. Love you too. "

"What else?"

"I love you more than a pony costs plus a bushel of gold."

"Me too, honey, more than a bushel of gold. Guess what?"

"I'm scared to ask. What?"

"Tomorrow we are going to Sylvia's mom's house."

"Why?"

"I'm going to learn how to make red beans and rice."

"Hope it's as good as the cafeteria's. I love their Monday beans."

"This New Orleans' cookin' is the best cuisine I ever tasted. I can't wait to learn Cajun cooking"

Laughing healed and bonded our marriage. We pulled into our driveway with the anticipated respite in our comfortable little apartment.

The next morning, the alarm rang way too soon. Denny, a man of routine, left for his morning jog.

I enjoyed chicory coffee, thinking how at the Cafe' Du Monde people of every type gathered to drink this warm brew. People from all over America and Europe visited the cafe established in 1862. Sometimes there would be a table filled with women in glittery dresses, or men in business suits would share a table. Half the enjoyment of visiting this famous tourist place was eavesdropping and people watching.

Den and I made a point of going there at least once a week. We had created some traditions we both enjoyed. Pouring my second cup of coffee, I recalled last evening, I had wearily plunked on the couch after dinner and napped on and off till bedtime, leaving the dinner dishes for morning. This was another pattern I'd developed. On Friday nights, I became a napper if we were home. It was interesting how our new habits became our rituals. *Teaching seems to have a way of both stimulating and sapping my energy.* I cherished the idea that Den and I were creating our own little niches together.

While Denny jogged, I relaxed with coffee and straightened the house. A refreshing long shower and thinking of going to Sylvia's mother's cooking session gave me reason to search for blank recipe cards. Filled with excitement, I looked forward to our Cajun celebration.

Soon Denny and I were back on the Mississippi Bridge. I threw a kiss at him, and he returned his love by rubbing my knee. This Saturday filled us with joy, and we chuckled about how much we liked our little apartment and our neighbors. We were silent for a while. *I wish our relationship could be like this all the time. Happy.*

We arrived at Sylvia's mother's home where the aroma of garlic and shrimp made my stomach growl with hunger.

"I smell the hot sauce and shrimp. Yummy." Denny gave Sylvia's mother a hug. We met her dad and brother, and they seemed as kind and gentle as Sylvia.

Her mama had prepared po' boys and stacked them on a large platter. Heaping mounds of shrimp with creole sauce filled the French baguettes. My mouth watered looking at our lunch of potato salad and a bowl of dark green collards and filled pedestal glasses of wine. Sylvia motioned us to sit at the dining room table, decorated with a well-used tablecloth and family style dishes.

"Have you ever tasted anything this delicious?" I asked Denny.

He shook his head no because he couldn't answer with his mouth chucked full of goodness.

Sylvia's husband gave a sexy grin and teased. "Mama is why I married Sylvia."

After his comment, everyone agreed that was a good reason to get married.

"After lunch Mama wants to teach you to make roux, first."

"I don't even know what rue is. Rue? We have to lament before we cook? I don't understand." My statement initiated more chuckles from Sylvia's husband, Adam, and her brother, John.

I helped clear the table, and the men excused themselves to the living room to watch football. Sylvia's dad turned on the small television. As I peeped through the doorway, I could see Denny grinning from ear to ear. Football and great food were his ingredients for a perfect day.

Sylvia tied an apron on me, and Mama beckoned to follow her. She handed me an onion, a green pepper, a few stalks of celery, a handful of garlic cloves, and a knife.

"Now, chop these vegetables 'bout the same size. Not too big and not too fine."

I did as Mama directed, wondering if my pieces were the right size.

"You doin' fine, baby. Never forget onions, green peppers, and celery. These are the holy trinity of all cooking."

"Here is the jewel of Louisiana cooking teaching how to make roux as her first lesson." Sylvia hugged her Mama and called her "My special jewel."

"First, honey, take two heapin' wooden spoons of lard and bring it up to hot."

Next, I watched Mama add flour to the steaming lard. She stirred it into a smooth, brown sauce. "This is the beginnin' of red beans, jambalaya, shrimp creole, and gumbo."

*Why that looks easy. I can do that.*

"Mama, how about giving Sandi a try at making a batch of roux?"

"I'm ready." In my eagerness, I grabbed another iron skillet, dumped in an over-heaping spoon of lard, and started cooking. The grease got hot too quickly, so I hurried to add the flour. It burned and smoked. Mama grabbed the skillet. "This first step is difficult."

"And I failed."

"No, child, you learned the first lesson. Don't burn the roux." All three of us cackled loud and strong at her comment. She wiped out the skillet with salt. "Now, try again."

I took my time and measured two heaping tablespoons of lard. She stood by and watched as it heated. "Now, baby, add the flour."

I did as she said. Then she took the spoon and stirred constantly. "See, use the flat side. Keep a stirrin'. Make it slick and shiny."

We added the chopped vegetables to the roux, and those delicate flavors simmered together.

"The beans are a boilin'." She had soaked the beans overnight and, after lunch, had put them on the stove to cook until the ham hocks were tender. Now, she turned the beans to low and removed the hocks.

"Add the chopped vegetables into the beans. Next, add sliced Andouille sausage and let the soup simmer. We be eatin' those beans later."

*What a great day I'm having. Sylvia's family treats me like family. It's like I'm one of them. Her Mama's directions are simple and clear. She has filled me with the love of cooking. It's easy with her as my mentor.*

After cleaning the kitchen, we joined the guys in the living room. Denny and I enjoyed our visit to a home complete with warm hearts, good food, and laughter. We thanked Sylvia's family for feeding us and teaching me to cook Cajun. Denny and I left with contented hearts, full bellies, and a container of Mama's red beans and rice.

Each time we experienced this New Orleans' hospitality and love, Denny and I became more comfortable and ingrained into the culture. *Perhaps, this is where we belong.* I learned to leap over roadblocks or remove obstacles through alternative ways of thinking about the circumstances, trying to find a road which suited me.

I, like Huck Finn, was "learnin' and adaptin'" to the ways of Louisiana.

## LESSON 24

A change came over the spirit of my dream. —Lord Byron

The weeks passed, and I appreciated the cooler weather as we moved into the middle of October. We scheduled our weekends for exploring the city and its historical places as well as sitting in Jackson Square, one of our favorite tourist attractions in the French Quarter. The square, located across from the river, provided walking paths, lovely foliage, and Andrew Jackson's statue. We often walked from Jackson Square to nearby Café Du Monde for a cup of chicory coffee and their famous beignets smothered in powdered sugar. These fried fritters were so tasty but also messy as most of the powdered sugar ended up on our clothes and in our laps.

"Why do we love this mess so much?" I asked Den.

"Because we are learning messes are as much a part of our marriage as our warm and cuddling times together."

Den's remark surprised me. It was romantic yet profound. *Was he turning into the romance novel husband I hoped for? Was he really working to make our marriage life smoother?*

Watching the tourists amused us. Local guides would explain the history of Pirates Alley while artists painted the view on their canvases. We could not afford one of their oil paintings. I wanted one so much but our budget, or lack of, said no. Eventually, Mom and Dad visited us and realized how this square had become a frame for our romance and new love. Before they left, they gifted us with a painting of Pirates Alley. We hung the painting in our living room. Each time I passed it, I remembered our special kiss and being in Denny's arms. We had meaningful dialogues we shared on our special bench. Maybe this was a visual symbol declaring I was loved.

We held hands and focused on each other. Before we were married, we chose New Orleans because we wanted a magical city to romance us as we romanced each other.

On the Square, we listened to a Black poet recite "Dreams" by Langston Hughes as a blues player moaned on his trombone the powerful line, "He did a lazy sway, he did a lazy sway, to the tune of those Weary Blues." The sadness of those notes spoke to my soul. I saw the life of a "broken-winged bird cannot fly" each day. Skin color crippled my students. Dark skin was a genetic cage in America. How could they become what they desired? Their dreams rotted in the sun. They could exist in Magnolia Project and Third Street, but they were constrained there and never allowed to trespass onto the White man's side of the street.

As I listened to blues and poetry, I remembered my student, Joan. She explained to me one day about her accepted areas. "We stay on our side of the street. We not allowed on the White side. Know our boundaries, and we keep to ourselves. On Washington Avenue, we walk on the Black side and don't talk to the Whites on the other side."

The music conveyed to my heart the weariness of the Black man's plight, living in America "with a dream deferred rotting in the sun like a raisin." Langston Hughes had known a rotting dream and voiced it well in his poetry. His words and my observations created a permanent heaviness in me. *Why couldn't my students have the same privileges as the White kids?*

"What are you thinking?" Denny leaned close. "You are a thousand miles away."

"I know. I can't stop thinking about Joan's words. She is talented and bright. Yet, she might as well be in a straightjacket the way White society has confined her choices."

"Come on, sweets, lighten up. Let's go." Kissing me sweetly, he whispered, "I love you. Be happy."

As we walked toward the river to watch the ferryboats, Denny disclosed he had to tell me something. We found a bench, and he started to confess a failure in his class. "I blew it. I was so embarrassed."

"What? You know how to teach and are comfortable with your team."

"Not on Friday. It was my turn to oversee of the students. I led them to the auditorium to start the day's film. Each gym teacher takes a class to supervise while the other three go to the lounge."

"You mean the other teachers have free hours while you stay with the kids?"

"Yep, and this was the first time the staff left me alone with over a hundred kids. I thought it an easy task. I watched the staff supervise for a month. I turned out the lights. Instead of the kids watching the movie, they started throwing spitballs. This led to loud laughing, slaps, trash talk—and soon I lost control."

"And how did you regain class order?"

He looked at his feet. He spoke slowly feeling his way. "I really blew it. I couldn't pull them back, so I left the students and ran to the faculty room. I got LeBlanc, and he came into the room, flipped on the lights, and bellowed, 'Sit in your seats, now.'"

158 | SANDRA BAKER BARON

Still looking away, Denny rubbed his hands together. I could see how much this upset him. "I don't have respect from the kids. I want it."

I put my arms around him and hugged him big and hard, like Sylvia's Mama had hugged me. "It'll come, honey. It'll come."

His disclosure exposed a lack of confidence. Denny seldom acknowledged his true feelings. He tucked in his thoughts like a handkerchief in a lapel pocket. He wanted to look good and be right.

"Well, I'm not using spiders like you do to hold my students' attention. I hate those crawly things." We both gave each other a suspicious sideways squint and choked on our laughter. We needed the tension release. I was grateful when Denny shared his deeper expectations and disappointments. I wanted to know what his thoughts were and what pleased him and gratified him.

*On our date nights, we both enjoy romantic movies like* The Graduate *and* Camelo*t. I desire his affection. I want him not to care if I don't pick up my makeup from the bathroom cabinet or hang up my clothes. I desire surprises, flowers, and unexpected lovemaking. Maybe that is Hollywood and not reality. How do I learn to separate truths from expectations?*

Denny hated my magazines on the table and other clutter. He seldom breathed deeply other than jogging. I knew why. Breathing long calming deep breaths allowed his feelings to surface. Relaxing yoga breaths created opportunities to let down walls he had built for our protection. He buried hurts and disappointments. He prioritized wearing a strong outer garment, and losing control in class Friday defeated and upset him.

The lonesome sound of the riverboat horn reverberated. Its rhythmic lament reminded me of my bellowing. Crying was easier than changing.

We had an enriched weekend, and I learned more about my husband. Self-disclosing and date nights were my favorite activities. When we left our bench in Jackson Square, we promised we would return soon.

# LESSON 25

As a young African American boy, I learned that a teacher was the one person I could trust. Knowing there would be peace and help each day at school was great comfort when the world around me grew chaotic. My teachers gave me courage, hope, and strength, which sparked my imagination. They helped me think and dream beyond myself and gave me the confidence to know that I could be as good as anyone else in my class. —Reverend Gregory S. Dyson, Vice President for Intercultural Leadership at Taylor University.

Monday already! Teaching duties called, as did the Mississippi Bridge. Each time I saw the twins, Lily and Millie, they grabbed my heart. I wanted them to stay motivated and realize an education could create a new world for them and their family.

During class time, I worked with Lily each day, but she wouldn't speak out in class for the first few weeks except to smile and say, "Yes, ma'am." I discerned talents lay dormant within her. I hungered for her to find confidence to rid herself of her uncertainties. I hoped to chase away her fears and timid spirit of insignificance with small victories to create self-esteem.

Lily had impeccable handwriting and followed assignments exactly. Her work mimicked her grooming. Each dark kink of hair tucked neatly into a little bun on the back of her head. This sleek hairstyle accentuated her large timid eyes. Her precise demeanor and posture reminded me of a marionette dance. I hoped she could become secure and find an honorable career.

"Do you want me to write these sentences over?" I looked at how Lily's tiny hands contrasted with a normal size 2 pencil. In her hands, the pencil looked enormous.

"No, they are legible."

"What you mean?"

"*Legible* is accurate, cursive writing easily read."

"So, I am legible?"

"Your writing is."

"Thank you, ma'am." Lily did her marionette dance, stiff legs in perfect synchronization, over to the wooden tray and deposited her assignment. Her petite ankles, stuck into bleached white socks, resembled a small toddler's legs. She peeped at me through the corners of her eyes and long, curly lashes. The combination of her features proclaimed beauty.

I adored her twin, Millie, delicate and beautiful but not assigned to any of my classes. Neither girl needed ornaments to adorn their loveliness. Millie's eyes sparkled as she talked. The excitement within couldn't be contained. She visited my room frequently and would secretively slip into Lily's assigned desk, hoping I wouldn't notice the exchange. Each time I gently told her to go on to her assigned class.

"I want this to be my assigned class, Mizz Bayronne," she said over her shoulder while running to class. Her joyful spirit doused my day with brightness.

"You go to your room, young lady. You can come back between classes and at lunch."

Lily frequently asked for help. She relied on Millie so much. When separated from her twin, Lily leaned on me. When she raised her hand, I would read through her paragraphs or descriptions and make a couple suggestions. Lily'd start another draft of her work as soon as she heard my suggestions. She diligently completed each task, regardless how difficult.

Today's bridge conversation surprised Den.

"Could the twins stay with us next weekend?"

"Of course, but their mother may not agree with the idea."

"I know, but I'm going to ask her. If she says yes, I'll take them shopping. Where else could we take them?"

"The airport, a movie, and out for ice cream after dinner at our house."

"I can't wait." I gave him a hug for agreeing to host the twins. I loved Denny's relaxed nature and willingness to go along with my ideas.

For once, I looked forward to Monday because I planned to visit the twins' mother after school. Most of my students lived in the Magnolia Project, located three or four blocks from our school.

No longer a prestigious place to live, Magnolia had become a necessary place to live. My students had their friends close around them. They played basketball in the yard. But, as rougher elements moved in, their teens carried blades, from a simple pocketknife to bigger and more dangerous knives. Lily said her mama's words were, "Run *from* trouble, not *to* it."

After the first-hour class, I stepped into the hall and whispered to Lily, "I am coming to your house after school to talk to your mama."

"Oh, what did I do wrong? I am sorry for whatever you think I did. Don't go to Mama."

"You have done everything right, nothing wrong. I want to go for a good reason."

"Why do you want to talk to her?"

"I want to ask if you and Millie could come home with us for the weekend?"

Millie was on her way to her next class and saw us talking. She joined us.

"Why hello, Millie, imagine you being here at just the right time." We giggled.

"You sure, Mizz Bayronne? I live in the last section." She paused a moment as if hesitant of saying her next thought.

"I'll find it. What is your apartment number?"

"Three hundred twenty," they answered in unison.

"While you are at choir practice, I'll stop by and talk to your mama. Will she be home?"

"Yes, ma'am. After three." Millie's eyes danced with excitement while listening to our conversation in the hall.

Mr. Bergeron directed the teachers to talk to their students about achievement on this day by way of another blue ditto casually called a memogram. First hour on Monday seemed like a poor time to motivate students to achieve. But I tried.

I asked what they hoped to achieve this year. Then the loudspeaker bleated, "Excuse me, classes. Due to inclement weather, we will not be using the park for physical education. Report to the gymnasium and remain there."

Loud moaning and complaints came from my class. Jerome clarified the complaints by saying, "Awww, we're havin' competition today."

"Do you think when you win a game in gym class it is an accomplishment?"

"Mizz Bayronne, you ask funny questions. That be a win."

I couldn't help but laugh at Jerome, and the class would chime in with their cackles, and I realized we were too loud. We were known as the noisy homeroom.

"Jerome, do you plan to win? Is it a goal?"

"Well, I ain't no loser."

"You aren't a loser."

My middle-class values and experiences created obstacles in understanding my students. I came from a home where my parents expected me to achieve high grades and partake in extracurricular activities. Unlike my students who had been thwarted too many times, they expected their daily fare would be disappointments and delays.

Without warning, a wave of grief washed over my heart. *Why shouldn't they be encouraged to reach their goals? Why should Whites belittle them and speak lies to them to discourage them? They are entitled to the same scholarships I received. I must be the facilitator of truth and hope to them. Please help me, Lord.*

I tried again. "Walter, do you set goals?"

"Yes, ma'am. Kinda. My mama sets a goal for me to go to school and not run around with trouble."

"Is your goal the same as your mama's?"

"I guess so."

"Help me. Tell me a dream or specific goal that you have."

"I want to be a singer and become a star."

"There you go. Being a singer would be your own accomplishment. Do you have a plan?"

"I guess. I sing a lot." His contagious smile forced the corners of my mouth to turn up.

"Did you receive a blue ditto to talk to us about goals? Lots of teachers throw those memos away. I think you should too."

"Well, thank you for your advice, Walter."

"No, ma'am, I'm not bein' smart. I mean those memos don't work. Why don't you tell us a story?"

"Be cool, Mizz B." Ellis decided to participate today.

"Let's sleep instead," bellowed another student.

"Heck, let's go home." Ava stretched her arms straight out and brought them together making a loud clap.

"I will tell you a story about the time I set a goal to be a teacher."

Instead, the end-of-class bell rang and interrupted my story. I had learned bells dictated not only teaching but my day. I could hear the shuffle and talking of students moving to other classes outside my room.

"Maybe another day for my goal-teaching story."

Education could not be applied like a formula. Instead, it was a constant experiment. College classes had created cut-and-dried curriculum suggestions. Educational texts taught formulas which sure didn't fit Carter G. Woodson. I often felt like a baseball batter striking out. But every once in a while, those swings got me to first or second base. I wanted my homeroom students and me to experience many home runs.

I breezed through my speech classes and worked in groups with my English students. When the dismissal bell rang, I couldn't wait to go to the project for my first time. I trusted I would recognize the twins' mother, Mrs. Garcia, since I had seen her at the parent-teacher meeting.

I packed my book bag and stuck a yellow note on top of the bag, to remind Denny I had gone to the project to meet with the twins' mother. My hands were shaking, and my heart raced. *Maybe, I'm a little anxious. Oh well, I will be calm when Mrs. Garcia agrees to allow me to take the girls home.*

As I walked the narrow streets, I looked at the familiar homes I had seen many times through my classroom window. I smiled at babies wrapping their legs around their mothers' waists, so they could be held longer. I waved at a grandmother rocking on her porch, watching the day's activities. As I moved through the streets, I recognized no one. Again, I was the only White person. I was lonely in my whiteness and became anxious. I saw a man peeping out his curtains, gawking at me. *Sneaking to look at me? Why?* Grateful to see a Woodson student in the street, I squeaked out a high-pitched, "Hi. How are you?"

My steps became quicker, and then, I passed a mother I had met in the office a couple of weeks ago. She gave a friendly wave of recognition.

"Good afternoon." I giggled, showing my nervousness.

The project's vastness and unfamiliar design confused me. Most apartments looked alike, so I could not understand or follow the directions Lily had given. I wandered behind a building where an old man sat on a crumbling step, smoking a cigarette.

"Watcha' doin' here? You don't b'long here. You better be goin'," he said in a raspy voice.

He frightened me, and I tucked my head and moved stiff legged, trying not to acknowledge my fear or chattering teeth. I could not look at him because I knew I could not stare down his hatred.

I walked faster when I recognized a student of mine standing in the doorway of his apartment. "Hi, Harrold. Can you show me where Millie and Lily live?"

"Why you be here?"

"Visiting."

"Go right past the blue trash can." He pointed. "The twins live in the first apartment."

Traditionally in the North, teachers visited students. Once I took a student's work to her while student teaching. Her parents were gracious and promised they would help her complete her assignments. A visit to a parent could make a great improvement in the young person's behavior. In my student teaching experience, I dropped by one student's home to ask his mom to remind him cuss words were not acceptable. A five-minute visit changed his vocabulary for the rest of the semester. I wondered if home visitations were common here. I hadn't heard a teacher talk about going to a student's home.

My familiar, warning voice began to talk. *I think you should have brought Denny. Maybe you aren't wanted here. Maybe someone will teach you a real good lesson about coming into the project.* I dismissed those thoughts when I saw the twins' mother standing in the doorway. She must have known I needed a little help finding her apartment.

"Hello, Mrs. Garcia."

"Afternoon."

"Your daughters bring joy to my heart. You've taught them well."

"Thank you, ma'am." She spoke the same soft voice as Lily. She had those big wistful eyes, which spoke wonders in this harsh, hard world in which she lived.

"My husband and I would like to take your daughters home with us Friday afternoon until late Saturday afternoon. Would you agree for us to keep them?"

"Sure you want those girls two days, Mizz Bayronne?"

"Yes, I'm sure. We want to take the girls to a movie, shopping, and a few other things, if that's all right with you. We'll bring them back around four on Saturday. Would you be comfortable with that?"

"Yes, ma'am."

"We'll take Lily and Millie to our house right after school on Friday."

"Yes, ma'am, on Friday I will send a bag with the things the girls will need for the weekend. "Yes, ma'am, my girls will be ready."

She must have sensed my uneasiness and showed me a direct street back to Woodson. She pointed to make sure I understood.

I walked as quickly as I could without appearing to be running or afraid. *Maybe jogging practice did help.*

Returning to my classroom, I found Denny waiting. "Sandra Lee, I am upset with you. The gym teachers told me I should go with you, but when I got here you were gone."

"I hurried out as soon as the bell rang." Disregarding his concern, I continued, "The twins' mother said we could take them. She said she would send their things with them on Friday. I can't wait, can you?"

"Sounds good." He touched my chin. "Next time, let's talk about your plan. Please? I worry about you."

## LESSON 26

When I was seventeen, I was invited to the home of my high school football coach. Once inside, I picked the closest seat to the door.

The coach's wife offered me a drink. "We keep tea in the refrigerator—the glasses are in the cabinet. Around here if you want something, you get it yourself."

Not only was I in the home of a White family, but she treated me like a member of the family. I knew this place was unique, but also knew when I returned to the rest of the world, I would be treated as before—different. I felt accepted by a White family in their home, not as a young Black man, but simply as a young man who was part of humanity. —Thomas Smith, Founder of Smith Academy, high school administrator, national and international speaker

On Friday, each of the twins brought a small paper bag filled with personal items for the weekend visit. They brought them to me before class, and I stored the bags in my closet until the end of the day.

As soon as the final bell rang, the girls appeared in my doorway. They were so excited about staying overnight as well as the thought of crossing the Mississippi. On our journey home, the girls looked out the windows, silently at first.

Millie broke the silence with her questions. "What's dat?" pointing at a barge. "Where's those boats goin'?"

"You live far 'way from Woodson," Lily chimed in.

The radio played "You're My Everything," and we sang along with the Temptations. Today, when we hit traffic snags, we didn't care. The four of us were in our own little world as we pointed out buildings and landmarks.

"Mr. Bayronne, do you like to drive with all these other cars in your way?"

"No, Lily, but I don't have much choice."

"Weeze faraway now." Millie's eyes were large.

"Have you been across the bridge?"

"No, ma'am." They answered in unison.

I had heard Blacks did not live or visit on this side of the bridge. I knew there was a wide gap between the Blacks and Whites in the South, but I had never fallen between the chasms until we moved to the Big Easy. I pictured the injustice as a woven piece of fabric with a checkered pattern in the middle. The black threads were controlled and in rigid lines in the middle. The white filaments created a wide border blocking the black fibers from moving anywhere. Those white threads controlled the design of the piece of cloth. The social differences in New Orleans declared city boundaries were larger and deeper than the Mississippi River.

When we pulled into the driveway Millie asked, "This where you live?" Her direct and inquisitive personality amused me.

I opened the apartment door, "This is it, ladies. Come on in."

Without hesitation, Millie entered first.

"Look Lily, they's got soft green carpet."

"All be pretty furniture here," Lily whispered to her sister.

I walked them into the spare room. "This is your room. This couch pulls out and becomes a bed. For now, put your bags in here."

We went back into the living room, and I invited the girls to sit on the sofa. They sat tight against each other as if still in their mama's womb.

"What's wrong?"

"Mama said not to be in your way."

"Oh my, you wouldn't be in my way. Mr. B. and I are so happy to have you here. Come on in the kitchen. I baked a special treat for you two."

In our small kitchen, Millie ran her small hands over the wood of the cabinets. "Look at all these cupboards."

Lily said, "This be a pretty table."

The very things I complained about, they saw as a treasure.

They stood by the table until I asked them to sit, and each pulled a chair and sat simultaneously. Many times, their movements were so synchronized they became one motion. Sweet expressions lit their faces when I gave them each a chocolate cupcake and a glass of milk.

I pulled out a chair and sat with them. We ate chocolate cupcakes and smiled at one another. As soon as they finished one, I offered them another cupcake.

"We can have two?"

"You can have as many as you want. This is your special weekend."

"Why you bring us here?" asked Millie with her unrestrained boldness.

"We like it," Lily countered in her gentle way.

"We brought you here to let you know how special you are. We are going to have fun, and Mr. Baron will be our date."

Millie wiggled back and forth on her chair.

"I didn't show you the bathroom." Rising together, they followed me to the bathroom. "Here you go."

"Look at all these mirrors sparkle." Lily looked at her reflection and tucked her head down.

"Pretty cabinets and shiny tile," added Millie.

"Big white bathtub." Lily ran her hand over the rim of the tub.

"I'll leave you two and go see how many cupcakes Mr. B. can eat." I shut the door behind me and could hear the girls whispering and talking about the things in our apartment.

Delighted with the cupcakes as much as the girls, Denny grabbed two. He was like a little boy tasting the icing. He grinned. "You are loving this, aren't you?"

"Yes, but I didn't realize how much we have and take for granted, including our skin color. The girls are redefining my understanding of being blessed."

"Did you ever think about all the privileges we have?"

"Woodson has shown me how easy my life is compared to theirs." Den grabbed another cupcake as he talked.

"The twins help me see and appreciate all this. I was given an education. All I had to do was go to class and complete finals. I wonder if they will have a way to get more education after they graduate? Lilly and Millie are a gift. They show me how blessed I am."

He put his arms around me and held me. "*You* are my gift."

Then the girls came in and cackled. They never imagined their teacher in the arms of her husband.

Denny and I scooped them into a hugging circle.

"Would you like to walk around outside and meet our landlords, Helen and Larry?"

Our duplex neighbors, Helen and Larry, had heard so much about the twins they wanted to welcome them too. Helen was from New Jersey and had lived in a diverse neighborhood. We enjoyed Larry's casual lifestyle and humor.

"Mizz Bayronne, I don't think we should go outside." Millie's sober expression included a worried brow.

"Why not?"

"It might cause trouble. We not s'pose to be here on this side of the bridge."

"We are keepin' you safe." I drew them closer to me. "Come, meet our landlord."

"You got to pay your rent today?"

Lily pushed Millie's shoulder trying to get her to stop asking questions.

"No, they are our friends."

"That be strange." Millie shook her head.

"Why do you say it is strange, Millie?"

"Landlords are mean, not friends."

Again, Lily nudged Millie to stop her talking.

As we knocked on the door, the girls huddled close into each other as if trying to disappear. Helen opened the door and welcomed us in. With a broad gesture, she beckoned the girls into the living room. Large eyes and snuggled bodies turned in unison. They looked at Helen's décor and remained silent.

"I hear you two are staying the weekend with your teacher," Helen said.

"Yes, ma'am." Lily smiled at Helen and looked down.

"I know you will have fun. She's a pretty fun lady and neighbor."

"Yes, ma'am. She and Mr. Bayronne are taking us to the movies, shopping, and to the airport." Millie extended her arms wide from her sides brought them together to do a couple of claps.

Helen's soft eyes reflected her pleasure as she welcomed them to her home. "Sandi's right. You are both beautiful."

Their eyebrows went up, and they looked at each other inquiringly but said nothing.

I intuitively understood their expressions. "My first name is Sandi."

Surprised eyes turned to smiling eyes, and both girls nodded in agreement.

"What are you doing this evening?"

"Lily and Millie are going to help me fix dinner, and then Mr. Baron is taking three dates to see *To Sir, With Love* at the Metairie movie theater."

"It is a great movie. Larry and I saw it last weekend."

After a little more of Helen's chitchat, the girls and I said our farewells and returned to our apartment. Once inside, the twins relaxed and became more like the sweet girls I admired.

"We know how to cook, Mizz Bayronne." Millie stood to show her eagerness to begin.

"Let's head to the kitchen right now and start dinner. You two can show me your culinary talent."

"What's that blue thing on the kitchen bar?" Millie pointed to my can opener.

"An electric can opener. I'm opening green beans for dinner." As I performed this rudimentary task, Millie leaned in so close I did not have room to detach the can from the opener.

"It moves all by itself. It stands there and opens cans for you." Millie put both hands on her hips and gawked at the opener.

"Nothing to it." I handed them lettuce and a colander. "Girls, will you wash the salad greens and cut them for our salad? I need to be excused a minute."

"Yes, ma'am," they said together.

I stepped into the living room where Den read the newspaper. "The twins were so quiet at Helen's. Her kindness made them feel comfortable, but her big dog frightened them. Larry put LaMancha in the backyard where he kept barking because he wanted to be with the visitors."

"La Mancha's greetings are overbearing even to me." Den nodded and told me not to tell Helen.

I hurried into the bathroom to freshen up.

"You won't believe what they're doing." Denny whispered on the other side of the door.

"What?" I cracked the door so I could hear him while I brushed my hair and applied lipstick.

"They are opening all the cans in the cupboard. They can't stop. Millie puts one under the opener and says, 'It do it again,' and both look amazed and reach for another can."

"Oh dear, I better hurry in there."

When I got back to the kitchen, there were several abandoned cans of opened vegetables. Campbell's soup cans lined up like little soldiers marching around the sink. The lids were all stacked, and the girls were having fun in their new world.

"Here, Millie, let's try one of these big cans of tomatoes." Lily handed her the can to open.

"Ladies, have you broadened our menu?"

"No, ma'am." The girls spoke in unison and looked at me then at all the cans they opened.

Our eyes met one another's, and we laughed uncontrollably. They realized they had been taken over by a can opener.

We put the opened vegetables and soup into separate containers and refrigerated them and continued dinner preparations. While the girls worked on their salad, I prepared chicken for the fryer. First, they thought it was funny I dumped the chicken in a brown bag. Millie rolled her eyes at Lily. Lily shrugged and they peeled potatoes while they watched me. Scraping the skins off the potatoes, they burst out laughing all over again.

"What is so funny, you two?"

"Are you mad at the chicken? Mama don't shake up her chicken. She rolls each piece in the flour on her biscuit board." Millie continued to eye my process and giggle at me.

"Mama has an iron skillet she uses to crisp her chicken. Mizz Bayronne has a shiny new fancy frying pan." Lily leaned closer to inspect the electric skillet.

"Mama's skillet sits on the stove, and the fancy skillet sit all by itself and is plugged in the wall." Millie picked up my plastic spoon and added to her narration. "Mama uses an old wooden spoon."

While the bread baked, I asked the girls to help set the table.

"I never seen a tablecloth with purple pansies." Millie smoothed the cloth before setting the yellow pottery dishes and utensils in place.

When our meal was ready, I called to Denny. These words fell on silent ears. He had drifted into a deep afternoon nap. I kissed him on the head to awaken him.

Once again, the girls snickered as they watched their English teacher smooch on the gym teacher.

As we sat around the table, Lily's eyes glittered as she looked at fried chicken piled high on a yellow platter. Millie clutched her hands to her chest as she studied the mashed potatoes and gravy, green beans, tossed salad, applesauce, and garlic French bread. Our little, green table was crowded holding all the bowls of food and dinner place settings.

As usual, Millie asked Lily's question. "Are more people comin' for dinner?"

"Only us." I realized I took a hot meal with lots of extra dishes for granted. These sweet students were teaching me thankfulness.

We ate as if we had been working on the farm all day.

While the girls finished their dessert of banana pudding, Denny removed the clean dishes from the dishwasher, placed them into the cabinets, and loaded the dirty ones into the dishwasher.

"You put dirty dishes in a cupboard?" Millie watched what my husband was doing.

"This is a dishwasher," Denny explained. "Dirty dishes become clean inside here."

"What he say?" Lily brought her dishes from the table.

"This is how the washer cleans our dishes." The girls almost bumped heads, peeping into the dishwasher as Denny put Lily's empty plate inside.

"No water. Can't wash dishes without water." Lily's close proximity made it easy for her to pinch Millie for her abrupt words.

"Yes, but when we push the outside buttons, the washer comes on. Hot water, suds, and the agitation created by the motor clean and sterilize the dishes." He stood looking proudly at his accomplishment.

The girls shook their heads back and forth, amazed again at such an automatic machine.

"My big sister and mama won't believe us when we tell her nobody washes your dishes."

We hurried to see the seven fifteen showing. The girls had never attended a public movie. They had gone to the theater in the project but never outside their neighborhood.

Denny went ahead of us and bought four tickets. We hurried in and got settled while Den went back to buy popcorn and drinks. Denny and I were naïve to the fact Blacks could not attend public theaters in the South. Perhaps, because the twins were so small and light-skinned, no one stopped us as we found our seats in the full theater. We sat the girls between us and chomped away on the salty, buttery delight, oblivious we were breaking social rules.

Sidney Poitier acted as a teacher in *To Sir, With Love*. The Lulu song caused a little toe tapping, but other than crunching and tapping, the girls were silent throughout the film. Again, something I took for granted became a novel event for the twins. I learned far more than the twins during their weekend visit.

We made our way through the crowd to our car. "Oh, did you see how those kids treated their teacher?" Lily climbed into the back seat.

"Kind of like Woodson kids." Millie slammed her door hard and kept chattering.

"I loved their teacher. He be so handsome," Lily said dreamily.

"You look like Lulu 'cept you have those big blue eyes. The boys think you a witch 'cause your eyes are so blue." Millie leaned up to look closer at me.

I bopped her on the head. "I am not a witch, and don't forget it."

"Gosh, girls. We spend all week at school, and then we take you to see a film about a teacher and his difficult students. We four must like school." I turned and looked at the girls in the back seat and clapped to their swaying and singing songs from the movie.

The twins continued to repeat the song they had memorized by the end of the film. We chimed in with them and hummed the melodies from the production.

"He be like you, Mr. Bayronne,"

"Yeah, 'cept you be White, and he be Black," Millie stated the obvious.

"People are people," I put in. "All want to learn. All want to love."

"Thank you, Mr. and Mizz Bayronne for taking us to the movie." Millie tapped us both on the shoulder.

"You are most welcome. I had the prettiest dates in the place."

The girls burst into giggles and started singing again.

When we arrived home, I showed them the extra towels and toothpaste and asked if they were ready for bed.

"Lily, fetch our bags from our room."

She returned with their paper grocery bags, and they went into the bathroom.

Den and I cuddled on the couch and talked about the girls' reactions.

"Why are they slamming cupboards?"

"Not sure. Better go see." I knocked on the door. "Girls, what do you need?"

Lily opened the door. "We can't find no hair grease."

"White folks don't use hair grease. I don't have any."

Like two bookends, they stared at each other. They dramatically shrugged their shoulders.

"Maybe you can help each other with your hair until you return home."

"We can do that. We can make do the Woodson way. Sorry we forgot our hair grease." Millie politely closed the door.

I was surprised Millie knew the phrase too and breathed a sigh of relief the problem was resolved.

Lily and Millie stayed a long time in the bathroom, bathing and enjoying the newness. While they finished their bath, I prepared the bed and laid two new books on the pillows. Before the twins retired, they told us good night, but not before thanking us for the most wonderful time ever.

With undeniable gladness, I pondered our time with the twins. I imagined how their eyes would light up in wonder and delight, seeing the new books laid on their pillows. Tomorrow would bring even more excitement and pleasure.

# LESSON 27

White fragility is based on the theory White people don't experience racism, and therefore, have not built up the stamina or ability to productively talk about racism. W. E. B. Du Bois' theory of "double consciousness" is further defined by Blacks living in a world while in another world—the White world. Blacks, then and now, navigate their own Black world to survive and succeed in the other world. Double consciousness: Black parents instructing their children how to respond to White people, so they won't be harmed.—Dr. Joan Holmes, Special Assistant to the President for Equity and Special Programs at Hillsborough Community College, retired

Dressed and ready for their day, the girls came into the kitchen. "Those pancakes smelled so good they woke me up. I thought I was dreamin'." Lily rubbed her eyes.

"Good mornin', Mizz Bayronne."

"Why, good mornin' back 'atcha, Millie. Go ahead and sit."

As I gave them their plates, I looked into Millie's warm, brown eyes. They were sparkling from her soul. I hugged her a quick hug.

"You be so nice to us." Lily was always grateful—she thanked me for anything I did for her at school.

"That's easy with you two. You are wonderful, bright ladies. How about going on a girls' shopping trip after our breakfast?"

"Hey, ladies," Denny greeted us in the doorway.

"Good mornin'," they answered in their usual harmony.

"I hear there's a shopping trip today."

"Sorry, ladies only." I gave him an exaggerated wink.

The girls winked back at me, and we ate bacon and pancakes with thick, rich maple syrup.

"This be better than grits," Lily said.

"I don't know, Lily. I love grits best for breakfast, but Mr. B. prefers pancakes. He doesn't have Southern roots like us."

"Can we watch the dishwasher clean our plates?" Lily watched Denny load the dirty breakfast dishes.

I slipped away to put on makeup and freshen my hair.

"I put soap in this little cup holder, close the door, and press a button." Denny's sweet voice drifted into my room. "They'll be clean in an hour."

"I can't wait to tell Mama," Millie said.

"Me either. Mama will think we are jokin' with her."

"Girls," I called from the bathroom. "My makeup is almost on. Are you ladies ready?" I felt four eyes staring at me. I grinned at their curiosity as they scooted closer. "Y-e-s-, what is it?"

"We want to see how you make your hair stand up," Millie said.

"I take a comb and tease it like this. Then, I smooth a little hair over the ruffled hair. Spray it like this. Done."

"White people's hair be different than ours," Lily observed.

"Yep, but inside, we are all the same, right?"

"Yes, ma'am." Millie continued, "But all folks don't think your way. Wish they understood like you and Mr. B."

Their sweet comment instigated a giant embrace from me. "You two are so special to me."

As I put on earrings, I directed the girls to get anything they would need from their room. I grabbed my purse from our bedroom and checked I had our new charge card. In the kitchen, I kissed Denny good-bye.

The twins were waiting at the front door.

"Let's go."

The shopping center was near our home, so we didn't have to cross the bridge. In my rearview mirror, I saw the girls look big-eyed at the center lined with stores and then shrug at each other.

"You ladies been to a shopping center before?"

"No, ma'am, we just go to Canal Street with Mama," Millie answered.

I pulled into a space. "What should we look at first?"

"What you mean?" questioned Millie.

"Which department do you want to go to first? Shoes, dresses, or underwear?"

The girls were silent in the back seat. Not a giggle, not a "yes, ma'am"—nothing.

"This is Harvey's shopping center. It is not near as big or busy as Canal Street, but the big department store has many styles and choices. You'll like it, I bet."

Again, silence.

"Lily, Millie, why are you so quiet?" I turned off the motor and turned around to look at them. Cuddled together, gentle tears softly ran down Lily's cheeks. "Darlin', what's wrong?"

"Lily be missing our mama."

"Of course, you miss her. This is your first time away from home, isn't it?"

Lily nodded.

"I understand you miss your mama. You love her so much. You'll see her soon, wearing your beautiful new dress. Now, dry those tears and let's go shopping."

We got out of the car, and I hugged Lily to me. She retuned my hug.

"She be born last," Millie confided. "That's why she misses Mama so much. She was in her longer."

I laughed. "Now, I've never considered that concept. The longer you stay in the womb, the more love you have for your mother."

They shrugged and walked on each side of me, close and quiet. We went in the door nearest to the junior wear.

The girls were tiny, so we looked at the smallest sizes. Because they were so knitted together in and out of the womb, they wanted look-alike dresses. We found several duplicate styles and crinolines to go under the skirts for the girls to try on. I showed them where to try on the selected dresses.

In a short time, they whirled out in unison from their dressing room. "We decided, Mizz Bayronne. We like these green ones." They spun around in the mint green dresses. They patted the crinoline underneath the gathered skirt. The shirtwaist dresses had pearl buttons with a matching small belt. Sweet smiles and bright eyes reflected their joy.

"You look spectacular."

"It be perfect for dress-up day at Woodson and church. Mama will love them, too won't she, Lily?"

"Give the dresses to me and while you change into your clothes, I'll go and pay for them."

"Wait on us," Lily pled. "We be fast."

"Don't leave us." Millie's voice had an urgent tone.

"I'll stay right outside your door. Don't worry."

Within one minute, Millie popped out of the dressing room with her new dress. "We ready." Lily followed her sister carrying her petticoat and dress.

"Great, let's pay for these. But first, I saw cute necklaces right outside the fitting room. I think you should each choose one for you and one for your mama."

"Really?"

"Here they are on this counter." I pointed to the selection.

Lily and Millie reached for identical gold hearts on tiny chains and selected a long pearl necklace for their mother.

A deep voice snapped, "What do you think you are doing?"

Startled, I turned to see the clerk bent forward snapping her fingers in front of the twins' faces. "You girls don't belong here." She glared at the twins.

"They do belong here because we are shopping together."

"Ma'am, *you* are welcome, *they* are not." She reached toward the twins. "You nigra girls know you don't belong here."

Her ugly words were like kindling to the fire within me. "I want you to call your manager," I demanded.

While these words spilled out of my mouth, a tall woman in a business suit appeared before me.

"I *am* the manager." Her thin face and small lips were tightly drawn. "Remove those girls, *now*."

"It be fine, Mizz Bayronne." Millie pressed herself against my side. "Let's go."

My face grew hot. I couldn't believe this was happening in 1967. "I am appalled." I spoke with new-found authority. "I would walk out right now, but I am not allowing you to ruin our day. I want to buy these dresses."

I looked her in the eye like my mama used to look at me right before she exploded. The manager grabbed my charge card, rang the purchases, and threw the dresses and jewelry in a bag.

"Now, out." She pointed to the door.

Two White women watched the whole transaction.

They clucked their tongues like hens. "Why would anyone bring those girls into this fine store? That White woman is no better than them. Why is she with those colored girls?"

Grabbing the girls, I turned so fast we twirled as if we three were one and stomped out of the store. I wanted to scream profanities at the clerks, the White women, and the South. Their superior, White-world mentality caused bile to rise in my throat, and I wanted to vomit in their department store.

Instead, I hugged the girls. "I'm sorry those women acted ignorant. You belong there as much as I do."

"Come on, Mizz Bayronne," Millie coached. "We knew we'd be yelled at in your White store. I thought you knew what you was doin', so we went in with you."

"You deserve much more. You keep getting your education, and you can buy your own store."

We climbed into the car. We were covered with sweat, not because of the New Orleans' humidity but because of the lack of humanity. How dare the hourly wage clerk and mousy manager treat us with disrespect. I wanted to bury my head in my hands and cry like a hurt five-year-old. Instead, I took a deep breath, "Freedom is sunlight."

"What you mean?" Millie asked.

"It's like Martin Luther King Jr. teaches at the rallies. We want freedom for all mankind because freedom is sunlight because it puts hope into your souls."

"Say it again, Mizz Bayronne."

"Sunlight is freedom. Freedom is hope. That's what you deserve whether you are shopping, eating, riding a bus, or getting a drink of water. We all need sunlight, no matter the color of our skin."

# LESSON 28

Don't judge each day by the harvest you reap, but by the seeds that you plant. —Robert Louis Stevenson

Still in silence, we arrived at our home. I didn't discuss the ugly prejudice because I feared I might start crying. I could not imagine how the twins felt.

Freedom to me was like oxygen. It was everywhere. Shackled ankles stopped and impeded Lily and Millie from achieving opportunity that existed right in front of them. Did they feel that way? I didn't ask because I thought it might be a painful conversation. The girls went straight to their room and opened their bags to look at their new dresses. In the kitchen, I pulled things out of the refrigerator for lunch.

I called to the twins to model their new dresses for Mr. B. In an instant, they emerged from their room and stood in the doorway, a green vision of youthful symmetry. In unison, the girls spun as Denny applauded. They were cute and happy, despite our bittersweet shopping experience.

Their beauty reminded me of a budding rose that prevails, although not recognized or affirmed. "Lovely ladies in green, you are beautiful."

"Thank you, ma'am," they echoed together.

"Everyone ready for lunch in five minutes?"

I tied an apron around my waist. "Change back into your other clothes, and we'll eat—then off to the airport."

Lily and Millie shaped my heart and thoughts for a lifetime. I loved these twins as if they were my own. I wanted our time together to linger, but I knew I must take the girls home soon.

"Airport limousine leaving in two minutes. Gather your bags and make sure you have your tickets," Denny teased.

I felt a loss, a loneliness after the biases and prejudices we experienced on our shopping trip. I wanted Lily and Millie's lives to be filled with opportunities, delights, and rewards. Their paths would be uphill with many difficult struggles.

Lingering, the girls touched the couch, the tables, even the can opener. The twins stood near each other, each holding two bags—one a wrinkled paper bag filled with old, faded, and worn jammies and the other, a crisp handled bag holding their new, mint-green dresses. This weekend together, we were forced to live the old New Orleans' way. I prayed our time offered the promise of a future without color discrimination. *Please, dear Father, show me how I can be used to help this dream come true.*

Arriving at the airport, we entered the parking lot. "Look, Lily," Millie pointed at the plane as it touched down nearby.

"It's a wonder they stay in the air," Millie exclaimed. "They be so heavy."

After parking, we walked into the terminal. The twins resumed their big-eyed and close-body language. At first, they were quiet and stayed near Denny and me. We showed them where people bought tickets and boarded their flights to destinations around the world.

"See," I directed their attention to passengers about to board. "The large group of people are traveling to France."

"I would be afraid," Lily said.

"I wouldn't. I would buy me a ticket and fly," said Millie.

Those statements pretty much defined their individualism.

"Mizz Bayronne, I want to see the big man."

"What big man?" I asked Lily.

"The one with that big voice saying the plane is leaving."

"Lily, he is on an intercom like our announcements at school. This system is much larger and much louder than the system used by Mr. Hughes."

We laughed and watched a few airplanes take off, one after the other.

"I want to go in one of those big planes. I want to see France."

"You keep learning, Millie, and making good grades, so you can earn a scholarship to college." I indicated the passengers boarding. "Then, you can fly wherever you want."

"Almost time to go, ladies," Denny reminded. We had promised their mother we would have the twins home by four. We had enough time to duck into the gift shop and purchase a little globe for each girl. I hoped this small token would represent new hopes. New dreams.

We talked of the countries on the globe as we traveled back. When we crossed Claiborne Avenue, the major thoroughfare in New Orleans, the girls read the street sign aloud which reminded me the students had taught me the term Vieux Carre on Monday during our "Create a New Orleans Dictionary" lesson. The more common name for this area is the French Quarter, but they liked Vieux Carre.

Many French phrases were used as folks spoke French and Creole in the city. I had learned from my reading that young people must come from established families if they chose to marry into old New Orleans' money. I did not understand the many social layers in this large cosmopolitan mecca, so I appreciated anything my students could teach me.

"Yes, thank you, girls, for teaching me about New Orleans."

"Thank you, Mr. and Mizz Bayronne, for what you taught us about New Orleans," said Lily.

We hummed to the radio's tune while Denny drove to Third Street to return the girls to the Magnolia Project.

As the girls inched their way out of the car, first Millie, and then Lily, gave me a heartfelt hug. The twins' mother walked out onto the sidewalk and asked if the girls had been well behaved.

"Oh, yes, ma'am. Your girls were perfect," I assured their mother. "Thank you so much for allowing them to spend last night and today with us."

"Yes, ma'am," all three said in unity.

That weekend, Denny and I were like children molding the uneven edges of clay, offering treasured and indelible experiences for two incredible, young girls. *Maybe these experiences would create a shimmer of hope in the twins.* We both understood the more we worked the clay, the smoother it would become. We, too, were being sculpted and refined under the wheel of the potter. *What comes next?*

## LESSON 29

If history were taught in the form of stories, it would never be forgotten. —Rudyard Kipling

For this Christmas season, I wanted to create a new opportunity for my students. Since so many of the children had talent, it seemed logical to propose a Christmas play. I asked Mr. Bergeron if I could order playbooks.

"Of course. For you, Mrs. Baron, anything." He had begun to say our name correctly as well as had a few other staff members.

My eyes widened and my underarms grew damp. His charm was magnetic. His green eyes searched mine as he patted my arm. I needed to hurry to my first period class because being close to Mr. Bergeron initiated uncomfortable jitters. I could smell the spices in his aftershave, beckoning me closer. I could feel his warm breath on my face.

*Jiminy crickets, I need to move away and out of his office. Why am I standing close and not moving? I've heard rumors of him being a womanizer. I assumed they were rumors but maybe not. My whole body is warm. I bet my cheeks are red, too.*

"Excuse me, I need to hurry to not be late for my class. I will peruse my play catalogs tonight, and put my order on an invoice tomorrow. Have a good day."

"You do the same, Mrs. Baron. Please bring that invoice."

I did a skipping step to the breezeway. In the open halls, I soaked in the day's sunshine and warmth, a mini outdoor recess to me.

Edna walked past. "You look like you've captured this day." Her fitted gold skirt accentuated her trim figure. Her modern coiffure framed her determined expression. I admired her professionalism and intelligence.

"Mr. Bergeron gave me permission to buy playbooks for a Christmas program."

"Really? I can help you."

"I'd appreciate your guidance, Edna. Students, who I don't know, will be trying out for parts. You'd be a great help."

We had reached our rooms. "I'll let you know when the playbooks arrive."

My room looked brighter and cleaner today. I straightened my desk and opened my lesson calendar. On Mondays, we created a mini dictionary. My students spoke a diverse language derived from their kinship, locality, or a blend of both. Some spoke Creole with words new to me. Many spoke an inner-city lingo mixed with Cajun phrases. This language, with a few unacceptable words, gave new meaning to vocabulary.

"Hey, Mizz Bayronne." Jerome drug out my name with his southern drawl and his playful, teasing style. He grinned broadly. "I've got a word to teach you today."

"I'm sure you do," I teased back.

One by one, students entered. Many cleaned up for the day, while others came with unkempt hair and wore old, wrinkled T-shirts. Lily entered dressed in a checked skirt with a clean white blouse that matched her tennis shoes. I could tell her mother had been busy with the bleach bottle over the weekend. As the heat of the day rose, her shoes would leak the smell of Clorox. Since she sat in the front row to be near me, the bleach scent wafted past.

She smiled in her sweet, admiring way. "Good morning, ma'am."

"Hello, Lily." We exchanged a lingering look at each other acknowledging our recent shared experience.

I glanced to my right and tiny Josie came through the door and approached her desk. My heart skipped a beat. "Josie, it's so good to see you back at school. Thanks for sending your lessons from the hospital. I'll help you complete today's assignments. and you'll be caught up with the class. You're here in time to hear Jerome's singing."

Our favorite class clown interrupted our moment. Singing and spinning created Jerome's daily entrance. His dark skin glittered from the humidity. "Hey, the man is here, all should fear." He chanted to his own beat.

He intended to talk with each of his buds before sitting. My intention was different. I wanted quiet and control. *Maybe I should hand him a ditto and ask him to fill in the blanks.* My inner smile spilled over into my actress mean girl look.

"Jerome, take your seat."

He picked up his chair. "Where you want me to take it, Teach?"

I'm sure he would never tease Mr. Foster, the Physical Ed instructor, who had the reputation of being the hardest paddler in the school. I, on the other hand, had to come up with my own classroom management ideas.

"Jerome. It is Monday. We all are tired but you. I'm going to use your energy for my benefit. Pass out these papers to your classmates. You have one second to give each person his paper and your wisdom. No more, understand?"

Other children would have responded, "Yes, ma'am." Not Jerome.

"Sure, White lady, I'll be your energy."

Jerome passed out clean paper for our dictionary project. As he went back and forth in the rows, he sang to the students. "Cool baby cool, love your lips sweet lady, brothers forever, and gotcha now." Using his own musical jive he completed his job and made us laugh. To my surprise, Jerome returned to his seat after passing out the papers.

I called the roll to keep them focused. They responded, "Yes, ma'am," or "Here I am, ma'am." Their Southern manners of always saying "ma'am" reminded me of my upbringing in the South. Living in the North during junior high and high school and then going to college in the Midwest had swallowed my "ma'ams." My Southern aunts would be appalled at my Yankee choppy words and fast speaking pattern.

"Class, please set up this paper like we do every Dictionary Monday. Write the word you want to teach me, followed by the accepted definition. Be sure to use the new word in your sentence. I'll be checking for end punctuation. Please write clearly so I can read your sentences. This isn't a fire drill. Take your time," I explained.

Lily grinned. She must have considered her word before coming to school because she began writing while I gave instructions.

Jerome raised his hand.

"Yes, Jerome?"

"Now, you aren't going to suspend me, right?"

"Jerome, I'm looking for words you use each day, but not the overused, colorful words you use as a crutch. Those words are boring, repeated, and show a lack of knowledge."

"What you say?"

"You heard me, Jerome. Now write."

Most of the students enjoyed this assignment, and it really did help me. On the first Monday I tried this lesson, my directions were not clear, resulting in many cuss words and expletives written and defined. Although entertaining, I reminded them each Monday those colorful words were unacceptable expressions.

My middle-class life seemed as foreign to them as their lifestyle did to me. We had to merge our cultures. Sometimes we clashed, other times we laughed, but we were gaining understanding.

I walked up the aisles patting a shoulder or rubbing a short-cropped hairstyle. I watched Walter write each line. His cursive was executed with preciseness.

He looked up. "How am I doing?"

"You are doing well. You always do." His grin broadened.

I wanted these kids to succeed but understood it wouldn't be easy. When I walked to the park, I looked at Third Street. The houses needed repair, paint, and roofing. Most folks worked for minimum wages or had relief payments from the government. My students, who were writing definitions, needed to be eating eggs, grits, cheese, and milk. Instead, hunger stole their focus and robbed their thinking. Growing up, I had been blessed with access to comfort food and any snacks I desired. In the kitchen, Mama kept a plate filled with fresh oranges and avocados. I could only imagine gnawing pangs of hunger, but I knew I didn't understand the pain.

"Yo, Mizz Bayronne. I can't write this word in a sentence. It be French." Alfred was small with a whimsical smile. As he talked, his long, lean fingers did a ballet in the air matching the rhythm of his cadence.

"You don't know French, Alfred. You can't use it," shouted Maurine. "You be stupid."

"You try to stop me, bitch." He pointed those long fingers in Maurine's round face.

"Hold on," I interrupted. "We are learning, not confronting each other."

"Does confronting mean having stupid fits?" Jerome looked pointedly at Maurine.

"Listen to me. We don't need to fight. Words give us power to say what we want to say without hurting another person. Confronting means to be in someone's face to challenge them. This lesson is not about challenging. It's about learning the power of words. Understand?"

"I know Jerome ask stupid things." Maurine's frown matched her belligerent remarks. "That's what I decide."

"Maurine, can you say something positive to Jerome? It would encourage his writing."

"Nope."

The class erupted in laughter. Fearful of losing control again, I redirected their energy. "You have ten minutes to finish this assignment. Teach me your words. Make your sentences as clear as you can."

"That's what I want to do," shouted Jerome. "But you won't help me use machete in a sentence."

"Put your pencils away and listen to me. At five years old, I would go into my father's garage to watch him paint signs. His skill earned his salary. The words on those signs were a mystery. I watched as he placed each letter in a sequence with his skilled hand and controlled paintbrush."

"Ma'am, you sayin' your daddy painted signs for money?" asked Walter.

"That was his profession," I continued. "I wanted to learn what those letters said. I thought those words must be important if people paid Daddy money for them. So, Daddy painted the word *indubitably* on a scrap piece of wood using neon orange paint. My Daddy told me, 'Go find the meaning, and use it in three correct sentences, and the word will be yours."

I ran next door to ask my aunt, "What does this mean? My Aunt Lottie responded, 'Let's look in the magic book and see.'"

I interrupted my story. "Who knows what the magic book is?"

The eyes of every student were focused on me. By telling a story, I had captured their attention. "Who knows of such a magic book?"

Lily raised her hand. "I think it be a dictionary. That's the only place I know to look up words."

"You are exactly right. Thank you. So, my Aunt Lottie looked up the word and explained it meant undoubtedly.

"I sulked, 'I don't know that word either, Auntie.'"

"You do, honey," assured Aunt Lottie. "It's another word for *sure*. You know something is true or sure or without a doubt. I love you indubitably. Now, run along and use your word in a sentence with your daddy. He will be so surprised."

The bell rang, but the students remained in their seats. Jerome spoke up, "I want to hear the end of the story."

"Tomorrow, bring me your finished assignments, and I will tell you the end of the story." Students pushed out their chairs and hurried to their next class.

*Today, I discovered a way to keep my students actively engaged—a classroom management technique that is the oldest one in history. Storytelling. If it worked for Jesus, it works for me. It is an indubitable fact I am concerned about taking the playbook invoice to Mr. Bergeron's office.*

# LESSON 30

In 1968, desegregation in public education was not practiced throughout the United States even though in 1954, the Supreme Court deemed segregation by race unconstitutional. The historic school race-desegregation case, Brown v Board of Education, concluded with the Supreme Court's decision that separating children in public schools based on race was unconstitutional (Turnbull et al., 2020). Their argument was the essence of simplicity: "Students are students, regardless of race." (Turnbull et al., 2020, p. 39). This landmark case ensured equal opportunity in education for all and sparked the Civil Rights Movement. In the early 1970s, litigation continued to be a powerful force in settling cases for exclusion and misclassification which violated students' rights to access to an appropriate education under the U.S. Constitution (Turnbull, Shogren & Turnbull, 2011)—Dr. Lucinda Barron, Retired Professor and author

"Mizz Bayronne," one of my students announced, "the office has a package for you."

"Thank you, I'll check during my break."

"Hey, Teach, go now. We'll be good," proposed Jerome.

"Yeah, go see what it is," encouraged another student.

"You are kind, but I'll wait to do it after class. Today you will need the notebooks we are keeping on *Huckleberry Finn*. Lily, will you hand them out?" I had purchased composition books for each student of my first and last hour classes to write notes and reactions about Mark Twain's classic.

"Thanks for getting us these," Debra said.

"Can we take it home?" asked Jerome.

"Remember, we need to keep them in class, so we have them accessible when we need them."

"There she go using big White words."

The class's laughter was music to my ears, though I had learned the administration thought silence was golden and a sign of learning. I didn't agree but submitted on the edge of keeping control. The rumors of standing up against Drake, being a spider handler, and reading *Huckleberry Finn* had brought me veneration. So, I went along with their system.

I read a portion I had read before.

> At first, I hated the school, but by and by I got so I could stand it. Whenever I got uncommon tired, I played hooky, and the hiding I got next day done me good and cheered me up. So, the longer I went to school the easier it got to be.

I finished this reading and directed the students, "Please react to this reading. Here are questions you might think about in your paragraph writing. Do you like school or hate it and why? Have you ever played hooky? If so, what did you do all day? If you got a hiding, why would you agree with Huck when he said the whipping did him good and cheered him?"

I asked these questions to better understand my students' thinking and lifestyle. I must have chosen appealing questions this time because most of them began writing.

I walked back to a boy who sat staring. "What's wrong, Eddie?"

Large and athletic, Eddie frowned. "I still can't write sentences. I can't make the thoughts in my head hit the paper. I can't write good." Though Eddie had many friends and was popular with the girls, he had a difficult time in English class.

"Sentences are words stuck together, Eddie. Write the words you can. Come to my desk and I will help you turn them into sentences."

Working quietly together, we formed a sentence from his words. I helped him choose and add punctuation. He smiled to see the sentence he had made, and his giant chestnut eyes shone with pride.

"Good job," I commended. "Now, go back to your desk and try connecting more words."

A knot formed in my throat, and remorse overtook me. I appraised Eddie's reading to be on a second grade level. Writing stretched him because the words were not familiar. School for him was another stamp of rejection. There were no special education teachers or classes to help him. His destiny was clear—unless something changed, he would be functionally illiterate. Maybe, with my daily affirmation, Eddie could experience progress by the end of the year.

Teaching meant much more than classroom management. On difficult days, I gritted my teeth so hard and long that my cheeks ached. Before my monthly cycles, I became nervous and reacted with sharp language and a loud voice. Day-to-day struggles left me exhausted and my compassionate heart was breaking into pieces. My most difficult classes reminded me of having a sharp stone in my shoe, which became more irritated with each additional step. I could not remove the stone of defeat from these classes. I had no extra time to tutor Eddie, no aides to assist me, and there were no field trips budgeted for the Black and inner-city schools. Eddie needed hands-on activities, new techniques, and experiences. The stone dug deeper each day.

"It's about time for the bell. Pass your notebooks forward," I instructed. "First person in the row please stack the notebooks on my desk. I will edit your work and return it tomorrow. If you do corrections, you can raise your score by one letter grade."

The bell rang, and the students hurried to their next class.

"Goodbye." Jesse was so quiet but always said goodbye to me. She was absent a lot, so I needed to make time to help her more on days she attended.

Since my first-hour class turned into my homeroom, I began to know each student as an individual. A rhythm developed in my teaching, and I paced my lessons more effectively. Near the end of October, I better understood my own naïve self as well as the intricacies of my impoverished students. I developed my own teaching strategies and was learning how to navigate my fledgling marriage.

During my preparation hour, I hurried to the office to check my mail and pick up my package.

"Good morning, Sandi." Edna spoke like a professional with well-chosen words. Her lean body fit into traditional business suits and dark straight skirts. She wore her hair styled in the newest coiffure—bleached, or tinted—but always short. Because of her sharp humor and quick retorts, the faculty liked her. I admired how she instructed her students and most of all how they esteemed her. I secretly wished I could be like her, coolheaded and firm handed. Edna's experience and skills helped her easily relate to her students. Even at the end of a hot and sticky day, Edna looked perfect. I wished to have class control like her, but it hadn't happened yet.

I reached into my bulging mailbox and saw a package from the publisher with my name on it. "Look, Edna, the playbooks for *Christmas Cheer* arrived."

"Girl, you are magic to pull money out of the budget for playbooks."

"I need your help. When can we do tryouts?"

Edna knew Woodson well as she had taught there five years. "Seven weeks before Christmas break. The kids will peak in time for the Christmas program."

"Sounds good to me. I'll shoot for the last week of October, but it is less than two weeks away."

"Who's going to be shot the last of October?" Mike grinned at us because he had been eavesdropping.

I hurried back to my room to edit the writings of my first-hour class. A few students wrote about school being the best part of their day. Others disclosed their hooky practices and happiness of sleeping late. Some wrote they felt sad or bored. Even though Eddie's writing was random with unconnected words, I understood how beatings *didn't* cheer him up.

I suspected receiving a whipping as a punishment was a way of life in most of my students' homes. I remembered how my mother's uncontrolled anger resulted in an unexpected slap to my face or a switching to my bare legs. Her harsh and degrading words humiliated and hurt me. I never felt cheered, only wounded and rejected. Huck Finn felt a relief from the hiding. Not me. I never wanted to punish a child by hitting. I never would.

# LESSON 31

When people show you who they are, believe them. —Maya Angelou

About seven weeks before Christmas vacation, tryouts for our Christmas program began. Throughout high school and college, I had done costumes and set designs and acted, but I had never directed a play. This being my year of firsts, I would add directing to my résumé.

Edna had offered to help, and I knew she would be an asset. She met me in the small auditorium filled with more than fifty noisy kids. I didn't know many of their names and was unable to stop their rowdiness.

Edna took charge in her quiet, commanding way. "If you intend to be in this play, remain quiet now, and show your cooperation."

Immediately, the students sat like little wooden soldiers at attention. Edna's experience brought instant control.

"Stand there, girl," she said to me, "and tell them what you expect."

I climbed the steps to the stage. "Look at the character descriptions on the pages I handed to you. Try out for the one that feels most comfortable. But we may see you in a better role, so do your best in your reading."

Edna gave me an affirming nod. And the students, still under her command, remained attentive. I never imagined these junior high kids in such a controlled state.

"We will start with Christmas Mama readings. If you try out for Mama, you must sing the song printed on the back side of the paper."

The turning of paper created an ocean-wave sound. I heard a few people humming. Several faculty members stood in the doorway watching as I fumbled through my first session of tryouts.

"I will start with those of you who signed up first. If you decided today to read for a part and are not on the preregistered list, advise me at the end. Debra, you are first on the list. I expect the rest of you to be a quiet and receptive audience."

In a flash, Debra walked on stage and began reading Mama's part with enthusiasm—then belted out the Christmas medley with the projection of an opera singer.

*Wow, that girl has talent. I can't stop looking at her.*

Edna realized Debra's performance had captured me in a time warp. "Next," Edna called out.

Singer after singer exhibited talent like I had never seen or heard before. These kids really had inherent musical talent. We continued until all fifty-seven participants had a chance to read the script for the role they wanted. I looked at my watch and saw the hands on six.

I returned to the stage. "You all did amazing. You all are talented. I'll post a list outside my door tomorrow. Thank you."

A noisy stream of excited students exited both doors. Edna turned to me. "Now is the hard part."

"What do you think?"

"A few of these kids have a history of fighting and getting expelled, so they would be a risk. They are great singers, too. You'll have to decide if you want to gamble."

"What would you do?"

It seemed Edna was reading my mind. "I wouldn't count on them behaving or not getting in trouble, if that's what you mean."

"Even if they have a lead role?" I asked.

"It's their way of life. Those kids have to survive, and sometimes, that means fighting to hold their ground and reputation."

I studied the names on my list. "I don't know what to do."

"The twins are a no-brainer. They can dance and sing and are so cooperative. They love you since you took them home with you."

"What? How did you know?"

"The whole Magnolia Project knows. Mrs. Garcia is so proud of them. Debra and Miranda are jealous and wondering why you didn't take them."

"I didn't think through repercussions. I just wanted to give the twins a wonderful weekend."

"You did give them a once-in-a-lifetime experience from the twins' reports to others." Edna's gentle look from her hazel eyes made me ramble more.

"I love them so much. They have so many problems and needs, yet they keep trying to learn, to improve, and to be all they can be."

Edna kept to the topic of the moment. "Joan will help you do whatever you need. James will be a star and a backup and never miss a practice. He has a lot of talent and thrives on attention. Those kids should win the key roles because they have earned a reputation for being responsible. Now, you take it from there."

"Thanks, I appreciate you setting the tone and supporting me."

"Yeah, yeah, tell me Friday night at the photographer's sponsored party. They will give us a big spread for using their company for our yearbooks."

"What? Here?"

"In the basement of their business. LeBlanc arranged it. You and Dennis need to show up. No tryouts. Be there."

Her devious smile made me laugh.

"Girl, you have the giggle of these young kids. See you tomorrow."

As Edna left, Denny entered. "Well, how did it go?"

"There is so much talent here. I will never be able to choose. I can't say no to any of the fifty-seven. I have a big problem. The script has eighteen characters."

"That is going to be a bit impossible, my dear."

"I can't cut anyone. This is all they have."

"It's like tryouts for a basketball team. Forty kids try out but only sixteen make it. Every kid hopes he is chosen, but it is not realistic."

"That's why I didn't become a jock," I said in my snooty voice.

"No, you didn't become a jock because you can't run. That's why you couldn't make the team. No matter how nice you are, you have to run to be on the team."

"I hear you." We walked to our car, and as I got in the car, I mumbled, "But I can't cut anyone."

Denny put our book bags in the back seat and started the engine and the radio. He moved through the dense traffic like he'd been living in a big city all his life. I had become a barge watcher and wondered how I could cut any of the kids on stage this afternoon.

At home, I quickly changed into something comfortable and concentrated on my tryout notes.

I considered how difficult it would be if I chose Alex who might choose trouble instead of his play script. He,

James, and Walter were the most talented boys and could carry the show. Debra Brown could sing, speak, and would have the spunk to carry any role. Joan's talented stage voice surprised me. The twins were a given.

The problem wasn't that I had too many students who wanted to participate. The play didn't have enough parts. I could write, and I could act. I needed to make this play longer with more minor characters. I wrote character parts.

I pulled out my portable typewriter from college and typed. First, I added a number of dancing elves with one or two lines. Miranda would love this part. The toy soldiers' lines were brief and to the point. I created another main character, so James could play opposite Alex. If either of them got in trouble, I could adapt the play back to one character. I presumed my solution could work. The play would make a big enough difference to Alex that he would not deliberately invite trouble for himself for the next six weeks. *Please, Lord, guide me, and show me whom to choose.*

Denny came into the room. "Are you going to type all night?"

"Have to. Have to post the list tomorrow. You go on to bed. I'll see you when I see you." As I spoke, he leaned over my shoulder, trying to kiss me.

"You sure you don't want to go to bed for a little while?" Teasing but still trying to coax me into bed with him, he gave me one more kiss.

"I am on a roll."

He slumped back into the bedroom like a denied child, and I ignored his body language because I had to finish writing additional parts.

I typed until three a.m. and then finalized the list of fifty-seven kids and their roles. It would be posted on my door. At four a.m., I climbed into bed, and at six, the alarm rang.

"Short night?" Denny patted my matted hair.

"I can't wait to post my list. I have to hurry."

"My little all-night writer, you better get a wiggle on it or we are going to miss first hour."

I grabbed a favorite linen ecru skirt and pulled on a dotted Swiss blouse. I reached for my bag of makeup, picked up my book bag, grabbed a banana, and rushed out to Denny waiting for me in the car. I did my makeup and hair as we crossed the bridge. Except for smeared lipstick caused by the occasional jerk of the car when Den had an unexpected need to brake, I looked presentable when we arrived at school.

"Good luck, babe. Post your list, and I'll see you at lunch," he said after a kiss.

"You are so sweet, and I love you." I blew him a kiss and ran to tape my list on the wall by my door.

In my rush to run out of the house, I had grabbed the wrong shoes. I knew my feet on these high wedges would be tired by the end of the day. *This is Friday, and I need to look cute for the party. I will have to break my shoes in little by little today.*

As I posted the playlist, Edna, standing behind me, read it.

"Oh, girl, you are a crazy woman. Where'd all those parts come from?"

"Wrote a few parts last night."

"Looks like all who tried out got a role. A cast of fifty-seven will wear you out." At her classroom door, she looked back at me. "You look pretty, even if you didn't sleep. See you tonight at the party."

I went into my room and found a part of *Huckleberry Finn* I could use today. Weary and sleepy, I would ask my students to read and respond in groups of three. The better readers could help the weaker ones. Each group would have one book to share.

Outside my room I heard all kinds of squeals, laughter, and "oh, baby" shouted as students discovered their names on the roster.

Mr. Hughes tromped down the hall. "What's going on here? Move to class right now."

"I got a part, Mr. Hughes. I got a part," Albert explained.

"Me too, Mr. Hughes. I am a dancing elf."

"I know you're excited but go on now before you are tardy. No tardiness at Woodson, remember?"

I managed to post the attendance and assign reading groups before talk of the play began.

"Mizz Bayronne, when does play practice start?"

"Monday after school. I know you're eager, but let's try to understand Jim's plight of finding freedom."

They were quiet when I began the paragraph where I wanted them to begin. I omitted the N-word Twain used so much in his novel and hoped they would follow my modeling. I then put them in groups of three and handed a novel to each leader. "Readers, help your group down the river." I walked around and listened as pupil's read and reacted. I chose not to ask my weaker students to read aloud. They got their grade by contributing in the discussions and reciting to me one on one. I was more confident and enjoyed my classes each day. I recognized how different classes responded in new ways to the material and my teaching style.

My speech students were getting quite proficient in their presentations. Listening to their speeches gave me new insights into their priorities and lives. Even if I did spend endless hours grading on school nights and weekends, days like this affirmed all my efforts.

I realized practices each day after school would increase my workload. *Can I balance being a director, wife, teacher, and new kid on the block? My confidence is increasing after two months into this first semester. What is happening to Huck and me?* I smiled to myself and thought the same thought as Huck. *Ain't nowhere else I'd rather be.*

# LESSON 32

Helping those who are underserved and discriminated against is purposeful and fulfilling. It was rewarding to teach my students to advocate for themselves since I believe that being a self-advocate promotes self-determination.
—Dr. Lucinda Barron, Retired Professor and author

Walter's broad smile lit his face and brightened my day each time he entered the classroom.

"Good mornin', Mizz Bayronne." He sounded sincere. He squeezed the most out of each moment, using his hours like an orange—peeling back and savoring each section.

"Let's sing our lessons today, Mizz B," Walter sang. "Listen, a verb is be. It be used too much. Too much, wrong way. Not what you should say. Says Mizz B., Mizz B." He sang the words to a clever beat.

Giggles from Lily and Jesse started a wave of laughter, created a crescendo of delight, and the class howled. I leaned on their laughter to diminish my classroom difficulties. Their joy became my joy.

"Let's think about Walter's song. When do we use the *be* verb?"

"All the time," piped up Joan.

"Let me explain how to conjugate this verb." I wrote on the board:

- Present tense: I am
- Past tense: I was
- Future tense: I will be

I had explained this concept one on one and corrected it countless times in their writings. I hit a wall at each attempt at teaching the conjugation. I thought maybe focusing on one more example might clarify the use of be.

"Choose me, choose me." Jerome did his usual starfish wave in the air with hands spread wide.

"You have a question?"

"Nope. I have an answer and evidence, as you say. Mama, all my neighbors, and sports stars all say *be*, like me. *You* be wrong."

"Good point, Jerome. However, sometimes we learn a word and continue to use it incorrectly out of habit or from what we hear around us."

"So, why would it be wrong?"

"If I say, 'I ain't happy,' is that wrong?"

"Nope. Sorry, Miss Bayronne, you ain't happy."

"It would be better for me to say, 'I am not happy.'"

"Don't worry, I understand you be sad either way." Jerome wasn't being disrespectful. He didn't understand the concept. He simply modeled the words from his home and culture. *Ain't* and *be* were his correct.

I handed practice worksheets to the students. They would have to put the correct tense in the blank and name the tense. I had used similar worksheets four times already, trying to teach the verb tense of *to be*. I couldn't understand why they weren't grasping it.

A window opened in my mind, and imaginary fresh air removed the cobwebs. Implementing countless hours of worksheets had little impact on their understanding. This teaching method didn't work. Why continue with what isn't working? My obscure thinking became like Jerome's with the *be* verb. Because I was smothered in dittos and worksheets, I had grown oblivious to their inefficiency. As a student, I remember filling in the blanks and getting my A, but often I did not understand the concept and had learned little. I did this rote and isolated activity because I wanted a good grade. I knew how to write and look up the right answers. Because this had been my educational model, I'd repeated this technique in my teaching.

I realized many of my teachers chose not to delete worksheets in their education model. I understood in my first two months of teaching filling in the blank could be an easy avenue to classroom management. I let my students finish the worksheets because it kept them focused. That's what real learning looked like according to many of my previous teachers. Deep within, I felt ashamed of my lessons today.

I sat at my desk and gazed out my door as a seasoned teacher passed with a stack of worksheets to grade. Carrying those stacks of papers home to grade gave her a hunched-over posture. Whenever I looked into her room, the students were always bent over a page from a workbook or a ditto she provided. Seeing the students and the teacher hovered over worksheets created an image of an unkept garden. There is a need of weeding. If the garden is to be reformed, then I must lend a hand in the weeding. I would not hover over worksheets my entire career.

*Am I destined to be like this older teacher or many of my college professors? Help me, Lord, to stop rote activities which could stunt learning. Let me be a weed puller to show your beauty of learning to my students. Help me not become entrenched in a practice of teaching nothing but quietness in the classroom.*

Walter handed in his paper first. "Mizz Bayronne, your eyes look real sad. Are you disappointed in us?"

"I am not disappointed in any of you. Maybe me but not you."

"You be kind, Mizz Bayronne."

The bell rang and the students walked like well-trained cadets, putting their papers in the tray labeled completed.

*Have I chosen the wrong profession? Maybe my thinking is blurred or perhaps I am not a thinker. Maybe it was a mistake coming to New Orleans. Who am I?*

Right now, I was an unsuccessful teacher and wife. My constant lateness continued to be a battle. I left my toiletries and makeup spread across the bathroom counter every morning because I rushed. When we returned home, Denny complained about the mess in our bathroom.

Monthly, we argued about my overspending. I dreaded when the charge card bill came in the mail. When Denny sat at the old green table to pay bills, my heart would speed up. I would grit my teeth and wait for the lecture.

"Sandi, I don't have enough money in the checking account to pay this bill."

"Pay the lesser amount it suggests."

"Can't do that anymore. The interest is eating us up."

"I'm sorry. I'll do better next month. I promise."

"That's what you said last month."

By now he was yelling in frustration. To escape his harsh tone, I stomped into the bedroom. I removed myself in hopes the argument wouldn't escalate. My reaction became my defense.

As I sat on the corner of our bed, I could see Denny slumped over the stack of bills. Neither of us were competent money managers. We needed to add another skillset to our marriage toolbox.

We even disagreed where to keep kitchen utensils. We had a power struggle over everything but lovemaking. *Listen little lady, you'd better pull your act together. You are wasting money on clothes and shoes. You are causing this stress in your marriage. It's all your fault.*

I loved Denny regardless, but sometimes I didn't like him. I tried to find fault with him to justify my own shortcomings. He hurt my feelings, especially when he didn't focus or act like he was listening to me. I needed my husband to look at me, to respond when I shared my thoughts with him. I wanted the same enthusiasm Denny showed at the Saints' games. I wanted to be cherished. *Is that too much to ask?*

I guess Walter had read me well. My eyes couldn't hide the sadness in my heart. In the housing project, he had lived with despair and depression all around him. Yet, he chose to become a stringed musical instrument that played a compassionate melody. He recognized heartbrokenness in others and focused on serving them with his melody.

*Why can't I learn from him? He finds joy amidst oppression. Can I?*

# LESSON 33

God meets us where we are. He sees the individual. Watch how amazing He deals with others as He is completing something in us. —Matt Carder, Pastor of Commonway Church in Muncie, IN

Excited voices. Laughter. Dramatic renderings of lines. All these sounds welcomed me in the auditorium after my sixth-hour class. The cast, using their usual junior high school energy, wanted to begin. "Cast members. Please take a seat."

They sat and shushed one another with "Be quiet," and "Listen to her."

"Thanks for your cooperation. Let's read through and block the first act this afternoon."

The kids were excited to be a part of something bigger than their daily routines. They grabbed an opportunity and aimed to be their best. Opportunities were scarce for most of them, and a role in our Christmas program meant success. Some students had succeeded in the well-known Carter G. Woodson marching band, but that required being able to rent and play an instrument. Achievement in the play meant showing up and memorizing dialog.

By the end of the first week of practice, most students had memorized their parts. I thought back to my theater days when we would procrastinate and kind of know what to say until the director threatened to replace us.

Not these kids. They were quick to remember blocking positions and were, overall, cooperative. I had chosen Jason, the playground bully, to be my stage manager. Edna thought I was insane. I suspected with some modeling from me, Jason could do it and learn to manage people in a new way, rather than shoving and hitting.

"Jason, please show the Christmas singers where they should stand." I pointed to stage right.

He herded and pushed our cast together as if he were moving sheep. They didn't mind being urged forward or scrunched. The cast found their designated stage positions with Jason's push-and-move forward technique. While Edna helped the singers with their dance moves, I asked Jason to sit beside me.

"Jason, you're doing a good job, understanding where people should be standing."

"Thanks, ma'am."

"When we block the next scene, could you *show* them where to stand and not *push* them into place?"

"Do you mean standing in front of each other?"

"Blocking in theater means deciding where each person will be located on the stage. I determine the spot where all the audience can see them."

"Yes, ma'am. So, after you decide, how can I make them do what I want without leaning on them?"

"Could you stand in the place where you want the person? Then, ask the student to please stand where you are on the stage?"

"Yes, ma'am, but I don't think that will work."

"I would appreciate if you tried a new way." As he returned to the stage, he mumbled.

During the blocking of the next scene, Jason darted to the spot where he wanted the actor to stand. "Here. Want you here." Then, he jumped high with his body tense and stiff. Because of his long, lean body build, his jumping reminded me of a pogo stick. I couldn't help but smile at his efforts.

"Here, be here." He would do a springing jump, but he didn't jam anyone into their assigned place on stage. Jason was working out well and had the high-spirited energy and determination to take charge and oversee his peers. Perhaps, the kids still had a little fear he would slip back into his bully role and pop them one, so they stood wherever Jason hopped up and down. I named him Jahopper. He accepted this name as an affectionate title, and he responded well to my requests. I noticed his usual frown and grimace relaxed at rehearsals.

One day after school when I came into the auditorium, a small boy with a large Afro hairdo was sitting in the front row. Chewing a wad of pink bubble gum as big as his head, he stood and approached.

"Great White lady, can I watch this show?"

"What's your name?"

"Jimmy."

"Where do you live?"

"I stay in the project. I'm in fourth grade."

"Do you want to be an actor someday?"

"Nope. I want to watch."

"Okay, Jimmy, but no gum in the auditorium, and keep your feet off the chairs."

"Yes, ma'am."

He threw his gum into the trash can, took his seat, and watched the whole practice without saying a word. The next afternoon, he was sitting front and center with a friend. "Great White lady, he be my friend, and he know the rules."

I smiled at Jimmy and his friend and proceeded with practice.

Debra Brown knew her lines as a giggling gaga. Her cackle, shrill and infectious, made all of us laugh. Her large deep-set eyes glinted with joy.

Adding a horselaugh and dramatic lines to James's already animated face created a strong stage presence. "Stay in character. You ain't the gaga," Jahopper voiced to others in the cast who were chuckling, too.

Jahopper paced back and forth behind the stage, reminding the cast to stay in their roles. But, when they saw me wiping tears of mirth from my eyes, they began laughing again.

"I said, be your own character," Jahopper shouted as he walked behind the other actors.

Debra could outdance and outsing anyone on stage—except James. He had all the right moves. He knew the exact pacing of his lines, stood tall, and stayed in character. James was light-skinned, and his beautiful long lashes lined his round eyes. Many of the girls were attracted to him. They wanted to talk to him and be next to him when not on stage.

When James and Debra were opposite each other in a scene, neither Jahopper nor I had much work. They were naturals. With Debra's and James's combined energy and talent, their captivating performances entertained and ignited the whole cast. They inspired me every day.

Each afternoon, Jimmy arrived with a few more friends, a growing and engrossed audience.

"Afternoon, Jimmy," I said.

"They know the rules," he said.

Jimmy's eyes were dark black and set in his head like giant orbs. His lashes curled on the end, and his teeth were perfect, white, and gleaming. I wanted to grab and hug him but knew I couldn't because he was a big boy and a leader in his age group. He kept his friends in perfect order. The cast greeted Jimmy and didn't seem to mind their audience was increasing.

"Dancers and singers, hit it. Give me all you got in this scene." I was surprised when Miss Bryant, the new music teacher, volunteered to choreograph and practice with my students. Having come on faculty in November, she wanted to know the students better. I had not seen much of her because she had such a challenge to get the students and her curriculum together.

*Thank you, Lord, for sending Miss Bryant. I didn't know I needed her, but you did. Could you help me with this conversation with Jahopper?*

"Jahopper, come sit by me, please." I beckoned him over.

Jahopper came right away. "I didn't threaten nobody. I didn't shove nobody."

"I know you didn't. You're doing so well and helping this play happen."

"Yes, ma'am."

"Now, watch this scene and see if anyone is blocking another character from the audience's view."

Edna had choreographed the dancers and practiced backstage while I had rehearsed other scenes. To my amazement, the dancers spun and bopped and moved in synchronization like the Rockettes. When they finished the scene, my awe drew me up and out of my seat. I clapped so hard my hands burned.

Jimmy's friends turned their heads toward me at the same time as if directed by a compass pointing north. I couldn't speak because tears were flowing, and the words were stuck in my throat.

"Watcha want me to do?" Jahopper panicked when he saw my tears.

"Mizz Bayronne, what's wrong? What we do wrong?" On stage, Debra's usual happy face melted into a compassionate big-eyed stare.

I continued clapping and smiled despite my dribbles on my cheeks. Perhaps my students had not seen many happy tears.

Speechless, I could only wipe the continuous, warm droplets from my cheeks. Jimmy's crowd clapped, too. The stage kids hugged one another and folded together like an accordion. They were one. They were successful, and they knew it.

Every now and then a man's mind is stretched by a new idea or sensation, and never shrinks back to its former dimensions. —Oliver Wendell Holmes Sr.

Daily practices were wearing on me but not the students. Attendance and participation were one hundred percent. These kids taught me a new meaning to the word *dedication*. Day after day, they uncorked their bottles of energy combined with passion to create their stage personas.

Watching them dance with fervor to *Rock Around the Christmas Clock* generated vitality into my moments of weariness, especially after a long day in the classroom. Seeing these kids' earnest and total commitment spoke to my heart. They were no longer stuck in the rudimentary life of repeated everyday activities. The new lifestyle included a concrete and attainable goal.

As I entered the auditorium each afternoon, I smiled at Jimmy and his gang and gave them a little bow. They beamed and nodded nearly in unison. Each day, even before I called curtain, Jahopper would direct the cast to their correct spaces on stage.

Amazingly, no playbooks were needed after the first week. Lines were memorized and skills became more polished each day. Near the end of December, the well-rehearsed cast needed few corrections, allowing our daily practices to fly by without a hitch. With much excitement, I announced we were finally ready for dress rehearsal.

"Mizz Bayronne," Lily looked concerned, "what if someone forgets their line?"

"Don't worry, you have known your script since the first week. Someone near you could lead you back to your conversation by repeating his or her last message with a cue word in it. You have worked so hard and studied your playbooks until they are raggedy. Jimmy and his crowd have been a built-in followership. Your stage presence is amazing. You are ready as your mama's grits in the morning. In fact, you are rich and smooth like them. Come ready to perform and share your gifts for Woodson tomorrow."

Squeals of laughter and loud recitation of lines filled the air backstage. Girls fixed each other's hair and put on ruffled red aprons with their green bobby socks. Edna tied perfect big red bows. The young ladies looked like an image on a Christmas card with their starched white blouses and red hair bows contrasting against their dark hair.

Magnolia Project mamas assembled fifty-seven costumes. Many of these mothers volunteered their sewing skills. Cheerful, willing faculty members donated parts of costumes or purchased crinolines or shoes from thrift stores. Everybody pulled together to be a part of something bigger than themselves.

After school during the dress-rehearsal week, students decorated several donated Christmas trees. Lily and Millie brought handmade red and green paper chains and a popcorn garland for the tree handmade by the neighbors from their block.

"We sit outside my door while my sister made a big kettle of popcorn. The smell called in the neighbors, and they came a runnin'." Millie's dark eyes twinkled with excitement as she told me of the fun. "We kept givin' them needles and a big, long string. They'd eat a little and string a little. My sister would bring out more corn. We kept eatin' and stringin' until we had enough garland to decorate the Magnolia Project."

Lily nodded and smiled, looking at her sister with the memories dancing in her eyes. Sharing this moment of fun with their friends and family brought delight and joy to the twins. Once again, the twins defined true happiness to me.

To my surprise, Jahopper brought an ornament from home. Even though the angel looked well used, he wanted to hang it on one of the front limbs.

"This be my place," Jahopper said. "I be the stage manager, and this be my decoration." He hopped in front of the limb.

As Jahopper hung the small, frayed angel on the tree limb, James reached to hang his ornament at this same spot. I watched as Jahopper frowned and then puffed up like a frog. Up on stage, behind a motionless mask of anger stood a young man who had learned a new, proper perspective by replacing his rage with a spirit of giving.

"Oh, oh, they be trouble, Mizz Bayronne," Joan announced loud and clear.

Suddenly, the laughter turned to silence. All eyes focused on James and Jahopper.

Jahopper's body language said, "Move out of my way" to those around him. He stood his ground in front of the tree with his ornament on his tree limb.

James's body language changed. He stepped back and said, "Hey, man, that's your place. You deserve it. You've really helped us."

"No, man, you are the star singer. Put your ornament there." Jahopper reached to remove his angel ornament.

"Naw, look here, this limb be big enough to hold both ornaments," James suggested.

Jahopper's body language softened. His facial expression, usually frowning or blank, lit up with a big, genuine grin as he punched James teasingly on his forearm. After the amplified silence came laughter between them. The two actors were writing their own script and delivering their lines with perfect timing. Jahopper's now cheerful and lighthearted demeanor pulled the onlookers' faces into soft, broad smiles. Chuckling began to flow throughout the auditorium.

When I saw and heard this congenial transaction between the boys, tears welled up in my eyes. Jahopper knew success for perhaps the first time in his fifteen years. Instead of advancement by way of bullying, pushing, screaming, or controlling, as stage manager, he practiced working with others. Now his abruptness turned to courtesy. His stage persona transitioned into this character, and he approached everyday challenges in a new way. In six weeks of rehearsals, he had become the best of himself, an energetic and effective leader.

These kids had learned more than acting skills. Ironically, they had learned how to work with one another. At first, the actor considered only the significance of his role. Then the play created a life experience. Now his role, no longer selfishly motivated, turned the actor into considering the importance to the whole cast and the purpose of the play.

Debra studied my face, "Why are your eyes crying again?"

I put my arm around her and whispered in her ear, "Because I'm happy, girl, because I'm happy."

Others brought one or two ornaments from home. I found a whole forgotten box—much like these kids—

stowed away in a storage closet behind the stage. The hanging of the greens was a turning point in my first year of teaching. I could feel the kids' consideration and watched them become strong characters on stage. Each one acted, danced, and sang with the drive and single-mindedness of an Olympic champion. Yet, they were one. They had been soldiers under Edna's command on our first recruiting day. Now they were authentic, a unit winning a battle.

The simple set included a table and a stuffed chair placed near the apron of the stage for dialogue scenes. With such a large cast, we needed all the room we could gain to accommodate the dancing and running with news of Christmas surprises.

A large record player on stage kept Joan hopping. She was in charge of keeping the records in order. Several times before the play she had checked the order of the stacked records. After cueing the music, Joan joined the back row of dancers and singers. At the end of each song, she spun and circled toward the record player and changed the record to the next song. She did it so smoothly I sometimes didn't even notice. Joan blossomed from her role as a dancing angel to accepting additional production responsibilities.

Before the Christmas play, Joan often stopped by my room to say hi. She enjoyed straightening my desk and organizing the stacks of student papers waiting to be graded. She helped with anything I asked, but rarely needed to be asked. Joan completed what she saw needed to be done. Each week, she matured more than the week before. Her responsibilities as part of the Christmas play gave her the affirmation she had needed. I knew Joan didn't have a mother. I cherished her friendship, even though I had been warned in my college classes not to become friends with my students. Joan was different. She didn't take advantage of our relationship, and I knew she never would.

Edna came up with yards and yards of red ribbon. Walter's mom made red bow ties with Edna's ribbon for the guys. She had always been supportive of me. Walter told me about his first afternoon at home after he discovered he had a White teacher.

"I told Mama I had a White teacher," he said.

"Was she surprised?"

Mama stopped ironin' and sat by me at the kitchen table and replied, 'I want you to give this White teacher the same respect you would give a Black teacher.' She patted my hand and went back to her ironin'."

"You followed your mama's advice well."

Walter's mother had done a great job rearing him. His manners were impeccable, and he worked hard at the task before him. His gentle nature built him into an easy student to teach and love. Our relationship had grown stronger since September. He entered the classroom with a big, easy smile. Even though he didn't realize it at the time, Walter increased my confidence in becoming a better teacher. His class responses were honest, and he was willing to participate even if unsure he understood. He taught me about being Black in the late 1960s. He took pleasure in sharing his stories with me before and after class, in his essays, and now after play rehearsal.

He shared that he wanted to have a chocolate sundae at Kresge's Five and Ten, a favorite drugstore at that time. "I would sit at the counter every Saturday. I'd sit a long time, and then, I'd ask the clerk, "Why won't you serve me?" He ignored me and waited on the White folks at the bar.

"I'd spin on the stool, trying to grab his attention. 'Excuse me. I'd like an ice cream sundae, please. Sir, I would like a sundae with hot chocolate on top. A cherry, too, please. Here's my twenty-six cents.' I was plenty mad.

"This Saturday, a boy came up to the bar and sat beside me. He ordered what I'd asked for, even the cherry. So, when the clerk set the sundae in front of him, I swished it right over to me on that slippery counter. I took one big bite, includin' the cherry and all the ice cream I could put in my mouth. I never tasted nothin' that good.

"'Boy, I am calling the cops,' the clerk screamed at me.

"The little White boy was still staring at his half-eat sundae, and I took off a runnin' like a train was coming toward me. I was so scared."

I watched Walter through eyes filled with love as he told me his heart story. I wanted to tell him I would buy him all the chocolate sundaes he would ever want.

"I'm so sorry. So sorry for all those Saturdays without sundaes. I'm apologizing for that ice cream clerk who was born and bathed in ignorance."

"Oh, Mizz Bayronne, you didn't do it to me. Don't apologize. I wanted to tell you a time I tried to stand my ground in New Orleans. You see, I knew my place but wanted to be someone different that day."

# LESSON 35

Nine tenths of education is encouragement. —Anatole
France

Dress rehearsal went smoothly, and I felt intoxicated
with admiration for these hard-working kids. I handed
them a simple playbook and the students turned the
outline into a lively production filled with music, well-
executed lines, and joyful dancing. Each of the young men
and women who began as a simple dandelion magically
turned into a hybrid flower. Magic stardust washed us
all. We began as separate units and merged into a united
body reaching toward the same goal. I never anticipated
directing my first play could bring this much joy and such
a close connection with the students at Woodson.

Jimmy and his squad of friends gave the cast a standing
ovation. Watching the big guys of the neighborhood
perform influenced those tough little guys. Jimmy's crew
watched how the older kids followed directions and did
their best on stage each afternoon. This play was the
format for learning love and admiration for all ages.

"Great job, kids. I'm so impressed with your talent and
your unity," I said.

When my voice cracked, Debra said, "Here she goes
cryin' again. Those tears show us God is washing her with
love."

The cast gave me group hugs.

"Cast, if you perform tomorrow in the assembly as you did this afternoon, you'll knock their bobby socks off."

Everyone laughed and cheered and hopped. Debra giggled. The twins grinned from ear to ear, and Walter gave me the biggest, warmest hug.

"Are you pleased with us?" Joan asked.

"Honey, *pleased* is not strong enough. I am poppin' with pride. But let's give Miss Bryant a hand of applause for her help teaching us the songs and making the music explode."

"Yes, thank you." Their eyes brightened when they looked Miss Bryant's way.

"Let's give Miss Bradley a big thank you applause. We couldn't have done this without her help with costumes and choreography."

"Thank you, Mizz Bradley. You are great. You are an answer to prayer," announced Debra.

"You showed me how I can make a career of dancing and singing," James said.

Edna's eyes looked misty. This contrasted with her usual calm and non-emotional state.

From his front row seat, Jimmy stood and came up to me.

"Yes, Jimmy?" He had never approached during the six weeks of rehearsals, so this caught me by surprise. "Great White lady, I really like these shows, but they be awful lot alike."

Jimmy's band of boys served as our built-in fans, quiet and respectful. I didn't realize, though, each day they expected to see a different dance, a different song, *and* a new story. I pulled him into an embrace. Small but muscular, he resisted at first, then fell into my hug. I looked forward to these little kids coming to daily rehearsals after they got out of school. Nevertheless, they kept coming to see if anything new would happen.

Laughter reverberated across the stage. Debra and I bent over with laughter until, breathless, I had to sit. Thinking of Jimmy's guileless, forthright critique of the play, I could not stop my ongoing, animated laughing. Rehearsal fatigue vanished, replaced by comic relief, and energy renewed with overflowing joy.

Regaining my composure, I slowed the lighthearted snickers of everyone with an announcement. "Kids, Mr. Baron and I'd like to host a cast party for you after our final performance. We'll set up the music and food in the cafeteria after the evening performance."

They were quiet and looked at me. As I peered into those gorgeous brown and black eyes, I wondered what they were thinking.

"Mizz Bayronne, you mean all of us?" Jahopper asked.

"Yes, I mean all of you—everyone involved—those who helped with lights, costumes, staging, and acting. You achieved jointly. Never could it have happened without you working together."

With his face lit up, Jahopper hopped in place while James sang out a hallelujah. The choir repeated his chorus, and the dancers bopped in the aisles. Our cast party had already begun.

Denny watched from the doorway with Mike Leonard. Their amusement from our joyous whoops produced applause from them. I caught a wink from Denny and knew he approved of my efforts because of the students' merrymaking.

"Let's call it a day. Two productions to go before we can party."

One by one, they returned props and costumes to the storage room. The cast and stagehands left in small groups, reciting lines, or singing their songs.

When all the students were gone and the lights were out, Denny whispered, "Let's go have a drink." He slipped his hand into mine, and we walked from the building, smiling inside out. *I wish we could freeze this moment in time and wander forever in this vision of love and success.*

# LESSON 36

From the start it has been the theater's business to entertain people ... it needs no other passport than fun. —Bertolt Brecht

That evening, parents of the cast came, as well as local folks, and packed the audience. Standing at the door, I welcomed all who came into the auditorium and recognized many of the same faces I had seen during my first parent-teacher meeting.

"Child, you are loved by these kids," one mother said as she embraced me.

"Walter thinks you are the kindest woman he has ever known." Mrs. Jones patted my face like she would do to a four-year-old.

"Girl, you have made these mamas happy," Sylvia said.

"Hey, why are you here tonight? You saw the play earlier. You're going to be reacting like little Jimmy this time," I said.

Sylvia chuckled. "I came for you and to watch again. I love seeing the kids doing their dream."

"Thanks, I don't know who has enjoyed this more, them or me."

Joan broke the laughter and quieted the auditorium by turning on the first record, which signaled all to be in their places on stage or in their choir positions. This all-school performance excited the cast, and they wanted to perform their best for their peers.

Lights blinked, and the cast froze in their places. The performers were in rare form, showing their families their talent and gaining self-worth in their success. The audience reacted by becoming a wellspring of tapping, clapping, and snapping to the beat of the Christmas melodies. Their reactions, coupled with the performers' passion, became a torch that lit the auditorium.

In a whirlwind, their dances began. Their excitement projected to their peers. Woodson students watched and clapped to the beat as the cast transported merrymaking and amusement to them.

Suddenly, the music stopped. Each character on stage stared at the silent record player. Joan stiffened. She didn't know what to do. Even James exhibited stage fright. The scene looked like children playing freeze on the playground.

"O my gosh, Edna," I whispered. "What's happening?"

"Be calm, girl. Look." She pointed at Jahopper.

Slinking to the back of the stage, Jahopper tried not to be noticed. He bent and unobtrusively plugged in the cord. The record player jumped back to life. The cast returned to their singing and synchronized dance steps as if nothing had happened. The play moved forward. They pushed all their excitement and nervous energy into their first performance.

Invigorated, the audience snapped their fingers and tapped their feet. The entire auditorium burst with Christmas joy.

Mike Leonard performed his own little bop in the corner.

Sylvia's smile beamed as she moved to the beat.

When I caught the principal's eye, he gave me the thumbs up as he sang along with the choir.

The choir had gone through a difficult transition this year when the New York teacher left. Their new teacher had reached out to them as individuals and earned their admiration. Miss Bryant had rehearsed the singing parts in her music room while we practiced lines on stage. This cooperative effort worked well, preparing the students for their performance.

I watched each beautiful face as they sang, danced, and acted in perfect harmony. This opportunity to perform gave them confidence. Their peers' interaction of praising and moving to the beat showed they were enjoying themselves as much as the choir.

As I sat in a corner seat, I appreciated Debra couldn't see and call me out for crying again. Although many of the spectators had lived with hardships and poverty, they could put that aside and become transfixed on the moment where radiance rested. They knew the importance of teaching their children to grab the moment and rejoice.

At the end, the audience stood and applauded long and loud. The cast members were like lightning bugs on the stage.

Another milestone had been achieved in my career. I directed a play successfully. My Midwest theater classes gave me a sound foundation. This training, coupled with the kids' innate talents to grab the moment and move forward, produced an outstanding event.

After a standing ovation from the onlookers, Mr. Bergeron expressed his gratitude to the performers, Miss Bryant, Miss Bradley and me. Dancing, snapping fingers, and singing *Rock Around the Christmas Clock*, the students exited the stage. Sylvia gave me a big hug as did many other staff members. This marked another day of feeling accepted and loved.

"Oh, Miss Garcia, you should be proud of your twin girls. They are talented and beautiful," said a woman who sat near her.

"Oh, girl, you brought up your boy right. He acted and sounded professional," another mother said to her friend.

The kids hugged me to smithereens, and I wore smeared makeup and wilted hair as evidence of being loved. I didn't care because this play fulfilled my dream too. My first production achieved a win.

I caught Joe's eyes looking at me as he came in to clean the auditorium.

"Hi, Joe. I hope our cast or visitors haven't left you too much work."

"It's fine, Mrs. Bayonne." His eyes shone with joy. "You made a lot of people happy tonight. You served them well. That's what's important."

I hurried to the cafeteria for the cast party. Sylvia, Edna, Mike, and Denny had set out the food. Den and Mike had spent the afternoon preparing the cheese platter. I had cleaned pounds of produce the night before for the vegetable tray, complete with onion dip. Crackers were in place, and chocolate fondue warmed.

Colorful platters of fruit plates complemented the table. Sylvia filled large bowls with salty treats from the many bags of Cajun potato chips and thirty boxes of crackers purchased earlier. Frosty cold cans of pop were plopped in ice, so students could drink all they wanted. As soon as the two giant bakery sheet cakes were on the table, Edna cut portions for easy serving. Starving from dancing and moving on stage, the cast dove in. Jahopper brought the record player and plugged in our music. The cast ate, danced, and reminisced every scene, action, and cue.

"Jahopper, you save' the day when you fixed the record player," James said.

"Joan, you sure keep' us organized on stage. I didn't know you were so talented," Walter's comment spurred her to complete the compliment.

"You be a star up there. I think you goin' to be a movie star."

With this comment, Walter swelled with pride and his dream ignited. "I think you be right."

"This is great fondue." Debra selected a berry. "My favorite is sticking strawberries and those little pieces of cake into the thick chocolate pot."

"This is the best party ever. Thank you." James did a spin and toasted me with his Pepsi.

The twins were side by side, entertained by dipping fruit in the fondue.

"This be the best." Millie complimented me between fondue dips. "Thank you. Mama liked our play a lot."

"When will we have another play? I want to be the stage manager again," Jahopper added.

"You were a great stage manager, Jahopper, and I couldn't have done it without you." We applauded.

His peers helped him along the path of learning how to give to others and reap joy. He wrote a new chapter in his life story. Jahopper had exchanged his title of bully for the stage manager who had saved the show.

Edna stood by me and whispered, "You were right, Sandi. He was a good risk you took."

# LESSON 37

Marriage is a feast where the grace is sometimes better than the dinner. —Charles Caleb Colton

The next week, all the joy from my success evaporated as we returned from grocery shopping. "You can't keep shopping," Denny ranted. "Our charge card debt is ridiculous."

"Maybe you could learn from Jahopper to quit bullying."

"I know you're tired from the play. But these bills are eating me alive."

"Way to ruin our weekend." I glared at my bully.

"Stop charging everything you see, so we can stop fighting."

"I'm tired of you yelling, and I want to go home." I pressed close to the door on the passenger side of the car.

We arrived at Mary Poppins and pulled into our driveway. I got out of the car and slammed my door as hard as I could. I dug through my purse for my house keys. By the time I found them, Denny had unlocked the door and smirked. I tromped my feet on the floor all the way into our bedroom. I knew why Flossy Mae, the playground bully, stomped. The action demonstrated her anger. Now I tromped too. My anger on the inside fueled by resentment exploded through my pounding feet.

I threw myself on the bed and cried and cried until I fell asleep from exhaustion. Denny had learned from our past fights not to try to comfort me, but to let me process my anger. I wanted to pound on him if he came near. He became my enemy instead of my beloved.

I awakened two hours later, showered, put on my robe, and came out to the living room. There was Denny, watching an old Western movie. It amazed me he could watch the same Lone Ranger series over and over. I guessed he used Lone Ranger as a comfort from his youth. I sat next to him on the couch.

"You feelin' better?" He rubbed my back softly.

"No, but I'm not so mad at you anymore."

"Whew, what a relief." He took me in his arms. "I hate for us to fight. I love you so much, but when you strike at me like a cobra, I'm frozen prey."

"I'm sorry."

"Awww, baby. Let's try not to yell at each other so much."

"Or shop so much?"

He kissed me on the top of my head.

"We have a lot of problems, don't we?" I leaned my head on his shoulder as evidence of my submission.

"Not a lot."

"I know I shop too much, especially when we're fighting."

"Why's that?"

"Shopping gives birth to a new me. It imitates joy, and I come home fixed."

"I'd like to fix you right now. You smell nice and look sexy in your robe."

"I understand, but let's talk a little more."

"I'm listening, so keep sharing your thoughts, girl. But the next time I kiss you, we're doing more than talk."

"Marriage is harder than I thought. We don't communicate enough."

"I know." He sighed. "The guys at work say their wives are always complaining about their men not communicating with them. Maybe it's a guy thing."

"I still don't know how to handle a lot of situations. I don't know how to be a good wife. Sometimes, I am selfish."

"We both need to work on giving in more. Like right now." He kissed me long and hard, and our conversation ended.

Later, I lay in his arms. "I like making love with you. Now, let's chat more."

He laughed. "You've got my total attention."

"Marriage is difficult and sometimes perplexing, but together we reach solutions, even if it's with make-up sex." I touched his cheek. "But teaching is more complicated and harder than I expected because it's layered with frustration. And fear."

"What are you afraid of?"

I swallowed back the tightness in my throat. "I'm scared there will be a girl fight in my room. Those are awful. I expect to see Drake standing in my door with a knife, even though no one has seen him for months. I fill with panic when the class gets out of control."

Denny leaned on one elbow. "Henri Todd is so esteemed that when he says stop, they do. Foster knows where the students are coming from because he struggled with obstacles and hardships. I learn so much from these guys at work. We're one big team of teachers. They help me with discipline when I'm getting in trouble."

"That's the difference. I'm alone in my room." In that moment, I realized how deep my fear went. "I'm trying to figure out how to teach and discipline."

"I know it's tougher for you."

"Some days, I want to run away," I confessed.

"From me or them?"

"Both."

He patted my arm. I think he patted when he had no words.

"I feel challenged because I've lost control of my life," I continued. "I don't know how to take your outbursts of anger or theirs. All my life, I wanted to escape Mama's screaming and anger. Your anger and theirs take me right back in the middle of it, especially when you yell at me."

"I'm a hothead. I get mad, and it's over." He gave an exaggerated shrug. "Don't take my words as threats. I have an anger issue. I need to be more sensitive to my volume control."

"I need to talk it out and understand why you are mad."

"Loving each other and learning to live together is difficult. We're going to make mistakes. We have learned to wait and agree to agree. We've learned to listen to each other's perspective when we cuddle and reflect on why a conversation turned into a screaming match. Our skills will grow like our love. I want to stay together always." After his thoughts, he looked at me with a smile that sucked me into his soul.

"You can always squeeze a smile out of me. I hope you always will."

"I *know* so." Denny sat up. "May I take my bride to our favorite Italian restaurant?"

"I don't know." I felt self-conscious. "I'm lookin' pale and sad."

"Put on something cute, and let's go."

Following Denny's directions, I dabbed on a little makeup to cover my blotchy face and did a quick outfit change. *I guess we aren't going back home. Lots of weeds in my life, and I had better start pulling them so the flowers can grow. It is the Woodson way. Make do, and find something good in today.*

"I have a surprise for you." Denny gave a sly smile.

"You do? I love surprises." I turned from the mirror to face him. "Tell me."

"Let's go to dinner." He touched my nose. "And then I'll tell you."

*At last, my world feels safe, and I'm in love with Denny. How can I swing from deep despondency to such glee? I don't understand myself, nor does he.*

We entered our favorite local diner hand in hand. We ordered their specialty, white lasagna with a blend of white cheeses melted on homemade pasta. Their discreet seasonings were not loud and bold. I was awed at the blend of cheeses and gentle spices. As we ate, I understood why they called it Italian comfort food. Each gooey bite calmed me and soothed my stomach.

"Time for your surprise," Denny said with a glint in his eye. Den paid the bill with me begging to know my surprise.

"I saw that you still had that advertisement about the lady selling basset hounds. I've been thinkin' maybe you need one of her pups. You've always owned a pet, and a basset hound could create a warmer home-like atmosphere."

"Are you serious?"

He held the ad in front of my face with the address highlighted in yellow. "See, I have the address. It's across Lake Pontchartrain Bridge. Let's find it."

"You are the best husband ever." I squealed and applauded.

"We'll go explore. This might not be the one," he cautioned.

"We will check out their health and their mother's appearance." I knew full well looking meant buying.

We sang with the radio and life bubbled warm and secure once again. Nothing mattered now except finding that puppy. As we pulled onto the street, my heart pumped hard in my chest.

"This is the address." He parked in front of a small home.

He knocked on the door. An older, rounded lady answered.

"I called you earlier in the day about seeing a basset pup."

"Yes, sir, come right in." She opened the door wider. "You and the missus."

Denny must have called her when I napped. *He really does love me.*

She led us to a room in the back of the house where a large red and white basset greeted us. Her ears stretched as far as her milk-filled teats, both touching the ground. Friendly and willingly, she led us to her three pups.

They were funny little red creatures, tripping on their ears. All irresistible. Like miniature toddlers, they wrestled, played, and fell over. All three rolled their big brown eyes to see if we were watching. We were amused at their clumsiness.

"Go ahead. Pet 'em. Pick 'em up. These three are left from a litter of six."

I sat in the middle of the floor to cuddle and kiss them. Overflowing with bliss, I could only smile. Petting the puppies calmed me. Those soft velvety ears brought happiness through my fingertips. Denny knelt, and one of the pups scrambled to him.

I had been reared with dogs, and they were like another family member. Denny, on the other hand, never had but one.

Den's mother kept their house immaculate. Everything had to be polished and in its place, so his mom had insisted the dirty dog stay on a rope in the backyard. Alone, outside in the yard without love or care, Denny's dog didn't live long. I had guessed with Den's lack of a real pet experience, he could not understand my desire for a dog. He loved me enough to try something I wanted.

The little redhead girl puppy nuzzled under his chin. Den laid his head on top of hers and formed a funny clicking noise that seemed to soothe her whimpers. Her four white socks were all I could see because she cuddled so close into him.

I stroked the two who were a reddish—butterscotch color. All the pups were marked with a white sock pattern at the end of their wrinkled and bowed legs. The female Denny held had ears so long they appeared to belong to a larger dog. Denny kissed her on the head. That did it.

"We would love our sweet little girl my husband is holding."

"Yes, ma'am," the owner bobbed her head. "She reminds me of her mother."

Denny nodded to the other pups. "Are you sure you want this one?"

"She wants *you*. She picked *you*."

He paid the breeder, and she gave us enough puppy food for a couple of days. Den took the papers to send to the American Kennel Club, and we carried home our new baby, wrapped in a little pink receiving blanket the kind woman provided.

I held our puppy while Denny drove. "We need to find a vet to give her vaccines, but right now she needs a name."

"How about Susie?"

"She needs a long name to fit her ears." I held out an ear, which was nearly as long as the dog. "Look at these big, soft eyes looking at us. She loves us already."

"Maybe we should name her after one of our parents since she is their grandchild." Denny corrected, "granddog."

As we sang along with the radio, I held her close, and her warm baby smell of milk and grain brought memories of puppies past. Her long, pink tongue cleaned my chin.

Once we pulled into the driveway, I said, "Let's name her after your dad."

"We're going to call a girl dog Henry?"

"Henrietta," I explained.

He hurried to my side of the car and opened my door. He took the pup in his big hands and looked into her sleepy, brown eyes. "Welcome to your new home, Henrietta."

# LESSON 38

A man who has never gone to school may steal a freight car; but if he has a university education, he may steal the whole railroad. —Theodore Roosevelt

After Christmas break, we welcomed in 1968. With the play behind me and less grading to do at the beginning of the semester, my freedom beckoned me to pursue my favorite pastime, shopping. As I recalled Denny's recent plea to slow my use of the charge card, my shopping spirit had slowed considerably. Yet, I needed new makeup.

Denny pointed to the bill. "Our debt is so large I can only pay the interest each month."

I decided not to sit around the apartment and listen to his lectures. "I think I will go out for coffee. We need a little space from each other." I walked over to kiss Denny, but his rigid body and tensed shoulders muscles made it clear he didn't want to kiss. I grabbed my purse and keys and started toward the front door.

"Go entertain yourself with the shops," he shouted. "Put us in more debt."

With those words of warning, I slammed the door with a deafening bang.

At the small shopping center, I spotted a breakfast shop and parked. I needed chicory coffee to calm my nerves and added to my order a large cinnamon roll covered with roasted pecans. I sat at a small tin-topped table and smothered my anger and shame with my sticky treat.

The sudden sugar high gave me an immediate pleasure push, and the warm thick coffee soothed my troubled soul. On the wall hung a Maybelline poster, which portrayed a woman with dark, plush lashes. Her eyes were thickly lined with black kohl. She depicted the current makeup trend of over decorated eyes and pasty light lipstick. I wished I could imitate the new style.

The woman sitting behind me scolded her two girls for not acting like ladies. She promised there would be no morning donuts until they could eat them without making messes. This scenario sounded uncomfortably reminiscent of my childhood so, I paid my bill and left. As I stepped out the door, I noticed a small local store and went in.

*What harm can that do to his lousy old debt? I could see what new fashions might be in stock. It would help me look forward to spring. Perhaps I should look through a magazine or find some Mardi Gras decorations.*

A male clerk greeted me. "Look around, Miss. We have lovely and useful items."

"Thank you." In another area, I viewed bright yellow flowered tote bags. *Remember, you are browsing. No more purchases because I don't want Denny glaring at me carrying packages into the apartment. He is probably jogging now to calm his anger. I want us to make up and find a new adventure today.*

The makeup display featured the Maybelline mascara and lipstick I had viewed on the poster in the coffee shop. I picked up the mascara and read the application directions. I pretended to return it to the shelf but instead slipped it in my sweater pocket. Next, I looked at the newest pale colors of lipstick. I picked up a couple and studied the new almost white colors. Again, I pretended to return the lip color to the display, but instead I slid a pale pink lipstick into my pocket.

"What do you have in your pocket, ma'am?"

Frozen with fear, I could not move. I gasped for air. I had been caught.

"Give me the lipstick and mascara," the clerk demanded.

I had no words. Sudden perspiration spilled from every pore. My hair was as wet as if I had been in a rainstorm. *I have been caught shoplifting. This can't be true.*

I didn't deny it. I never intended to buy the items. On impulse, I had stuffed them into my pocket, thinking no one would notice. I can't remember why I did it, except I really wanted the lipsticks and makeup. Without reason, I thought I could get away with taking them. I heard a voice in my mind. *Take them. You want them. You don't have money. And you know you can't charge. So, take them.* To my surprise, I did. I listened to that mental prompting and entrapment followed. My pleasure turned to terror.

The Black community had entrusted their kids to me. With no strings attached, Woodson had offered the gift of hospitality as I walked through those doors. Now they would learn I was a thief. *Thief, thief, thief.*

"Ma'am, I am not going to say it again." The clerk demanded, "Come with me."

I followed zombie-like to the cluttered back room of the small store. My knees buckled and I sat and cried. I had not been to this deep place of hurt since my mother's unexpected slap of my face on a warm, sunny day. These hot tears and terrifying moment were the same. This catalytic day I cried equally hard and loud. Snot poured from my nostrils. I went from such a high to my lowest moment in New Orleans.

The man handed me a wad of stiff tissues. I wiped my nose and begged, "Please don't call the police. Please don't tell anyone. Here is the lipstick and mascara. They aren't open. They aren't hurt. Please take them back."

"Ma'am, it's not about the packaging, but the fact you stole them. If I hadn't caught you, you'd be opening those packages in a few minutes. Why did you come into my store and steal?"

I had no answer. I had done it, but I don't know why. This was not my habit or usual behavior. I had stolen a record in college from the bookstore, and once I got out of paying for one of my books. The new woman at the register missed adding the last book in my stack. I assumed other college kids had done the same and figured it wasn't a big deal.

"I am going to ask you one more time. Why did you steal these?" His intense stare and dark eyes created a frightening frown chilling me to the bone.

"I don't know." I began to cry hysterically and with a volume that could be heard throughout the store. "I think I'm going to vomit."

He grabbed a plastic bucket placed to catch rain from a ceiling drip. "Here, use this."

With no compassion, his furrowed frown grew more intense. His loud voice echoed in my ears, and the pain in my head pounded harder. I got up and paced. I needed to move.

I lifted my head and looked him in the eye. My fear had moved from my body to my conscience. My burning shame crushed my ego. *How do you think you are getting out of this mess? This will make Denny madder than using the charge card. Oh, God, why did I make such foolish choice?*

I wondered what my kids would think of me now. Any admiration I had gained would be lost. Feeling worthless and no good, I wanted to strike out like the bully on the playground. But, instead, the merchant marked me with a black mark of disgrace that could end my career in one phone call. No teacher with a record of stealing would be retained or ever hired again. Even worse, how could I tell my new husband his wife was a thief? All these thoughts swirled in my head as I walked back and forth in front of the manager. I couldn't sort them, nor could I organize words to come out in the right order. I am a felon at twenty-two. I stood and paced back and forth in a small area which made me lightheaded.

"What's your name? Stop pacing. Sit before you fall."

"Sandi Baron," I whispered as I sat back down.

"Where do you work?"

*How will I ever get out of this entanglement? My life is ruined.*

I began to cry again. "I am so sorry, so sorry. I teach at Carter G. Woodson. Please forgive me?" I jammed my hands in my pockets distorting the fit of my sweater.

"No White woman should be in a Black area." He rolled the lipstick and mascara in his large hands. "If you were Black, I would have already called the cops. Now, I find out you teach in an all-Black school."

Words tumbled out of my heart and my mouth. "Please forgive me for taking your goods and not caring about the money it provided your family. I still don't know why I stole makeup. I don't know."

"Ms. Baron, I'm not callin' the police. I'm not telling anyone. I think you're crazy to teach at Woodson. I don't even know why I'm letting you go."

I heard honking outside and the bell on the door ring as a customer entered. This wasn't a nightmare. I was awake and branded.

"Never walk back in this store again."

I looked up through my swollen and burning eyes. My face grew hot and my heart pounded in my chest. *Is this God's grace shaping me into a vessel more understanding of my kids' troublesome ways? More forgiving of how they ended up stealing? Fighting? More insight into uncompleted assignments?*

I thanked the salesman for his forgiveness and walked out of the store with slumped shoulders, mascara-stained cheeks.

I used my theft experience as an emotional whip to beat myself repeatedly. My embarrassment haunted me, and I felt ashamed. My ugly secret of stealing revealed my vulnerability. My personal growth was painful.

# LESSON 39

Duality was the Black person's ability to be whom they were purposed and predestined to be, while also being mindful that in certain settings and circles, they won't be accepted–especially in ethnic and cultural settings that differ from theirs. —Geoffrey L. King, Author, Pastor at Fellowship Missionary in Fort Wayne, IN

After the play performance, I accomplished more than directing. I now loved these kids with unconditional love. But I still knew I was not reaching many of them. Here I was, halfway through my first year, realizing I had so much English curriculum to cover.

I continued to struggle with how to meet state requirements and reach the whole child. At Woodson, I encountered many unrealistic and unattainable hoops inherent in an inner-city school.

I found it more difficult to cope with the myriad of needs and difficulties my students faced daily. Some were hungry and hauntingly thin. Some were angry because they had been shoved and not loved. Others were forgotten in the school system and denied special help for their individual needs. All these factors, coupled with learning how to live with Denny, drained me and crippled my usual positive, but sometimes naïve, rose-colored outlook.

Some days I wondered why Denny and I were here. *Were we achieving any success? Would I be a lasting influence on any child's life? Am I doing any good?* Because New Orleans chose merriment over educational improvement, schools were not a priority—at least, not the inner-city schools.

Woodson had been battered when Hurricane Betsy hit in 1965. The wind and water destroyed windows, detached the roof, waterlogged books and student records. The football equipment was strewn throughout the nearby area, and the stadium seats mostly destroyed. Worse than neglected repairs, the lack of staff and school supplies needed for our students reminded me of slow-moving caterpillars on blemished plants, steadily eating away their leaves. Plant by plant, each was being destroyed with no overseer or gardener to stop the garden's blight.

Even with our school's football championships under its belt, the school board deemed replacement and repairs out of the budget. The storm and low budget destroyed future opportunities and ignored the athletic program Woodson needed.

Some areas of the roof and the gym had never been restored. Desks stolen by Betsy's winds were replaced with ones rejected or found in other city schools. The staff seemed to accept the school board's decision. They were used to living in their place, as Walter had stated, and didn't seem disgruntled or angry. I couldn't understand it.

*Perhaps the faculty never discussed their discontent in front of us. Maybe I am not aware of the board working toward a goal. Maybe the board's lack of provision is beyond their control.* At least, I hoped these thoughts had some truth.

I struggled to find a way to teach students to reach for more. To not settle. To refuse the place society had created for them.

On a Sunday at the beginning of February, in my spirit of discontent, I sat in our little home and pondered.

Perhaps, my sullen mood could be attributed to living daily with my students. Their indifference existed because they had too many challenges to enjoy youth or have dreams. *Junior high students should be developing their dreams. They need aspiring goals to create secure and rewarding futures. Instead, these teens fight for their food, space, and existence.*

I flipped on the television as a distraction. My eyes froze on the news clips showing the racial riots in Detroit, Atlanta, and Birmingham. The streets were exploding with the anger of Blacks who wanted to choose their destiny, not settle for man's place for them. Emotions grew tense in the entire nation.

I listened to news anchor Walter Cronkite explain that Martin Luther King Jr. was known as the champion of nonviolence. King planned to travel to Birmingham, Selma, and Montgomery, where thirteen years earlier the same journey had started his rise to world acclaim. Cronkite said King's revisit would gather support for his Poor People's Campaign, which hoped to reverse the drift toward violence in America. *How can America be violent? Why are hundreds of young men protesting the military draft to serve in Vietnam? Is our country dividing? Why am I just now aware?*

I listened to how Martin Luther King Jr. offered solutions to racism by nonviolence. Other Civil Rights leaders like Rap Brown stressed Black Power and self-defense. I stared at the news clips from the riots in Detroit and Cleveland. *Will these riots come to New Orleans? Are Denny and I in danger? I guess I should be scared.*

I could not listen to more pessimistic news. I did not like the ifs my mind conjured. Negative thoughts inundated me concerning my students' hopeless lives. And now this? I walked over to the TV and turned it off. *Are Denny and*

*I still unaware? Are we viewing this news through biased eyes? Has the staff protected us from their true feelings?*

It eased my anxiousness to know there were no riots in the streets of New Orleans—at least not yet. Again, I sensed a different attitude here. Perhaps, in New Orleans they digested what Martin Luther King Jr. preached because they wanted change through peaceful actions. I too wanted change.

Woodson provided me a microscopic view, a real-life understanding of being Black in the late sixties. I detested how the state neglected the educational needs in the inner-city schools. Even with my limited classroom experience, I recognized these kids needed better provisions to inspire them. Was it any wonder I was emotionally depleted and physically exhausted? My students were deprived of what they deserved. And I couldn't change it, even though the world dramatically evolved and changed around me.

New technologies like satellite broadcasting provided detailed television coverage. Media images of the Civil Rights Movement and the Vietnam War could be transmitted worldwide within hours. *Is this good or bad? It certainly does create new political awareness for viewers.*

I hated my melancholy moods. They made me cynical. Tired of pleasing Denny, I needed to be me. I wanted to go home because I needed Mama to cook for me, take care of my needs, and take me shopping without a concern for money. Marriage was a daily effort. If I spoke my preference, it could cost me a weekend of tension, or at least, a cold shoulder for an evening from Denny. Not cleaning or keeping things in immaculate order initiated a confrontation with Denny, which in turn sent me into a pity party and rage I couldn't overcome.

*It's so easy to focus on what's wrong with my life. Instead, I need to write what is right in my life. I need to look for more silver linings and focus less on the dark clouds that hang over my head. Maybe I need to look more above the clouds and see a godly realm.*

With our new credit card, I overcharged our budget. I was thrust into the bait-and-trap quandary—I see things I want and use the charge card. Then the arguments escalated about money and responsible spending.

While shopping, I experienced the same high as when I drank those fancy drinks on Bourbon Street. I had done irreparable damage purchasing new pillows, bedspreads, knick-knacks, and anything else that allured me. Our apartment was filled with evidence of my overspending.

We had been married six months, and each month we spent far more than we made. Our charge account facilitated both of us dining with gourmet chefs. Denny wanted to see New Orleans jazz clubs and try new restaurants every weekend. He flipped out the charge card for these entertainment expenses because it was an easy and fast way to pay. The calorie-ridden Cajun foods and French bread and butter were our daily fare. Our taste buds hungered for more of that delightful New Orleans cuisine—with the unfortunate result of extending our waistlines. *Will Denny still like me if I am a round wife? I wish I didn't love food.*

As I sat thinking on that Sunday, February 11, 1968, I reminded myself of Rosalind in *As You Like It* when she said, "O, how full of briers is this working-day world." I missed the bubble of college days of parties, Coke dates, and dances. I craved carefree time when my biggest pressures were an exam or a late-night writing of a term paper. I now realized I no longer could find the expected romanticism in New Orleans, instead it needed to come from us. I could not see a glimmer of my college beauty in my mirror. Instead, it revealed a pudgy belly and limp, frizzled hair.

Plus, my heart grieved for Walter, Lily and Millie, and even playful Jerome because I could not change their world. How could anyone not have positive feelings about these young people? I loved Debra's fire and persistence to bring all she could out of her life. Of all my students, I knew she would succeed. Her grandmother's values had saturated her soul. She knew God so early and appreciated life. In my heart, I knew Debra would never settle for the place society gave her. She would reach out and help others find their destiny.

Out my window, the pouring rain and endless gray skies persisted. The dark clouds hung on me. I needed to quit worrying about my kids and, most of all, finish my pity party and start grading. Student essays and dictionary assignments awaited my red pen.

Only little Henrietta understood. She always loved me whether I was grumpy, sleepy, or bored with grading papers. Her kisses greeted Den and me when we returned from school. She loved Denny's cuddle time as well as his trying to teach her to sit up. *Who tries to teach a long-spined basset to sit up? It's good we don't have children.* We were practicing on sweet Henrietta, who grew longer and clumsier each day.

I hugged Henrietta. "You are my only bright spot tonight, girl. Thanks for always being here when I need you."

Denny did errands and picked up puppy food. My dismal moments were difficult for Den to understand. His dad had taught him to shove feelings inside and laugh on the outside, make a joke, or tease. Activity and teasing were his coping devices. Mine, on the other hand, were to power shop or sink into deep thought and analyze each action, word, conversation, and element of life.

I considered his motivation and wondered why he acted as he did. *How can two such different people ever stay married? Will I make it to the end in this labyrinth I have chosen?*

# LESSON 40

In a comfortable classroom setting, a teacher can challenge the students' mindsets. But the teacher needs to look at things from the Black perspective. They know their place in the White world. —Geoffrey King, Author, Pastor at Fellowship Missionary Church, Fort Wayne, Indiana

The first glimpses of the great city of New Orleans looks romantic because most areas have been historically preserved. The beauty of the antebellum homes on St. Charles Street, and Pirates Alley's cobbled path lined with ferns at Jackson Square created a European landscape. Hawkers at the entrance of striptease joints lured customers to come and see. Famous jazz players like Billy and Dede Pierce, Harrold Dejan, and Andy Anderson performed in Preservation Hall. Hay bales were used for seating, as they are to this day. In earlier years, Louis Armstrong played at the wooden shack. For one dollar, we heard famous bands at Preservation Hall. We favored this cheap date over most events.

Entertainers and musicians sought money and tips while they filled the air with rhythm and blues on street corners. Many tourists, as well as Denny and me, enjoyed Pat O'Brien's Hurricanes, which were a drink that smeared the edges of reality off dirty streets and masked the urine smells in the French Quarter.

The Carnival Season begins on January 6, which is King's Day or feast of Epiphany. Mardi Gras parades in 1968 began their journey on February 27, but celebrations and balls had begun two weeks beforehand. Fat Tuesday ended the festivities. Den and I were surprised schools would be closed for a week and nonessential businesses closed on the days of the big parades. Young and old experienced the holiday of Mardi Gras. Families brought picnic baskets and coolers and set up for the day to watch parades and catch tokens, stuffed animals, and beads thrown from the parade floats.

Private, nonprofit Carnival Clubs called krewes created the decorative floats. The year before the next Mardi Gras, they decided on themes, the décor, and hired dressmakers to create costumes and masks. Other krewe members ordered trinkets and candy to be thrown to onlookers on parade day. With more than fifty parades, I understood why the Big Easy was a city celebrating everything.

Originally, in the mid-1800s, balls were private affairs for krewe members and their invited guests. However, in the late-1900s, public dances and formal celebrations were held in the Superdome and Convention Center with top-notch entertainers. Mardi Gras is big revenue for the city. The *Times-Picayune* chronicled photographs and descriptions of the krewes' galas. These events would elect kings and queens and other royalty titles, and their formally attired guests were invited based on social status in the Crescent City.

The higher status Blacks, both socially and financially, were a part of the Zulu krewe and the Mardi Gras celebrations. I heard LeBlanc and others discuss their activities in the lounge. Of course, Denny and I were not part of any krewes, so I would peruse the paper to glimpse at the inside secrets of their traditions.

Since we weren't a part of the celebrations of Mardi Gras, we splurged and made reservations at the Corrine Dunbar Restaurant, a quaint old mansion known for outstanding food and service. The prices were extravagant even with our combined teachers' salaries, but we decided to go anyway. Denny put on his best dark suit, and I wore my too-tight, ankle-length black dress.

The night skies poured rain so hard our umbrellas were useless. We parked, walked as fast as possible, and rang the brass doorbell. We looked a bit drowned, but the butler welcomed us. The smell of Chantilly Paris perfume and Tweed Mist permeated the Victorian furnished parlor. Tucking my wet hair behind my ears, I noticed women in expensive haute-couture garments by Parisian designers. Other ladies flaunted their legs in mini-skirts and the popular A-line dresses. As they sipped mint juleps, we waited in the parlor together. Men wore bright shirts, suits with wide lapels, and flared-leg pants.

I recognized the women's Louis Vuitton leather purses and Italian leather shoes and wished I could hide my scuffed black heels. *How come their hair isn't wet? Why don't their husbands' suits look wrinkled like Denny's suit? Why am I feeling like we don't belong?*

When our reservations were honored, we were ushered into the blue and gold dining room and seated at a small table. Old-fashioned china trimmed in gold accented the linen tablecloth. We ate a seven-course meal for the first time in our lives. We savored gumbo, then Creole Daube, a boneless chuck roast created with beef stock, hickory smoked bacon, and dry red wine. Denny and I devoured stuffed cabbage and a basketful of fresh breads smothered in herb and orange butter.

Taking my last roll, I looked up to see the party of six who had waited in the parlor with us. Those ladies sat with perfect posture, sipped wine, and ate a few bites from their plates. I'm not sure if I heard the "oh my" cluck from their tongues as they looked over at me or I imagined it, but I recognized we were eating with the heartiness of peasants compared to their aristocratic, balanced bites.

Finishing an almond torte and flan caramel, I sighed. "Have you ever had a better meal?"

"No meal has been this tasty nor have I ever been this full." He reached for my hand. "I wonder when the bill will come. I hope we can pay it," he said a little too loudly.

One of the servers came to our table and asked if we would like to order wine.

"No, thank you, but we would like our bill now."

"Sir, at Dunbar's the bill is paid at the Dutch door at the end of the hallway."

"Thank you." Denny's eyebrows lifted like a fast-moving elevator as he whispered in my ear, "What is a Dutch door?"

"I think it's a horizontally split door. Not sure. Let's go." *What is one more faux pas this evening? Why is my skirt hiking up in the back? Oh no. I have gumbo on my dress. Those other ladies look perfect and in the height of fashion.* As we scooted out our chairs, I could feel the scrutinizing eyes of the table of six.

As Denny paid the bill, his still-wet suit fit tighter and seemed shorter in the legs. His trousers pulled at his bulging calves. *Had the rain shrunken his suit?*

While making this observation, the table of six came up behind us, ready to pay their bill. One woman tittered and said to her friend, "Seems like JC Penney suits aren't made for the rain."

"Where can I buy tight-legged trousers like those?" One man whispered loudly to his friend. "Maybe the Salvation Army?"

My face felt red and hot. I would not let their eyes meet mine. I was too embarrassed. We didn't belong at this restaurant on St. Charles any more than in one of the fine mansions with groomed landscaping. Nor did we belong in the projects on the other side of the river where my students lived. *Where do we belong?*

Every new experience taught us a little more about the city. We understood many things, but the secrets of the streets, the balls, the old money, and the working of the city politics were a mystery. Now, we would enter into Mardi Gras season like thousands of other tourists. We would embrace the celebration, never knowing the secret underlying messages.

The Big Easy beckoned Mardi Gras revelers to come play and dine. When Denny and I would walk down Bourbon Street, we could not believe every kind of desire and sexual fantasy was displayed or hawkers encouraged those walking to step right in and see Champagne Girl. They had a street named Desire, and the infamous Bourbon Street provided entertainment that would give Sodom and Gomorrah competition.

The glamorous facade of New Orleans, which engaged the visitor's view, had awed us. Large, restored cathedrals added a sense of grandeur. Quaint Parisian shops and art galleries provided a strong European influence. We enjoyed learning the history about each section through walking and carriage tours.

However, those who lived in the city recognized the corruption in the city government and knew the hospitality workers made the fine dining and high-quality service possible. We learned from our staff several Woodson mamas were part of the underpaid seamstresses who started on the elaborate dresses and costumes a year ahead of each Mardi Gras celebration. Mike Leonard explained the well-kept homes in the Garden District and on St. Charles Street were pristine because Blacks and Hispanics were employed in a life of cleaning and serving others. Without garbage collectors and clean-up teams, rats would overrun New Orleans. How much were they paid to do this filthy job daily? News stories reported this injustice caused the terrible riots in Memphis.

Because of this complex infrastructure, a visitor never realized Mardi Gras rested on a network of humans and social classes. We were no longer visitors, so we didn't belong to that category either. At least the Blacks, on the surface, accepted us, and we were developing deeper relationships as they had extended politeness. Most Whites did not accept us because we taught in a Black school—as unacceptable as marrying a Black in 1968. Southern prejudice had ingrained the concept of no mixing of races in the people's minds.

My mental chanting began. *Where do Denny and I belong in this city? Are we rich or poor or somewhat poor or maybe lower middle class?* We have family in the Midwest. Our families are our identity, and I looked forward to Denny's folks visiting for Mardi Gras. I realized how important it was to belong to a family unit.

"What New Orleans' food do you want me to prepare for your parents next week?"

"Red beans, of course. Sylvia and her mama taught you well."

"Red beans and rice it is. What do you think they'd like to see?"

"Mom would love the carriages and vendors at Jackson Square because she's never seen an historical area. Dad will enjoy the free prizes thrown to onlookers."

"I'm so looking forward to being with them."

Denny kissed my neck. "They'll love being with you as much as I do. You smell sweet like the jasmine blossoms."

"Keep with the plan, man. We are designing our Mardi Gras agenda. No kissing now."

"I can do two things at once," he joked.

"Let's give them a tour of the Big Easy. A trolley ride to see St. Charles Street and then show them the Garden District and Bourbon Street."

"They would like meeting Helen and Larry," he said.

We were ready for a break from our intense schedules and marriage doldrums. Denny and I needed the fresh laughter his parents would bring. In exchange, we would create a game plan for entertaining them at Mardi Gras with New Orleans's Cajun food, Bourbon Street drinks, and fascinating sights beyond our imagination.

# LESSON 41

Intelligence plus character—that is the goal of true education. —Martin Luther King Jr.

Every Sunday evening, I dealt with my new reality—teaching English was a two-edged sword. Denny would go off to jog and visit with our neighbor Larry. I graded papers for hours. Prioritizing writing, I wanted to give my students the opportunity to express their ideas. Thus, I assigned one essay each week for every student in my four English classes. This seemed like an ideal plan until I found myself taking home more than one hundred essays each week to grade every Sunday.

Every Monday, I returned the graded essays. I used a correction system for students to improve their grade. If they rewrote the essay, making the suggested corrections, they gained a twenty percent increase. Few students settled for their initial grade and grabbed the opportunity for improvement, which in turn created more papers to grade.

I had finished reading *Huckleberry Finn* to them and used the story as a starting point for many writing assignments. Through classroom discussions and studying this novel, I learned much about my students as well as myself. As I sat propped on the couch with sweet Henrietta at my feet, I felt more like Huck Finn than I wanted to admit. He wanted to honor his and Jim's friendship, but a biased society complicated his efforts. He chose Jim over money or proper rearing from Miss Watson. Huck never quite fit in anywhere—not with his drunken dad, not with the widows trying to make him clean and moral, and certainly not with the Southern feuding aristocrats who took him in. However, under Tom Sawyer's leadership, Huck had been a faithful follower, yet he still was not confident enough to know where he belonged without Tom's guidance. Being only thirteen, Huck needed time to mature and find his identity.

I felt that way. Young and inexperienced, Denny and I had been hoodwinked by the New Orleans recruiter like the duke and dauphin in *Huckleberry Finn,* who took advantage of Huck and Jim. The recruiter had needed two White teachers to integrate the schools to meet federal guidelines. We were naïve enough to believe he wanted us for our educational training. And even though Den and I strove to honor our position as integrators of Woodson, I, like Huck, spent my time surviving—Huck on his raft down the Mississippi River, Sandi in the river of Carter G. Woodson. Being only twenty-two, I needed time, like Huck, to mature and understand who I was—not only in the classroom, but in the streambed of marriage.

Some days, I wanted to be cuddly and coddled by Denny. Some days not so much. Each day of marriage required effort. This difficult balance composed rhythms that were off beat. We either loved and laughed or pouted and yelled. I needed to face it. I wanted to escape and be free like Jim.

*Free from what? Oh my, I am such a melancholy girl on this Sunday evening. It must be the winter blues of February.* I decided to lose myself in the essays of my students.

Debra Brown's mature writing used interesting details to support her ideas. Her essay was titled, "Granny's Teachings."

I felt the pressure at school to not do well in my studies. Popular girls weren't always concerned with their studies, but I had pressure from my granny.

She said, "You do good, child, you do good."

I love my granny, and she always knows what's best. She cleans for a rich, White family, and they have a daughter near my age. I go to work with Granny and play with Yvette. We play together so often I became her sister. It felt normal when we were inside their house. But not outside. When I go to the store with her, shoppers would stare mean at us for holding hands and being giggling little Black and White girls together. We would buy and share our candy. Other shoppers scorned our every action. Granny said to pay them no mind. They didn't understand needing a sister. Granny's ideas grabbed my mind. My Granny is the best person I know. The End.

This week's assignment was to write about an influential, respected individual in their lives. As always, Debra's succinct writing provided interesting examples of support. She wrote or talked often about her granny. Her granny owned her own home. She took Debra to church and taught her to love and follow God. Debra's parents lived nearby, but she preferred living with her grandmother who taught her there were no such things as boundaries as to what Blacks could do. She gave her a foundation of faith and a backbone. I knew Debra would not fall into the patterns of some of my students. They were content where they were. They didn't have a vision or a future goal. They submitted to peer pressure. Not Debra. Because her loving support came from her grandmother, Debra used her talent and faith to succeed. I knew she would do well.

Joan's essay said:

My father was a military man. I respect his devotion to his job. He never pushes me to go to school. He says it is my choice where I land in this world. I live with him, and so maybe I don't see all he is.

Joan wrote a short essay, and I needed to put some tutoring time with her on how to expand her thoughts. Since she loved organization and enjoyed helping me, I would ask her to hang posters after school on Tuesday. We could talk more about her goals and writing.

Each essay made my heart hurt a little more. I wanted to extend support and teach more. *How do I help my students to mature and set goals? Can I give them overcoming strategies? How can I do something significant for these one hundred kids?*

In addition, I taught two speech classes. Teaching, like marriage, could be overwhelming if I thought too big or too long. I did not want my students to be unaware. I needed to teach them the longest night ends with the dawning of a new day.

My eyes became heavy. I cuddled with my eighteen-pound baby basset, who had become our furry child.

Weary from my pensive mood and tedious grading of my students' essays, I anticipated that next week's Mardi Gras celebration would remove my despair. Until then, I needed a nap—a long night's nap.

"Come on, Henrietta, I will help you up on the bed. Good night, baby girl."

I tucked in with Denny.

# LESSON 42

It has been said that a Scotchman has not seen the world until he has seen Edinburgh; and I think that I may say that an American has not seen the United States until he has seen Mardi Gras in New Orleans. —Mark Twain

Purple, green, and gold banners decorated the fine homes on St. Charles. As we drove past the neighborhood, I looked at the magnolia wreaths on stately front doors. The grand white columns, wrapped in purple and gold décor, called attention to this royal holiday.

During my prep time, I relaxed and sat in the lounge awhile. Decorated in purple and gold banners, the lounge buzzed with conversations about float designs. To the staff, Carnival embraced a rainbow of promises and celebration of long, learned traditions such as the King Cake that appeared in the lounge each day.

This day all the talk in the lounge revolved around Mardi Gras—parades, parties, and a week out of school. The parades continued for two weeks, but the big krewes like King Rex, King Zulu, King Comus, and other traditional krewes were scheduled the same week we were out of school. Every day produced a reason to celebrate.

"Honey, you've never seen a Mardi Gras party." Sylvia advised, "You better start figuring out your costume and make it sexy."

Henri Todd smiled. "You'll be wading in liquor, baby."

Edna came into the staff room. "Has Mardi Gras started?"

Her seductive smile gave everyone a reason to tell stories of Mardi Gras celebrations past. The energy sparked gaiety among the staff. February not only birthed the Mardi Gras season but the signs of spring with pink hibiscus, soft violet dogwoods, and the amazing iris. However, a few days could still be cold in New Orleans. Today, I shivered, even wearing a heavy sweater. Henri Todd handed me a cup of chicory coffee, and the cooks brought nuts and sweet caramel rolls. I grabbed a handful of nuts.

"You like those, Mrs. B?"

"I love nigger toes." The words spilled out before I could think what I was saying. Choking on the Brazil nuts, I gulped some coffee.

The lounge filled with hilarious cackles.

"I am so sorry. Forgive me. I didn't mean to say that." My vision blurred with tears of embarrassment. "Please forgive me."

"Girl, we call them the same thing. It's all right." Sylvia confided, "Dennis and you have cramped our style. Before you two came, the guys in the PE department called each other nigger all the time. We all have had to be careful when we talked with you White folk."

We knew the dismissal bell would soon ring, but no one seemed to care. Henri Todd could not stop laughing. Mr. Gritton, a history teacher, gave me a little hug. The students liked how he framed what was happening today and showed how it would become history tomorrow. His quiet voice was soothing and melodious. I appreciated his outward gesture in front of the faculty.

Different faculty members offered words which were comforting and forgiving. My lack of thinking caused my embarrassment. I could not believe I said the N-word.

My whole life my mom had called Brazil nuts by that derogatory term, and I never noticed until today. What a day of learning the hard way.

Still choking and sweating, I removed my sweater. More snickers. "Guess it's not as cool in New Orleans as you thought," Mike Leonard teased.

As the bell sounded, the staff left the lounge to attend their third-hour classes, but we remained in good humor. Saved by the bell had a new meaning.

I entered my classroom to greet my smallest and quietest class of the day. Like the staff, they were talking to one another about next week's Mardi Gras break.

"We be gettin' lots of candy from the floats."

"No school. No English lessons, no math homework," said Joan.

Where did this year go? How could it be February 23 already? I had not completed near what I intended. Because so many of my students were struggling, I slowed each lesson to a snail's pace, not to leave anyone behind. The stronger students were grouped together part of the hour to help one another continue forward.

I needed to move faster and help them polish their paragraph structure and correct that darn *be* verb. *How could I complete this—in three months—by the end of the school year?*

Only a moment had passed when Jerome walked to the chalkboard and drew masks, beads, and an Indian complete in feathers. Jerome could sketch anything. I liked his drawing because it gave me the opportunity to ask some specific questions about the week ahead.

"Jerome, why did you draw an Indian?"

"Mizz Bayronne, Mardi Gras is 'bout the Indians. They come near the project, and we all run after dem. The Wild Magnolias meet the Wild Tchoupitoulas. They come right into the project all dressed in purple, yellow, red, and green feathers. They look right into each other's faces and yell."

"Yes'm. They be covered in beautiful feathers. Wish I be an Indian princess," Miranda said.

"You be beautiful enough, girl," Jerome affirmed. "You got a jar of pretty you smooth on your skin?"

I smiled to myself. Yesterday after school while cleaning my boards, Miranda told me she could twirl two batons at once. "Only majorette that does that," she said.

Miranda's extracurricular activity built her self-worth, and she embraced the prestige it gave among her peers. She told me she never felt pretty until chosen to be on the majorette squad.

"Miranda," I asked, "what's the best part of Mardi Gras?"

"My mama cook a big pot of red beans, and they smell wonderful. She cook fresh roasted peanuts, and people stop by our house all day to eat. Every year she buy me a brand new pair of Sears and Roebuck jeans for Mardi Gras."

"That sounds like a special day," I answered.

"The tribes show off their new costumes and headdresses," she continued. "We dance around and follow them from street to street. Lots of drummin' and dancin'."

"Me, me, choose me." Walter waved his hand. "Do you know about the coconuts?"

"Teach me."

"We always be teaching you. We teach you our words, our ways, and now all about Mardi Gras. When Mr. Hughes delivers your check to your room, I tell him to give it right to me."

"Drum roll for Walter," another student bellowed.

"I be teasin' you. Mizz Bayronne."

"It is all right, Walter. Teach me. But you're not getting my pay check."

"When the Zulus come around, they throw coconuts into our house. They be sure we catch them. That be their toast to us. The Indians in Louisiana helped the slaves. Sometimes, they hid them from their owners. Did you know?"

"Thanks for teaching me." I looked to the other side of the room. "Debra, what do you want to teach me about Mardi Gras?"

"Well, we go to Jackson and St. Charles and see the floats and try to catch some trinkets and beads," Debra shared. "We allowed in one area. Granny says not to go any farther from home."

I frowned. "Doesn't the parade krewe toss beads to everyone?"

"You see, they really be throwin' them beads to the White kids standin' on ladders and bleachers behind us. The float riders look right at the White children and shout, 'Here'. With the krewe's hands filled with gold and green beads, they stretch to reach the children on the platforms. Sometimes the beads slip through the White children's hands. That's when we catch the missed beads."

My heart wilted. My skilled and talented students were content to collect the missed beads. They got the used books, the leftover furniture, and the missed beads. Yet they were content, they appreciated anything all the time. My students taught me more than traditions and vocabulary.

I visualized the boy Denny had told me about sharing his orange, pulling apart the juicy segments, and handing each one to his friends. When on lunch duty, I often saw the girls trade red beans for pudding or bread for rice. At times, they pulled pieces of caramel rolls and gave them to each other. Girls shared their new lipsticks, and boys shared their candy. Cajun potato chips were a favorite snack. Slender brown fingers reached into a shared sack and took one chip. That salty sour flavor was licked off the chip, and the crispiness savored for one delicious moment for each child. They existed in moments.

# LESSON 43

The optimist proclaims that we live in the best of all possible worlds, and the pessimist fears this is true. —James Branch Cabell

The Mardi Gras break produced more merriment and fun than we anticipated. Our little duplex welcomed Denny's parents, Deanie and Hank, with an over-the-door banner decorated with green, gold, and purple balls and greenery. Our weary parents were hungry. After we showed them their room, I put dinner on the table and told them everything was ready. I had decorated our little green table with fresh flowers and Mardi Gras ribbons as a table runner.

"This is pretty fancy, Sandi. Looks good," said Hank.

His mom looked at the table spread with bowls of beans, rice, and salad. Crowded together was a platter of garlic bread and butter, and small bowls of olives and green onions shoved between the other items.

"I've never seen this combination, and why are you using cloth napkins?"

"It's what we like, Mom. We think you're special and want to give you a nice dinner, New Orleans style."

"Let's quit talking about it and start eating it. I'm starved." Hank reached for the red beans.

Hank and Deanie gulped each bite. "This tastes great." I loved watching them refill their plates.

Denny winked at me. "Mom, I told you she was a super cook."

"Sandi proved you right." We chuckled at her comment and kept eating. It was a feast of family love and affirmation. Den and I needed their love and laughter more than we realized.

Each morning of their visit, we grabbed toast and coffee and joined the early bridge brigade. Parades and the historical sights of New Orleans awaited us. Street food venders stood on most corners offering fine restaurant quality food. After gravitating toward a muffuletta shack or po'boy stand, we chose our personal favorite and found a drink cart with every alcoholic creation imaginable. Geared up with food and drink, we made our way through the crowd towards the parades. With each parade, decorated floats crawled past like barges on the Mississippi.

At our first parade, the Hermes captain led the procession in full regalia on a white horse. Floats adorned with neon lights followed. A ten-foot lobster passed on a large float with the krewe throwing golden doubloons and strands of beads. Like children, we reached our hands to the sky, trying to catch a stuffed toy, doubloon, or beads.

Den's dad got into the festivities, and he ran beside the floats yelling, "I'm from Mississippi. Throw me a doubloon."

He learned the phrase from watching another man on the street. With pride, Hank returned with handfuls of gold coins and specialty necklaces because of his new-learned chant.

Children insisted on being lifted above the crowds. They squealed and shrieked to catch multi-colored, sparkling beads and hard candy. Carnival, the greatest free show on earth, provided all kinds of entertainment. Large floats decorated with flowers and greenery, banners, and huge velvet chairs held ladies dressed in plunging necklines and elaborate satin dresses. Masks decorated with rhinestones, sequins, and pearls completed their glamour. Men stood in long velvet robes, wearing specific crowns identifying the krewe's identity. They waved at the onlookers who reached to catch flying beads and doubloons.

Trying to negotiate the crowds, men hollered harsh words and women cussed under their breath. Drummers batted on their drums. The bands created their loudest bebops and boogie-woogies with creative flair. Police whistles made piercing sounds above the street noises. Horses pranced their clip-clop, clip-clop, clip-clop rhythms. Folks greeted friends with booming voices and warm, hearty hugs.

Even before mid-morning, parade watchers consumed gin, vodka, hurricanes, and beer. Their motto, licker is quicker, was embodied through their uninhibited crassness. The cacophony created by the horde of loud, obnoxious carousers and increasing crowds intensified. By midday, the liquor enhanced belly laughs, and crowd noises grew into one undulating sound.

Surprised by the many elaborate and thrown-together costumes in the crowd, I stared and gawked. Locals dressed like queens with dipping sweetheart necklines and scarlet lipstick that matched their designer gowns. Men with painted faces and yellow and black jester costumes bowed and swirled to the ladies in the crowd. Two children wore blue-checked dresses with white pinafores and fanciful masks. Some folks were not dressed up—they wore jeans and colorful shirts with layers of beads around their necks and unique masks. Looking up, I marveled at how the clowns on stilts could balance and maneuver their way through the throngs lining the streets.

The parades routed through Canal Street this day, but other days the paths took sightseers to St. Charles and various sections of town. No matter where one lived downtown, there would be a cortege nearby during Mardi Gras week. The Krewe du Vieux kicked off the Mardi Gras season by being the only procession allowed through the French Quarter. Because those narrow streets could not handle the enormous floats, Krewe du Vieux walked. Since parade schedules were printed each year, everyone knew where the floats would be and at what time.

During a pause in the parade, I observed how well the krewe had depicted a past historical theme on the next elaborate float. Among the dazzle and glitter on the gold and green decorations stood three southern belles with giant brimmed hats and dress designs from the Civil War era. Right out of *Gone with the Wind,* the scene enchanted me, and I smiled at an elderly white-haired man, dressed as a Confederate general, throwing candy to the crowd.

I remembered Debra Brown's missed beads story. I wondered if the tokens thrown would land on the ground. My stomach tightened. Revelers cheering on this float nauseated me. *How could they celebrate slavery and war with merriment?* Other float characters wore tattered Rebel uniforms. Women wore masks framed with multi-colored feathers of purple and green. Each belle held her mask by the wand handle in a flirtatious way that brought more applause from the crowd.

My senses were overstimulated. Even though I appreciated the detailed costuming and creative designs incorporated into each float, something tugged at my inner thoughts. I understood these parades commemorated the Old South, celebrating their traditions and experiences. The intricate construction designs fascinated me as did the floats holding characters in embellished costumes.

My emotions seesawed, flowing from breathtaking highs to heartbreaking lows as I watched the Southern Belles and White plantation owners enjoying their roles on the floats. From my perspective, they recreated this desired reality because they did not want reformation.

With little reaction from the crowd, a naked man ran past. A few comments of 'look at his costume' were the only remarks to his nudity.

Faces were shellacked with sweat, and the smell of liquor outweighed expensive perfumes.

Bodies pushed against each other and jumped to be the first retriever of green and purple beads. When people pressed against me, I could smell their toxic body odor. My standing space grew smaller and smaller. These were sights, sounds, and smells foreign to my senses. Mardi Gras revelers threw their drink glasses, beer bottles, and trash along the street without shame.

My first Mardi Gras day etched scenes in my mind and tugged at my heart. The sour smells of vomit and urine caused me to gag. The elegant sequined and feathered masks, golden fans, and southern-belle hats edged in lace and pearls spoke of wealth and the past. This indelible experience burnt into my brain. Masks and merriment showed me why there was no other city like New Orleans. Despite the less savory aspects, I was hooked.

Denny stood by his mom and explained the sights to her. Her sweet smiles reflected how much being with her son meant to her.

No matter how exhausted Hank was, he kept chasing doubloons. I could hear his continuous chant, "Hey, Mister, give me a doubloon."

Few Blacks stood on the area of Canal Street where we watched the parades. My kids told me most of Canal Street constituted an understood off area to the African

Americans. Not being surrounded by my sweet, happy, brown-skinned children felt strange. *Was I missing my students?* Even on my vacation, I could not stop thinking about them. By the end of the day, I felt loneliness even amidst the massive crowd and festival parade.

Our first parade experience concluded with eyes unmasked and ears opened to sights and sounds we never had encountered. We Barons began each new dawn in anticipation of what wonders and excitement lay ahead at Mardi Gras. New Orleans never failed to enlighten us.

Throughout Mardi Gras, the celebration of food, trinkets, costumes, and floats followed by loud marching bands continued. By the end of the ongoing festivities, the old Barons and the young Barons had bonded well. Before leaving the city for the last time, we decided to stop at our favorite restaurant to have Cajun gumbo and pecan pie.

"Hank, do you think you have enough doubloons to pay for your gas back home?" I asked.

"Enough blisters to last a lifetime. I haven't walked or run so much in years."

"Thanks for coming to see us. You were a trooper in those crowds." I kissed my mother-in-law's cheek.

Deanie hugged me good-bye. "I came to see you two kids, where you live, and New Orleans. You showed us everything, I think. Good thing I brought my comfy shoes."

We drove back across the Mississippi River, limp and tired from our final day of Mardi Gras fun and frolic. I took a deep breath, grateful for my Denny and his family. New Orleans did not disappoint and gave them stories to tell when they returned home. Our five days of sightseeing and six Mardi Gras parades exhausted us. After seeing Denny's parents off to Indiana, we relaxed on Sunday from our fast-paced spring break.

On my day of doing nothing, I lay on the couch with

Denny. "What was your favorite part of Mardi Gras?" I expected his answer to be he loved having his parents here.

"When women pulled up their tops and showed their breasts to gather more strands of Mardi Gras beads."

"Dennis Baron, wrong answer."

He took me in his arms and kissed me long and hard. Our day of rest climaxed into a much needed, intimate renewal after a week filled with parental love and new memories.

# LESSON 44

I don't have to be perfect. All I have to do is show up and enjoy the messy, imperfect, and beautiful journey of my life. It's a trip more wonderful than I could have imagined.
—Kerry Washington

Cool and rainy days were a frequent forecast until the 4th of March, my twenty-third birthday. I had taught more than one hundred and fifty days. Each day created more confidence and comfort. Humidity returned, and March brought spring blooms of foxglove and azaleas. Soft whites, yellows, blues, and purples exploded in the garden district.

I much preferred walking in the Garden District with no Mardi Gras crowds, enjoying these normal days. Life was good in this three-hundred-year-old city. This Mississippi metropolis offered jazz and blues, sensuous blossoms of spring in City Park, and Creole cuisine and culture. They wooed me. *I have found myself in love and ecstatic with this place called New Orleans.*

The Crescent City cuisine taught my taste buds to hum when Cajun spices were a part of the recipe. This ancient city displayed living landscapes of vibrant color all year long. As we drove on St. Charles Street, the baroque and pre-Civil War architecture featured beauty as well as history. I knew I could live here forever. *Laissez Le Bon*

*Temps Rouler*, as they say in this Mississippi city. Let the Good Times Roll.

The school staff told us Mardi Gras would diminish winter blues and cause emotions of glee to burst forth like the blossoms of spring. Once again, the Woodson way blessed our life.

Sylvia's natural charisma and kindness extended friendship to me early in the year. Edna's calm and defined teaching skills modeled effective classroom management techniques. Outside of the classroom, however, her lively and engaging personality led me to appreciate and experience New Orleans and its party life. Like watering a plant, Sylvia watered me with hope, renewing my optimism when I was dry, encouraging my growth as a teacher.

Mike Leonard's smile, friendliness, and constant offering of help along with Henri Todd's genuine wisdom influenced Denny. Their friendship impacted my husband as strongly as Tom Sawyer's companionship shaped Huck.

These were the people whom I had learned to love, and who generously loved me back. They suffered because they were limited by their skin color. They fought for any opportunity or promotion, often beaten out by someone White with lesser abilities. With his sharp mind and compassion for young people, Henri could easily have been an administrator. Edna's professionalism taught me more than any textbook. I owed my training to the staff of Woodson.

As I clutched these images close, I realized New Orleans had given us much more than we expected. She had matured my thinking and understanding of others. Denny and I both were now at ease in our new home and appreciated each other's gifts. We argued less and loved more.

I, at last, accepted Denny really did love me. I didn't require him to prove it every day. If he needed to take a football furlough and be with guys who understood the game, I was comfortable with his choice. My mistakes, my misgivings, and I merged into maturity. Perhaps, marriage is like a baby in the womb, needing nine months to develop and form a life-giving bond. Yet, the bond does not end with birth, for the baby requires years of nurturing—to become all it can be—through love and commitment, like my marriage.

This March, I celebrated more than twenty-three years of living on earth. Not only had I matured, but my perception of a perfect marriage had changed. I now understood that I was not the most important person in our marriage. Denny's worth and individual desires were as important as mine. I needed to give him honor.

My teaching style no longer mimicked my college instructors. With my skills, I designed challenging lessons that gave my students growth and hope. My classroom management was built on storytelling. My self-disclosing stories taught morals with the lesson of the day. Grammar time would have been better labeled, "Be all you can be, be you, and I be me." Literature lessons came straight from the pens of Mark Twain and Langston Hughes.

The children of Woodson had become my heart's love. Walter taught me through his smiles and stories. Joan demonstrated maturity through her ways of coping, and Debra brought intensity through her daily dose of energy and goal setting. I admired their daring and eagerness to learn and improve in writing and speaking.

My mindset renewed and reset. What used to be trials at Woodson were now my victories. When classes grew rowdy, I could settle them without yelling, anger, or meanness. My students respected my requests and me. Lily and Millie kept my days filled with smiles and questions. Miranda developed into a confident lady flowering into her own person. Jerome managed to find humor in my Northern ideas and ways. Knowing when to joke and when to stop, Jerome brought fun and laughter to my life. Jason didn't conquer his enemy by bullying—instead, he had learned to be patient and think before reacting. Best of all, his confidence improved. The play had reshaped his self-image, and by the end of March, he, too, handled conflict in a gentler way. Most days, Jason stopped by my room to share something that happened that day. Woodson kids showed me how to live and how ordinary things that fill my heart with joy can make a perfect day.

In spite of those initial classroom struggles, I gained insight into my ability to resolve problems. *I think I am a grown up. I wonder what scene and sequel will follow tomorrow? No more conflicts in my playbook please. I love my life. I am content.*

# LESSON 45

As a bi-racial woman with a Black father and White mother, I am incredibly familiar with otherness. Being bi-racial means that no matter what the ethnic make-up of a room, I am always other. Otherness means being painfully visible when I do not wish to be, yet completely overlooked when I need to be seen. May we all submit to the process of growth, no matter what label we are saddled with, and thereby, change the world. —Angel Dixon, CEO, Crossing Color Lines

Clusters of white blossoms on the Japanese apricot trees and flushed pink magnolias lit the city parks. From the Garden District to the University District, the seventy-degree temperatures created an almost ideal life. I embraced the uneven brick streets, the unexpected showers, and the constant traffic. New Orleans held me as one of her own.

As soon as we arrived home from school, Den went for a jog.

I had given up this torture and, instead, walked Henrietta around the duplexes to calm myself from the hectic day. The neighborhood's new homes had sprung to life from the winter construction. Cerise azalea bushes brought color to our Mary Poppins Street. Henrietta sniffed the amaryllis lining the sidewalks as we took our evening walk.

I was no longer a pilgrim on the wrong road. Rather, I felt a part of the whole, willing to accept the direction this new path would point me. Likewise, I hoped for opportunity for my students and wanted to believe the 1970s would bring freedoms and better choices for the Black community. *Please, Lord, allow my students to have all they deserve. Why did I pray so little this year? Am I afraid I would have to choose between God and Denny? Perhaps the New Orleans' party atmosphere didn't lead to praying or even attending church.*

I remembered when I asked Denny, "Do you believe in God?"

He rubbed his hands together. "I do believe in God, yet I don't believe. I think God is a crutch many people need to lean on. I don't need that crutch. That's how I live my life."

His answer challenged me. Unsure what to say, I didn't tell him how much I loved God. *I know God is real. Why didn't I pursue my conversation? I couldn't then. I wonder if I could now. When will we reach that point in our relationship? We haven't even been married a year.*

I rambled back to our duplex, coaxing Henrietta the last two blocks. Henrietta disliked walking quickly but favored stopping along the way to sniff. Once inside, I grabbed a glass of tea and collapsed on the green couch while Henrietta lapped cool water. As I dozed, Denny came bounding through the door.

"Honey, I picked up the mail and guess what's in it?"

"Ummmm, money from my mother?" It was close to Easter, and she always sent a holiday check. Her generous gifts lifted our spirits and our budget. *Am I missing my Mama? I am.* I snapped out of my reverie. "Show me the mail."

He handed me an envelope with a return address from Ball State University in Muncie, Indiana. "Open it. Your wish has come true."

"What wish?"

"Your wish to go back to a fine Northern school with all the supplies and benefits a new teacher needs."

"No, no, that's not my wish anymore. I used to wish that, but I'm changed now."

"You're always complaining about having dusty, dirty books, and no teacher's guide, causing you to create the next week's lessons every Sunday evening."

"That's me ranting. I don't want to leave."

"Read the letter." He smiled broadly.

Addressed to Denny, the letter had the embossed emblem of the Ball State cardinal. "We are offering you an assistantship to earn your master's degree." I let the letter fall to my lap.

"Honey, do you know what this means? They are helping pay for my graduate degree. Free money, baby."

"That's nice," I said through pouty lips.

"Nice? This means everything to my career in education." He raised his voice loud enough that Larry and Helen next door could have heard him.

*How could this be happening? I don't want to go back to Indiana.*

I knew the streets of New Orleans were not paved with gold or silver or even smooth pavers. My dream and my goal centered on reaching the Woodson kids and helping change their shattered world. In a room with this loving man, I had chosen to share my life with, I should be ecstatic.

Instead, I felt trapped. I wanted to crawl out a window and run through the streets of Jackson Square. I yearned to bask in the sun by the Mississippi River. I needed to hear the jazz at Preservation Hall. I needed New Orleans. *I want to smell the scents of garlic, onions, and andouille sausage in the streets every day, and that isn't going to happen in Indiana.*

I had chased away my fears of being weak and inexperienced. I had exchanged fear for confidence that I was reaching Debra, Joan, Walter, and many others. My students were my life, the blood in my veins that brought energy and laughter to each day. *How can I leave now? Who will watch over little Josie?*

"Thanks a lot for all your support, Sandi." Denny walked out the door. No goodbye. He slammed the screen door.

I reached for Henrietta. "Oh, girl, this is awful. I don't want to leave. You don't either. This is our home. We are Southern girls, right?"

Her droopy eyes said it all. I began to weep from a deep hurt within. The thing I wanted last fall had happened this spring. "Why, Henrietta, why?" My tears dropped on her long, velvety ears. My heart was pierced, and I panicked in my deep misery.

Denny returned after a while and turned on the TV. We didn't talk.

He watched the news, and reporters showed films of racial riots escalating in Detroit, Atlanta, and Birmingham. Martin Luther King Jr. was scheduled to speak on April 3 in Memphis regarding the ongoing sanitation workers' strike.

I watched the news clips of his speeches. I had studied his 1963 "I Have A Dream" speech in my college class. I realized I needed to take copies of his speech to my classes, so we could analyze his strategies. My students needed to hear more professional speeches from which they could model their own. They needed to understand Dr. King's words that their character should be their focus and expect being Black would not jeopardize their actions or choices in America.

Denny changed the channel to watch the Smothers Brothers. I wasn't in the mood for laughter, so I went to bed only to toss and turn all night in anguish.

*Will he leave me here in New Orleans? Will he walk out on the marriage?* I disappointed him because I didn't respond as he desired. His eagerness to return to Indiana matched his excitement when we came to New Orleans. *How can I become a part of his world? Who wants snow instead of Mardi Gras parades in February?* I stuffed my pillow around my head and imagined I was walking on a beautiful white, sandy beach.

When the alarm sounded the next morning, I wanted to rise. Although tired from my restless night, I wanted to keep my word and be ready to walk out the door with Denny at seven sharp. We both gave Henrietta a goodbye pat and closed the door.

# LESSON 46

No one ever told me grieving felt so like fear. —C. S. Lewis

On our way to school, I pretended to read lesson plans, so I didn't have to talk. I ignored the sights. I didn't want to appreciate the spring blossoms and pillars on St. Charles or acknowledge the poverty on Third Street. I remained distant. I didn't want to think about anything but seeing the twins today.

When Denny parked, I gathered my books and purse, shut the door, looked hard at Denny, and walked away briskly without comment. If body language could shout, I wanted mine to boldly communicate my thoughts. As usual, he ignored my drama, locked the Malibu, and went into the gym.

I hurried to my room, delighted to see the twins at the door to greet me.

"Hey, Mizz Bayronne," they said in unison.

"Hello, ladies. What's new?"

"We're havin' a waistline party on Friday night," said Millie.

"What's that mean?"

Millie's eyes lit up, "You don't have waistline parties?"

"Nope, don't think so."

Immediately, Millie grinned and started talking. "See, I have a tape measure and when you come to the door, I measure your waist."

"Now I know I'm not coming with my growing New Orleans' waistline."

"Aww, Mizz Bayronne, we think you be beautiful."

"Are beautiful, Millie, use the correct verb forms."

"See, you know you *are* beautiful." teased Millie.

That caused me to snicker, and the twins followed me into my room.

Lily put her things on her desk as Millie continued to tell me about the party. "If your waistline is twenty-four inches, you pay me twenty-four cents. Some of the boys' waistlines are thirty-four inches. I gets lots of money."

"You mean they pay to come to the party?"

"Sure do. That's how I pay for the pop and candy that's there," Millie shared.

"Do you save money for snacks for your next waistline party?"

"Yeah, or maybe my penny party," Millie answered.

Lily walked up. "I like penny parties. They be best because I don't like people measuring me."

"Me either, Lily," I said. "How does the penny party work?"

"People comin' and bring pennies. Everything in the room is a penny. Mama lets us empty the livin' room, and we put out Kool-Aid, penny candy, and she bakes cookies. Everything cost one penny. The music is free."

"You two are so clever. I think it's a great idea to collect the money for your next party."

"What?" asked Lily.

"So, the penny party fun happens because everyone has already contributed at the waistline party, right?"

"No, ma'am, they paid that day."

At the sound of the bell, Millie screeched, "I fail if I'm late again, Mizz Bayronne." and took off like a jackrabbit.

As Millie dashed out, Walter came in. "Mornin'."

On Walter's heels, Joan arrived. "Glad you be our teacher."

Almost every homeroom student greeted me in a special way, then took their seats without being asked. As the spring breeze cooled our room, I enjoyed this day.

The morning classes went well, but during my preparation hour I had way too much time to think. *Why do I feel guilty for wanting to stay and provide more opportunities for these students? Why shouldn't what I want matter? I have a career, too. Do you understand, Denny?*

Our marriage reminded me of a three-act play. Act I entitled, "Getting Married." Act II, "Learning to Teach in New Orleans," and now Act III, "Leaving New Orleans." I didn't like the ending. *Should I toss out the marriage papers and stay here by myself and continue teaching at Woodson? Should I leave with Denny? Society and the Bible say it's right to submit to my husband. Can I leave city life? Do I want to be his helpmate? What about me?*

"Hey, Miss Sandi, you're a thousand miles away." Sylvia often stuck her head in my door to check on me.

I blinked to bring myself out of my internal ranting. "I know. Thinking about thinking."

"Well, hope you're thinking of coming to the staff party next weekend. We're having a big thank you party to celebrate the closing of school."

"What kind of party?"

"You know. Good New Orleans food, music, drink make us a party any time. Are you coming?"

"I think so."

"You better know so, girl. Oh, there's the bell. See you later."

I put the attendance out for the office girl, pushed aside my latest ponderings, and asked for my first volunteer speechmaker.

Debra's hand went up first.

"Debra, these are five-minute speeches. Class, take out your evaluation sheets, and do your best to rate her delivery, not her cuteness."

After the crinkling of their evaluation papers and the movement of feet stopped, I started the timer.

"What is your goal today?" Debra began, "If you answered you don't know, you are the person that should listen to what I am saying. Now if you don't have a goal, how will you reach your goal? You need a plan. What will be the first step you take? For example, if your goal is to learn to cook, then ask someone to mentor you in making a recipe. Ask them for a date they can help you and come prepared with the recipe and ingredients. How else are you going to learn to make chocolate chip cookies? Make your commitment clear by reminding your friend about the time and date. Show up on time. You will come away with a batch of your favorite cookies and the experience to make it happen again."

She had exact timing, smooth delivery, and a relevant topic. Everyone applauded, marked their evaluation sheets, and passed them forward to me. *Debra's speech slapped me in the face. How can she be so wise at fourteen? How has Debra learned to overcome and plan so early?*

I loved this little lady and wanted to watch her mature into all she could be. It was my dream for so many of my students. I knew Debra would turn this dream into reality. She had God and her grandmother on her side and an urgency to grab everything good and add it to her dream goal.

Soft-spoken Josie walked slowly to the front. She chose sickle-cell anemia as her topic. She explained the cause and symptoms. I had instructed the class to speak on a personal topic to make it more impressionable. Josie did that today. I could still see her curled up in the bed of the Charity Hospital.

Her speech lasted four and a half minutes with a gentle but determined delivery. Everyone applauded her heartily because they knew how she struggled and could see her improvement.

*Will I ever know what happens to Josie? Will she be able to live through her next attack? What is her destiny?* As the students passed forward their evaluations, I looked into her soft eyes. I sensed if I took one step closer to her, I would be in another realm. She had an old soul and an experienced aura. She had endured much yet had shaped her suffering into kindness and compassion.

After the last speech was given, we verbally evaluated the strengths of today's speakers. We knew there were factors which needed improvement, but I wanted to build their confidence before my students gave their final speeches. On their evaluations, I praised them for what I saw as their strengths before listing what they could do better next time. I reinforced them any time I could.

The bell rang.

"See you tomorrow, teacher."

"Bye, Mizz Bayronne."

These were the same kids who used to stomp out and say nothing. We had a relationship now, but there were less than seven weeks of school left. Seven weeks. My heart drowned in grief.

*Why must we leave? Why? Why doesn't my husband understand I am devoted to these young people? And I admire how far they have come in spite of discrimination, neglect, and poverty? How can I live without them?*

# LESSON 47

Sometimes I have these premonitions and I don't forget them, so I will be prepared when they happen. —Isabel Allende, *Island Beneath the Sea*

For more than a week, I had been on time to school. Initially, I made the extra effort to leave on time to please Denny, but I realized I enjoyed my calmer mornings. We were less stressed and more kind to each other while crossing the Mississippi. I had time to read a little Scripture and count my blessings.

*What did my first year of marriage teach me? I give a little, and Den gives a little, and we meet between the sheets. I could compromise—but not on New Orleans and leaving my beloved students.*

I felt something uneasy in the air this morning.

"You're quiet. What's wrong?"

"I know. I am anxious for some reason."

"You'll be fine, don't worry," Denny comforted.

"What's today's date?"

"It's April fourth."

"I am so busy, I must not have had time to look at my calendar." I looked toward the river.

Barges struggled against the water's force in the Spring heat that arose as early as the sun. On this foggy morning, my usual landmarks on each side of the bridge were difficult to make out. Suddenly, Denny hit the brakes because the car ahead had slowed to a crawl. The mist blurred everything and contrived the surreal illusion of sitting on the bridge with no one else there. I listened for something as if putting my ear to a train track and hearing the rumble before I saw the train.

Quiet and motionless, I examined the shape of my hands and folded them in my lap. That prickly, panicky feeling rose within, and I did not like what I perceived.

My gift of discernment had sharpened through the years. The accuracy of my predictions increased, warning of wrecks, plane crashes, and death. I dreamt these happenings and awoke, wondering what I should do with this information.

As the newscaster talked of inclement weather, Denny switched the station. The music did not calm my tension. My senses were on high alert.

Crossing St. Charles Street, the clashing wheels of the streetcar seemed to shout at me. The sky above Woodson appeared dull and lifeless. Police sirens and screaming came from Shakespeare Park. Several kids with flying tempers brawled so early this day.

We parked. Denny kissed me good-bye and joined the other gym teachers in the park to calm the onlookers and move them toward the school doors. As the police took away the angry, fighting boys, my knees were shaking. Why did I feel so uneasy today?

Sylvia and Edna walked with me to my room.

"Girl," Edna looked sidelong at me, "you turn over a new leaf?"

"Why do you ask?"

"You've been on time for over a week."

"Is it that noticeable?"

"We thought you had adopted the Southern style, slow and easy," Sylvia said.

"Next time I'm late, I'll claim that. See you at lunch." I entered my room and saw little Lily slumped in her chair. Lily, small and light brown, blended into the oak color of the desk.

I went to her. "Why are you crying?"

"I don't know. I just be sad."

Had the everyday violence all around Lily permeated her feelings? Or could she sense the unease I felt?

"Everything will be all right. Don't be sad." I put my arms around her. "You're a special young lady with lots of love in your heart. You are smart and eager to learn. You're going to have a good future."

She looked at me through her tears, "If you say so."

I wiped her tears with my tissue. "I say so."

Lily, at last, smiled that sweet smile. The early bell buzzed. "Run to the restroom and wash your face. It's almost time to start class."

Morning classes were difficult to motivate. They were tired and not interested in putting forth energy to learn what I taught. Afternoon classes whined about the heat and were not prepared. Even Jerome had no teasing in him. The kids of Woodson had taught me so much since September. I knew when to be stern and when to back off. I understood their hunger and sometimes passed out hard candy, fruit, or homemade Rice Krispie bars when they were unfocused. I knew how they appreciated every laugh, treat, or new piece of learning. They were sponges for life, but I could not discern why everyone, and everything, seemed out of sync today.

# LESSON 48

What we need in the United States is not division; what we need in the United States is not hatred; what we need in the United States is not violence or lawlessness, but love and wisdom, and compassion toward one another, and a feeling of justice toward those who still suffer within our country, whether they be white or whether they be black.
—Robert Kennedy

Regardless of my mental anxieties and headache, I cast myself into the work I loved, caring for their hearts, and filling their minds with new truths. By the end of the day, my attempts to encourage and entertain them into loving poetry tired them and me.

My speech classes gave impromptu speeches. Students drew a paper from a basket of prepared topics and spoke on that subject. They were to announce the topic and speak on it for two minutes.

Miranda volunteered to draw first. "Role models is my topic." She composed her thoughts and walked to the front of the room.

"Without role models I'd have no goals or dreams." Her eyes went to Debra. "My friend Debra Brown is one of my role models because she always does what's right. She helps me not be tempted to break the rules. My teachers are role models. They help me know my goals and how to choose a path to reach them."

She continued with her need for and appreciation of archetypes and concluded right on time. The class gave her enthusiastic applause. Along with the confidence of becoming a majorette, her speaking abilities had blossomed.

Next, Debra drew from the basket of topics.

"Best day is my topic." She pulled herself into a confident posture and went to the front of the room.

"How many of you remember Miss Simms?"

Several students raised their hands.

I smiled because she had learned the importance of engaging her audience.

"Miss Simms gave us a social studies assignment. I prepared, practiced, and still felt nervous." When she called on me, I said, 'I don't have it.'

"Miss Simms said, 'You're not going to be a dummy in my class. Give your report.' Though I pretended not to pay attention, that teacher said, 'Debra Brown, I'm talking to you. Do you hear me?'

"'Yes, ma'am,' I answered.

"'Honey, I don't have time to play with you. Get up and give your report,' she demanded.

"I got up and gave my presentation, complete with examples and evidence. The whole class listened. I was proud of myself because Miss Simms said I did really well. That day changed my knowing. From that day on, I knew I could do what I wanted to do if I was prepared. I call it my report of self-confidence."

These kids were great at impromptus. They had gained confidence to think on their feet.

Debra's speech had lifted my mood. "You know what, Debra? Miss Simms was right. You did better than well. You are a born speaker. You have a gift."

My throbbing head and tense shoulders made it difficult to stay focused on the remaining speeches. At last, the class was over. "Great job today, kids. See you tomorrow, and we'll hear some more great impromptus."

My sixth-hour students seemed to sense my exhaustion and were cooperative. When the dismissal bell rang, we all seemed pleased to leave school. Because of my pounding head, I chose not to take papers home to grade. I grabbed my purse, closed my door, and hurried to the gym where Denny waited.

On the drive home he asked, "How's your day, honey?"

"Hard, but part of it is this splitting headache."

"Maybe that's why you had all those heavy feelings this morning."

"Maybe." I rested my head on the back of the car seat.

I slept most of the way home and then took a long nap. The aroma of yesterday's gumbo awakened me.

I followed my nose to the kitchen. "I appreciate you preparing dinner."

"Not too hard to warm up leftovers. Are you feeling better?"

"A little. My head isn't throbbing."

We ate at the little antique green drop-leaf table where we shared many cozy meals. I finished the warm bowl of gumbo, but my uneasiness prevailed. *What is happening or going to occur? I can't discern if trouble is coming to Denny? My mom? Me? Lord, please guide me on this intuition.*

We went into the front room. The television played in the background while we read our favorite sections of the *Times-Picayune*. Suddenly, Walter Cronkite announced a special news bulletin.

"Tonight at 7:00 p.m., Martin Luther King Jr. was assassinated on his hotel balcony."

"Oh, no! Oh, no." I held my breath, hoping it wasn't true.

Cronkite continued, "An unknown sniper's bullet struck him."

"The hope of the Black man's dream is gone." I moved closer to Denny. "How awful."

Denny looked stricken. "Henri and LeBlanc often used Martin Luther King Jr. as a role model to the kids. They encouraged the students to reach for their dream."

"Dr. King seemed to be the answer to my prayers for Woodson's kids' future." Smothering in sorrow, my soul grieved. "Dreams are dashed this day."

Denny rested his head in his hands. "I can't believe this has happened."

All night, special news reports talked of Martin Luther King Jr. and his achievements for the Civil Rights Movement. One of the most impactful quotes on the news was one Frederick Douglass declared to the country after Congress had passed a bill in 1850 that required Northerners to capture fugitive slaves and return them to bondage.

> Your boasted liberty is an unholy license; your national greatness, swelling vanity; your shouts of liberty and equality hollow mockery. Your prayers and hymns are fraud, deception, impiety, and hypocrisy—a thin veil to cover crimes which would disgrace a nation of savages. There is not a nation on the earth guilty of practices more shocking and bloodier than are the people of the United States, at this hour. It is not light that is needed, but fire; it is not the gentle shower, but thunder. We need the storm, the whirlwind, and the earthquake.[1]

The news report reiterated that Martin Luther King Jr. had continued that sentiment with his famous quote, "It is not light that is needed, but fire." Reverend King, a son of a preacher, had received a top-notch education. He not only knew right from wrong, but he also practiced it. In his final speech on April 3 in Memphis, King told the sanitation workers, "I have seen the Promised Land, but I might not get there with you."[2]

*Did Dr. King know his death was near?* As they played back this speech, I realized his discernment was as strong as his eloquent and inspirational speaking style.

Apparently, whether going to jail for righteousness or being slain, Martin Luther King Jr. believed in aggressive actions but not coupled with violence. I watched as the world mourned this great man's death, a young man's sacrifice for our nation.

Denny remained silent as I wept. *How could this happen in 1968? Who would kill such a pure and dedicated man?*

Further reports revealed rioting in the streets of Detroit, Birmingham, and Chicago. Businesses were looted and burned. Television brought teargas, police brutality, and angry protesters from across our land into every living room.

Denny reached for my hand. "There is a global reaction to his tragic death."

Late into the night of April 4, I sat on the couch with my husband. "How much do Blacks have to suffer before changes are made?"

We had no answers, only despair.

"Denny, what does this mean for us? Will we be safe at school? Should we go to school tomorrow?" I wiped my tears. "The Black man's world has changed overnight. Ours has too, Denny. Ours has too."

# LESSON 49

God may still be in His Heaven, but there is more than sufficient evidence that all is not right with the world.
—Irwin Edman

We left early the next morning. Denny's noisy yawn reminded us of how little sleep we had gotten. I had no words, so silence settled between us. As we turned onto Third Street, I could hear my heartbeat. My clammy hand touched Denny's knee.

"We'll make it, like we did through that first parent meeting." Denny patted my arm. "We'll find a way through this step by step."

I knew he was talking to himself as well as me.

As we walked toward the gym door, there were no coaches' greetings, none of the usual happy hellos. In unison to the faculty lounge, we gathered our mail. When no one spoke, my stomach tightened and sweat beads formed on my forehead. In small groups, our friends spoke in hushed voices.

Denny and I walked out the door and collided with Mr. Gritton.

"I'm so sorry. We weren't watching."

"Today is a day you should be watching. History is being made." *No hugs today from Mr. Gritton, just history.*

I went my way and Denny went his. I meditated on Mr. Gritton's words. He and his wife had experienced a lot of social injustices. My students would tell me about him in homeroom. What they liked about him was that he and his wife were one of the first renters in the Magnolia Project. He moonlighted evenings in the cleaning business that he and some of the physical education teachers owned. *Mr. Gritton has always been kind and helpful to Denny and me. What did he mean with that warning? What should we be watching?*

As I walked alone to my room, I understood isolation and the emotion it brought. Sylvia and Edna didn't choose to walk with me this day. Caught between two worlds, I tried to climb another glass mountain with no help or recourse. I opened my door, hoping someone would be there.

Inside my classroom, I looked at the torn tiles, the scarred and worn desks. I opened the splintered drawer that held my purse each day. Looking out my window, I could see neighbors huddled in tight circles as the staff had done. Perhaps the circling of people could protect them from the pain they were feeling at the loss of a great leader, a man who had promised how their world could be better. I heard mournful crying in the narrow streets. Perhaps the streets were crying too. I knew the Black community, overcome with sadness, had begun their grieving. This dismal day's sights and sounds cast a shadow of fear throughout the city and across our land.

I wished the bell to ring. I had never wished that before. I wanted my class to come in, but it took the bell to push them in. I needed to talk to someone. Maybe the kids would not see my whiteness as the cause of Martin Luther King Jr.'s death. I so wished he had not been slain. His dream was every Black man's dream.

In college, I had researched King and analyzed his "I Have a Dream" speech. I decided I would teach from that revelation today. I would try to pay tribute to him and share the beauty of his words. Afterwards, I would ask my students to share their thoughts in an essay assignment on the man, King, and what his death might mean. I rehearsed my day's plans over and over in my head. *God, I need your help on this day.*

The bell buzzed long and labored, sounding as if it, too, were grieving.

# LESSON 50

White guilt is the individual or collective guilt felt by some White people resulting from racist treatment of ethnic minorities. In *The Emotional Lives of White People*, Willard Gaylan describes the variety of feelings White people experience including fear, hatred, indifference, amnesia, anesthesia, denial, loneliness, anger, and hopelessness. Feeling guilty informs us we have failed our own ideals, "At its best, we care for one another and are responsible for one another." Because of their experience and pain living in a racist society, they may show empathy and compassion.
—Dr. Joan Holmes, Special Assistant to the President for Equity and Special Programs at Hillsborough Community College, retired

At the beginning of my sixth-hour, Mr. Bergeron announced we would leave school early today. He instructed the students to go to their lockers at once and return home.

Hearing strange noises rising in the streets, I recalled Mr. Gritton's warning, "Today is a day you should be watching."

Solemn and sober, my troubled students filed into the hallways filled with hushed whispering. Talking in low tones, they made their way to the project or nearby homes. With haste, I gathered my things and headed toward the gym. Mr. Hughes met me in the hall and escorted me to where Denny waited.

"You two must leave now to be safe." He watched until we were locked in our Malibu and leaving Third Street. We both sensed danger and chaos in the streets. Today, we were most definitely the wrong color for this neighborhood. As Denny drove us to St. Charles, we did not speak. He pushed through the traffic as fast as possible.

Once on the bridge, we both let out a big sigh. Slow bridge traffic gave us plenty of time to process our day.

"Today, I felt different," he said, "like a White guy in a Black school for the first time."

"Me too."

"The male teachers decided they would have a free day. We kept the kids as quiet as we could. Each hour, the female gym teachers had a memorial program for the girls."

"I punted each class but talked about King's 'I Have a Dream' speech. I let them share their thoughts."

"Good plan, Sandi." Denny's confirmation was important to me today.

"I hated my quiet lunch today. No one talked to me, but they didn't talk among themselves much either."

"Same here," Denny said.

For a few moments, we listened to news about the riots in Birmingham, Atlanta, Detroit, and other cities. New Orleans was filled with anger and static but no riots—yet.

"Mr. Hughes walked me to you."

"I know. I saw him."

"I think they were worried about us, and that's one of the reasons they let school out early," I said.

"Maybe."

As we inched across the Mississippi, our conversation was interrupted by the radio news releases. When we got home, Den changed into his running clothes.

"Gotta go." He pushed open the door.

I knew that jogging helped unravel Denny's frustrations and concern. Sleeping helped me cope. I became lost in my dreams. I lifted Henrietta onto the couch beside me, "Let's take a nap and walk later."

An hour later, I awakened to see Denny sitting in our new green and orange chair, our only furniture purchase in New Orleans.

"Any mail?" I queried.

"Well, there's a six-hundred-dollar credit card bill." His frown matched his words. "No more shopping trips. It's the end of the school year, and we've spent more than we made."

"What?" Since Denny kept track of the bills, I didn't have a grasp of month-to-month payments. At the start of our marriage, he began managing our finances. Since I hated numbers and bookwork, it seemed like a perfect fit.

"New Orleans has taught me lots of lessons. One is credit cards are dangerous," he said.

"Well, if that's the good-news mail, I don't want to hear the rest. And I don't want to make dinner or go out either."

"I'm not hungry either," Denny added.

I turned on the nightly news. Every network played Dr. Martin Luther King, Jr.'s "I Have a Dream" speech and gave updates on the search for the sniper. I had never known dread like this, except for our first week. My anxiety during that week, however, had been caused by exhaustion over how to schedule and manage my classroom. The uneasiness I sensed now derived from what looming danger we might encounter. The staff had been friendly to Denny and me from the start, but maybe they weren't our friends but associates. *Was I right? Wrong? Didn't understand?* All day on Friday, I felt alone.

"Denny, do you think Sylvia, Henri, and Mike are really our friends?"

"Couldn't tell it today. Too wounded I guess."

"I wouldn't want to try to talk to them right now. I wonder what they're thinking," I said.

"I have no idea. I do know we're in troubled times." Denny's acknowledgment of this scared me. This tragedy united us. We were a team of two right now.

I tried to put myself in Sylvia's place. What could she say to me? "I wish you weren't White like the guy who shot Dr. King"? I knew she wouldn't say anything hurtful. I guessed we all needed rebounding time. Henri and Mike loved Denny too much not to keep supporting us. I knew their hearts were pure but broken right now.

A Black man in another area of town would hate us because of our skin color. Spring brought wrath and storms on the city. I needed to be watchful, as Mr. Gritton had warned. *Who knew what would happen next?* Dr. Martin Luther King, Jr.'s death impacted the entire world, all colors, and all hearts.

I did know we would go back to Woodson and finish our year.

# LESSON 51

Whatever affects one directly, affects all indirectly. I can never be what I ought to be until you are what you ought to be. This is the interrelated structure of reality. —Dr. Martin Luther King Jr.

As we returned to Woodson on Monday, it became reality that Dr. Martin Luther King Jr.'s death had changed the world and the destiny of so many—including me. Within me, I experienced a new knowing like my student Debra had explained in her impromptu speech. This certainty is difficult to explain to others. It is like a statement with an exclamation mark. A consciousness that provides a light directed outward that will take me through the tunnel of understanding. God had given me a gift of intuition. I could only listen to find direction. Listening and waiting were difficult but necessary.

I opened my classroom door, and Joan had come early to straighten the room. "Good morning, Joan. Thanks for helping me once again."

She smiled. "Yes, ma'am."

Somehow, Joan's presence gave me hope that all would be well.

"I'm grateful you're here, Mizz Bayronne."

"Thank you."

"I mean your talks and kindness give life to my days," she said. "You've been good for Woodson. You've shown us favor when we could've all been bitter about White people forever. You came this year and showed us that all Whites don't hate Blacks."

Tears dripped on my cheeks. "Joan, I came because I love teenagers. You're my favorite part of the population. God and fate put us here at Woodson. I'm grateful we bonded."

She nodded and watched my tears dot my blue silk blouse.

"You and the rest of my students have shaped me for life. Woodson taught me how to cope with problems though love and laughter, and I appreciate that."

"Thanks, Mizz Bayronne."

"Thank *you*, Joan."

The bell buzzed and I dried my tears. Joan and I had a knowing of each other—a knowing that something was changing but that we would meet again, someday.

In class, I encouraged the students to work on their essays about Martin Luther King Jr. As I walked among my students' desks, I helped them to know when to start new paragraphs and how to use quotations. Some classes I took to the library for more research. They were eager to express their views on such a great leader. Days like today reassured me that I would teach as long as I could.

Young people have the ability to ignite life and energy into their teachers. Today, they did that for me.

The ultimate measure of a man is not where he stands in moments of comfort and convenience, but where he stands at times of challenge and controversy.—Dr. Martin Luther King Jr.

Earlier in the morning, I'd said hi to Sylvia on the way into class. "I'm so sorry. This is an awful blow to Civil Rights and to you."

"I know, but it's not your fault, baby. It's fine between us."

"You're still making the way for me. You made it so much easier for me. Thank you. Thank you."

She went into her room and I into mine. *Thank you, God, that Sylvia reached out to me. She is like you. She shows me love every day. Today is awkward, but she lessened the pain.*

On Tuesday, the students handed in their completed essays.

"I am going to be like him," one said.

"I did good on this one," another told me.

"He was a great leader," a student noted as he handed in his paper.

This assignment was a bridge to hope, to something bigger than their own small world of survival and rudimentary activities.

When we arrived home from school, I pulled the essays from my bookbag. Henrietta and I curled up on the couch to read them together. After school, she was eager for attention and cuddling, so I read the essays to her as I evaluated them. Each student took either a religious, biographical, or racial injustice slant.

"Listen to what Marcia wrote, Henrietta. 'Martin Luther King Jr. is a free man now. He done the work the Lord asked him. Now it's our duty to continue on his work.'"

"This one is good, too. I like Alex's beginning. 'Dr. Martin Luther King Jr.'s greatest respect was gained through nonviolence.'"

Harrison wrote the next essay in my stack. "We cannot let this man die in vain. If he gave his life for the cause, then we can surely give a little time and effort. We must join together and make his dream come true." *I like that he understood his part in the future task.*

Debra Brown wrote, "I don't think there is one human being who can or will replace him. But I do believe, 'We shall overcome.'"

Shiloh wrote on King's early life. "When Martin Luther King Jr. was little, the bullies would pick a fight with him, and he refused to carry a knife or stick. He believed as a child that hurting someone else wouldn't get you what you want out of life."

I patted Henrietta and asked if she heard that. Even as a child, King had been kind. I appreciated Shiloh's viewpoint.

I read on and on as my other students commented on their respect for a great man, and their sadness for the loss of a dream, loss of hope. But my favorite essay had no name on it. Teaching the kids to label their papers with their name and date was an endless task.

This student wrote, "King had a heart of golden walls where no hate could ever enter. He aimed at ending segregation and other discriminations against the Negroes." The essay ended, "But if we wish to fulfill King's dream, we must say, 'Father, forgive them for they know not what they do.'" The image of a heart with golden walls impacted my soul.

I graded before dinner, after dinner, and while Den watched TV. Grading consumed my life. I loved reading my students' thoughts and words, but sometimes I envied Denny's freedom to live life after school in the way he chose. Maybe with more experience, I would learn to teach English with less grading.

Henrietta and I took our usual short bedtime walk and looked at neighbors' lights and the faraway glow of the city. As we walked back toward the apartment, the night's stillness forced my thoughts to be loud and annoying. I thought of all the lessons the Crescent City had taught me. She gave me an understanding of Cajun culture and cuisine that I could never have known without living here. The Big Easy revealed jazz and art in a richly textured way from the talent of my students to the original jazz artists at Preservation Hall, housed between old galleries of art and antiques. She exposed Southern aristocratic tastes, St. Charles Street architecture, and the art talents of the Jackson Street painters. Bourbon Street unmasked nudity, homosexuality, and drinking to a level I could not measure. New Orleans taught us merriment and how to make a party out of any occasion.

Nonetheless, with the good teachings came difficult lessons—that using a credit card on too many entertainment nights busted an already tight budget. Enticing cuisines in a dive or fine restaurant added pounds and inches to my small frame. Those rainy mornings brought humid and sultry afternoons, ruining my makeup and poofy hairstyle. My thoughts rambled as I walked toward our door, pulling Henrietta. She was smelling New Orleans and her slow pace caused us to be outside longer than usual.

I heard the door open and Denny's voice. "Honey, I was concerned about you. Come in. It's late. We need to move out early, you know."

"Coming. Let's go in, girl." I left my thoughts and the blur of the city behind. I crawled into bed and snuggled close to Denny, accepting our future for better or worse.

# LESSON 53

The purpose of a storyteller is not to tell you how to think, but to give you questions to think upon. —Brandon Sanderson

As I wrote May 18 on the board, it forced me to acknowledge the school year was ending soon. I turned to my homeroom. "Does anyone need help today?"

I once resented the principal asking teachers to use the homeroom period to assist and tutor students, but now I saw this opportunity as the greatest privilege.

"Tell us a story," suggested Walter. "That would help us."

"Yes, tell us something about when you were young," Lily encouraged.

"Does anyone need help with homework?" No hands were raised, so I began my story.

"When I was six years old, my mom and dad decided to sell our Florida house and move to Ohio. Playing in the sunshine, going to the beach on the weekends, and visiting my Aunt Lottie, the schoolteacher, 'most every day filled my early years. So, I didn't understand why we were moving. Sad and scared, I didn't want to go. My daddy was a welder and painted signs to supplement our family income. When he was offered a welding job that paid twice as much as he was making, he took it because he wanted to make a better living for our family. Both of my parents' mothers lived in Ohio as well as many of their sisters and brothers. I didn't know those relatives well, but I knew there were passels of them. Relocating was Daddy's choice, and my mama honored his decision."

With those convicting words, this story became an epiphany for me.

"Mizz Bayronne, hurry or we won't hear the ending," nudged Walter.

"I entered a Northern school as a first grader. Unsure about this whole education thing, and because I was uncomfortable around new people, I didn't want to go to this new school."

The kids giggled, and Debra interjected, "You were shy?"

I told them I enjoyed school and liked my teacher, Mrs. Reed. I had fun writing on the blackboard and learning to read through Dick and Jane stories.

"There were so many cousins in Ohio. I never had anyone to play with in Florida because my mother wouldn't let me go out of our yard. I had asthma, and she liked me to stay near to her. My new-to-me aunts hugged and kissed on me to show their love. They made wonderful chicken and noodles and delicious seven-layer cakes. My aunts had plenty of time to share with me, chatting and even bringing little surprise gifts. Mama's mother let me help her in the kitchen and the garden. Grandma was stern, but I knew she loved me. Since Daddy's sister, Aunt Leona, had no children, she treated me as her own. She played dolls with me for hours and took me with her to Sunday school. My life held inspirational teachers who influenced me. I knew early on that I wanted to become a teacher like them. So, the thing I didn't want to do—leave my home—turned into a blessing, a wonderful childhood, and many lifelong relationships."

*Are you listening, girl? There is your lesson: Doing what you don't want will turn into a blessing. Remember when you wanted to leave Woodson? Staying has blessed you and given new life to you. Remember?*

"So, if you'd stayed in Florida, do you think you *wouldn't* have been a teacher?" Walter wanted to know.

"I'm not sure. But I'm pleased I became one, so I could teach here at Carter G. Woodson."

A warm glow generated throughout the room. The students nodded and applauded. These young people were so great. The bell rang, and they went on to their first-hour classes. Of course, most of them stayed in my room because they were in my first-hour English class. After I took attendance, they tried to coerce another story.

"No, it's time to practice our paragraph writing."

"Oh, Mizz Bayronne, we like your stories."

"I like your paragraphs more. Let's write. Choose one of the topics on the board. It's due at the end of the hour."

I watched as the students began their thinking charts. I had taught them how to brainstorm ideas to initiate material for their writing. A couple of students went to the "use mine" paper stack that I kept stocked and always available. They did not take advantage but used it when they had no paper of their own.

As they wrote, I went to the back of the room and looked out my window. I could see Denny in the breezeway sharing with Mike. Although the last couple of weeks had been rough, we managed to talk to our colleagues more and more each day. Dr. King's death dominated the news, but the staff reached out to us as they had always done.

Denny looked up, saw me watching, and waved. Mike gave me the thumbs-up sign. Then, they returned to the gym.

Denny's deadline to accept Ball State's offer was March 30. To my chagrin, he had sent in his affirmation. We tried to discuss the offer, but it always ended in a debate or screaming match. Denny let me work through my agony of leaving New Orleans by myself. He knew my self-care came from within. I would not allow him to comfort me because he caused my deep grieving.

I wondered if Mama had felt the same when Dad took his job in Ohio. She never let anyone comfort her and did everything herself. *Am I going to be like my mother? She honored her husband's decision to move on. Will I do that too?*

I turned to look at my class and saw Eddie's hand raised. He needed help turning his words into sentences.

"Eddie, come sit by me at my desk. Let's work together."

*How can I be so nurturing and kind to my students and so discordant to my mate?* I now understood that his acceptance of his assistantship gave us an alternative that we needed during these troubled racial times. I recognized God's timing and Denny's leadership.

# LESSON 54

Nothing is more difficult, and therefore more precious, than
to be able to decide. —Napoleon I, Maximas

On Tuesday, as we left the school for the day, I knew
my heart had softened. Ironically, my storytelling worked
on my conscience too. "Denny, can we talk?"

"Sure, that's what we always do on the way home."

"Let's stop at the square and share a muffuletta and
watch the riverboats."

"You got it, sweet pea."

We returned to our favorite bench on Jackson Square.

"Do you still love New Orleans?" I divided our sandwich.

"Of course I do. This place is in my bones for life."

"But you sent in your acceptance of the assistantship
in physical education."

"I had a deadline. I had to."

"Is it that you are missing your family?"

"We got a great offer that will help our finances." He
drank his sweet tea.

"Can we come back?"

"Sure. To apply for an administrative job, I have to
have a master's degree. Taking this assistantship makes
that happen."

I thought this over. In order for things in our lives to
get better, we had to take advantage of opportunities.

Denny hugged me to him. "Then, I will be in a position where I can be an advocate for Carter G. and other Black schools."

"That's why you accepted the offer? I am holding on to the hope that we can return. God will guide us."

"I don't want us to fight so much. I want us to be a team."

"I've never had team-playing modeled." I considered my parents. "Mama's independence manifested in a divorce after twenty-five years of marriage. She said she wanted independence. It broke Dad's heart, but she did it. She had dreams and went after them."

"They could have gone after them together," Denny offered.

"My mama never understood being a team," I answered.

"Are you that way?"

"Yes and no. I would like to come back here and continue to work in the inner-city schools. I'd like to keep an eye on Walter, Debra, the twins, Joan, Miranda, and the others. I'd like to be here when they graduate and stand up and cheer when they walk across the stage."

"We can do that, but we have to procure the education and then hire into better positions so we can help them."

I took my napkin and wiped the muffuletta drippings from his chin. He looked so handsome. The sincerity in his eyes and the gentleness as he touched my cheek reached into my heart.

"I have two more weeks to work with my classes. I haven't told anyone we are leaving. Have you?"

"No. I think we should submit our letters of resignation tomorrow."

"This is Tuesday night. I have papers to grade. I'll write the letters, and you can type them."

Denny kissed me. "Let's go home, teammate."

We held hands as we walked in the twilight to our car. Our first-year journey together had been tumultuous yet joy-filled as we learned the lessons of marital harmony.

As we walked, I heard in my mind Dr. Martin Luther King Jr.'s words so clearly, "We refuse to believe the bank of justice is bankrupt. We refuse to believe that there are insufficient funds in the great vaults of opportunity of this nation."[1] We believed that too, and we wanted to be a part of Dr. King's dream by sharing this story of hope.

# LESSON 55

The sincere friends of this world are as ship lights in the stormiest of nights. —Giotto di Bondone

"Last night a bullet killed Dr. Martin Luther King Jr. and his dream for America."

As if it were last week, I remember how the news report pierced through my soul on April 4, 1968. More than that, the memory brought to mind my former adolescent students whose hearts ached from the news of their fallen hero. Even though their skin color forced unwanted boundaries on them, those students showed this White woman what life in New Orleans looked like from their perspective.

Four decades later in 2011, I returned to New Orleans to interview my former students who had become the supporting characters in my story. After two years of searching for them, I found Walter and made an appointment to meet him. As Denny and I drove from Indiana, I visualized Walter's broad smile as a junior high student. Walter had radiated cheer each time he walked into my English class. I imagined he had experienced a lot of life in the past forty-five years including Katrina, the deadly hurricane.

We agreed to meet in an elegant hotel lobby. I watched the escalator with people coming down and listened to the grind of the rotating steps. The building held a lot of history as well as a musty odor. Of course, I was unsure how Walter would look forty-five years later.

*Has age stolen my youthful beauty so Walter might not recognize me or walk my way? Will he come as he promised during our telephone conversation? Will his memories match my mental diary?*

On the noisy escalator, I saw a tall brown man scanning the lobby as if searching for someone. It was late morning, so the room was not too crowded. As he looked at me, my heart beat faster.

I recognized those familiar doe-like brown eyes. "Walter, is that you?"

His kind face shone with recognition as he left the escalator. "Miss Bayronne?"

My heart sang at his pronunciation because all my students in New Orleans had pronounced it like a Creole name. The lyrical sound awakened memories of a young Midwest woman of twenty-two who went to the big city for her first year of teaching. We hugged, smiled, hugged again.

He shook my husband's hand. "Pleased to meet you." He introduced us to his wife, who came to meet this teacher from his past.

"We have a lot of catching up to do." I put my arm through his as we walked to one of the city's favorite Cajun restaurants. My husband walked and chatted with Walter's wife, because Walter and I were already lost in our past.

As we sat at the eatery, Walter shared that he still lived in New Orleans and worked in hospitality. His animated gestures kept me glued to his story.

"It was God who saved me and my family. Yes, ma'am, God was my refuge. I couldn't find my mother or other relatives for months after Katrina damaged the city."

I would be devastated if my family were lost in such a great disaster. I patted his forearm as Walter continued sharing about his family.

We talked about Carter G. Woodson Junior High, the school that introduced me to New Orleans in 1967. He remembered warm memories of the Christmas play I had directed. His tenor voice and gift of acting boosted my first attempt at directing a play. We laughed about the unexpected things that had happened at our Christmas pageant rehearsals.

"Walter, I wrote a book about my year at Woodson. You're one of my main characters."

He rubbed the top of his head. "Really?"

I reached into my purse for the wrinkled paper I had kept in my file cabinet for more than forty years. "Walter, I'm returning your essay that you wrote the Friday after Dr. Martin Luther King Jr.'s assassination."

His eyes misted. "I can't believe you kept this all these years." He held the paper to his chest. "I'll show my son and daughter. Mrs. Bayronne, you've worked hard to find me. I appreciate it."

As we finished our dinner, we shared remembrances about the cherished history we had made together in the 1967-1968 school year. Warmness crept into my heart as I laughed until my cheeks ached. We parted with a promise to see each other again and soon.

Thinking back to February of 1967, I recalled my husband, Denny, and I being recruited to teach at Carter G. Woodson Junior High in New Orleans. On our first day of school meetings the following September, we realized our skin color had gained us the job placement, not our training or résumés. This story has been a part of me for over fifty-five years.

Showing me discrimination in their everyday lives, the staff and students shaped my new perspective. I cannot pinpoint the moment my fate changed, but Carter G. Woodson pointed me to my future of advocating for Blacks throughout my career. I had struggled and recognized my own prejudices and realized I needed to make a difference in racial injustice.

# EPILOGUE

The fine line between fiction and creative nonfiction creates problems because of memories. I held this story in my heart for forty-five years. In 2011, I interviewed Walter, the first of my former students I was able to locate. The disaster of Hurricane Katrina in 2005 had uprooted people, destroyed homes and landlines, and relocated tens of thousands of residents to Atlanta, Dallas, Baton Rouge, and other cities.

We found Mr. Gritton, a retired Woodson teacher, who provided us with newspaper articles and school papers that he had kept to document what a great school Woodson had been throughout his career. Woodson's finest supporter still remembered it as the best school in New Orleans.

We came across a few other teachers who checked my facts and memories of Carter G. Woodson but are not in the book. In the winter of 2012, my husband and I revisited New Orleans to interview and return the students' *Dr. Martin Luther King Jr.'s Death* essays they had written two days after his assassination. My students shared many memories of the Christmas play we had forgotten. They recalled I introduced them to fruit salad and chocolate fondue. The twins remembered their visit with us and so did Joan, Debra, and Miranda, who wondered why we never took them home for a weekend as well. They told me stories of what they had done for entertainment at Woodson in their free time.

From these interviews, I recreated the dialogue in the story. Of course, I could not remember students' exact words, but I remembered the spirit and personality of the student and made up the dialogue from those memories. Since their essays on Dr. Martin Luther King Jr.'s death were in my files for forty-five years, I could quote directly from them. However, I could not locate all those former students, so I used fictitious names.

Sadly, I could not reach Sylvia again and am indebted for all she gave me. I understand she left Woodson after a few years to teach in another school and finished her career in New Orleans.

Lunching with Edna refreshed my memory on the fun and parties enjoyed by the staff at Woodson. She told me about staff members' lives as well as their deaths. Soon after we departed from Woodson, Edna exited too and finished her teaching career at a local college.

Ray LeBlanc served as athletic director for the New Orleans Public School System before being elected a city councilman in 1974. He was appointed King Zulu for Mardi Gras 2000. Although he had passed away in December 1999, he was the king in honor and name.

Emile Bergeron became New Orleans' first Black superintendent of schools. He began his career as an English teacher and then principal at Carter G. Woodson. After leaving Woodson, he moved into the school system as an administrator, overseeing child nutrition, security, and maintenance. He was instrumental in gaining the first property tax increase for the schools in more than thirty years. Mr. Bergeron was quoted in his obituary as saying, "I have tried to reshape this institution and redirect its resources so that the New Orleans public schools can educate the children of poverty with the same ease they educate the children of privilege."

When we visited in 2012, Adam Gritton invited us to his home for breakfast. He and his delightful wife answered many of my "did this really happen?" questions by showing us yearbooks and photos of Woodson.

We tried to find Mike Leonard on both of our interview visits but were unable to locate him. We never located Mr. Hughes or John Foster either, but others told us they were deceased.

In the late 1990s, Henri Todd and Ray LeBlanc met us and took us to the Zulu club for a social gathering to celebrate old times. Unfortunately, we never formally interviewed Henri because of his severe illness that extended through 2011 and 2012 when we were collecting research. Henri passed away on July 11, 2013.

Debra Brown Morton is a charismatic leader, author, visionary, and entrepreneur. She is the senior pastor of Greater St. Stephen Full Gospel Baptist Church in New Orleans, Louisiana, and co-pastors with her husband, Bishop Paul S. Morton Sr., at the Changing a Generation Full Gospel Baptist Church in Atlanta, Georgia. Debra earned the distinction as one of the first ordained female elders to preach in a Baptist pulpit. She has written many songs and produced an album, authored several books, and opened a troubled teen girls' home. Her sphere of influence expanded far beyond her local pastorate. In 1987, she founded the Greater Women of Excellence Ministry that nurtured thousands of women and hosted motivational conferences annually for over fifteen years. In Debra's office, we held a lengthy interview, and then she took us to dinner where she confirmed my memories. She added many details to help me understand the views and ideals of a young Black teenager in 1967.

Miranda Lee brought pictures for me to see how they looked as teenagers and filled in my understanding of what happened in her neighborhood at Mardi Gras.

Walter Jones is in hospitality and has a family in New Orleans. He and his wife met us for dinner in 2011 and 2013. I gained so many stories and a wealth of information from him as he retold his teen stories and helped me remember our time at Woodson. He described my actions and classroom attitudes, which helped immensely in developing my character at twenty-two years of age.

Joan Ellison Turner moved to California but returned to New Orleans as a Task Force leader for FEMA. She has been deployed to various hurricane disaster areas to help others rebuild their lives. She has used her organizational skills to help others. Joan graduated from Southern University in New Orleans.

Jerome is a fictitious name for a student I could not locate. As the class clown, he taught me how to laugh in the midst of frustration and despair. So, Jerome, if you recognize your character, thank you.

Jason is not this young man's name either, but I wanted to include him in the play. I did not have a last name for him or Jerome, so I could not trace them through friends or interviews. Jason was a student at risk, and I included him so other students could know it is never too late to change one's image.

Lily Garcia relocated to Dallas, Texas, after Katrina. Millie lives and works in New Orleans. Both these ladies have families and miss living in the same city since Hurricane Katrina uprooted and separated them.

This one-year assignment folded into a lifetime of memories for Denny and me. These characters directed my future teaching curriculum and expectations. The teachers cited had a profound influence on Denny and me. They taught us love, character, and compassion that enabled us to reach out to others who seemed different. I have made an honest attempt to recreate an experience artfully styled to show others the spirit of each individual as accurately as possible. I recognize that many viewpoints are those of naïve twenty-two- and twenty-four-year-olds experiencing the big city for the first time.

Because life got in the way, we never returned to teach in New Orleans after completing our graduate degrees. We had two sons, and I continued to teach English and speech. Denny coached and became an administrator. I taught and retired from Delta High School in Muncie, Indiana. Denny retired later from a successful administrative position in Muncie.

The writing of this book brought Denny and me closer. Denny accepted Christ in 1976 and has been spiritually on fire ever since. We have been married for fifty-five years and are active in racial reconciliation prayer groups, One Race, and support a nonprofit organization, Crossing Color Lines.

We bask in our memories of New Orleans in 1967 and 1968. We still know Dr. Martin Luther King Jr.'s ultimate sacrifice changed our lives and the lives of the Black community forever. Thank you, Dr. King, for teaching us all the importance of dreams and personal commitments.

Through this creative nonfiction, I share my experience. Because our racial climate has changed so slowly in America, I decided to bring Black voices along with me. My contributors shared their 2022 attitudes and stories juxtaposed with my narrative. Unfortunately, the contributors' voices reflected much of the same discrimination that I had witnessed in New Orleans fifty years ago. The strings of skin pigmentation then and now have tied up progress. We need to actively prevent further discrimination and understand our own biases. As we all seek peace in our world, will you be aware and intentionally stand in the gap to change our future?

# ABOUT THE AUTHOR

Sandra Baker Baron's passion is working with people and coaching them to better understand their giftedness, talents, and interests. She helps them discover why God allows us to make choices and have difficult days. Her intent is to lead participants into a greater awareness of who they are in Christ Jesus. Part of that awareness is grounded in creativity. Discovering who you are through creative outlets brings new understanding of self-worth, God's purpose for our lives, and how to reflect on the past to grow in the future. All of these activities guide people into a deeper relationship with God. Sandra is an oil painter and writer because those creative activities are closely related and bring her new understanding of the Creator.

Sandra, a seasoned teacher of education for thirty-five years, has a unique gift of influencing people through her writing and speaking skills. In the late 90s, she reached out to Kazak and Russian teachers, exposing them to strategies of teaching the whole child. On her vacations and summer breaks, Sandra led writing and teaching conferences in Taraz, Kazakhstan (2002,2004,2006,2009). Sandra continued to show her passion for teaching by traveling to Bangkok, Thailand, in 2008 to give ESL presentations. She shared life lessons she had learned working with teens and other cultures in her blog Sandi's Impressions 2009 to 2016.

She continues to address racial injustice through her involvement with nonprofit organizations like Crossing Color Lines, One Race, and Fellowship Missionary Church's outreach to the Black community in Fort Wayne, Indiana. She lives her life initiating conversations on exploring racial justice and offering ways to recognize one's own prejudices.

Sandra graduated with a BA and MA in education with majors in English and Speech. She continues to use her writing and speaking voice to point out the severe discrimination that our Black and Brown brothers and sisters suffer today. Her book was written with the hope and intent to offer a continued understanding of the heartache and limitations that result in a White preference society.

If you would like to contact Sandra, she can be reached at facebook.com/sandi.baron or her website and blog at sandraleebaron.com.

# QUESTIONS AND TOPICS FOR DISCUSSION

1. A theme throughout *Bridging the Mississippi* is survivability. With which characters did this theme surface? How did they survive?

2. What was the most important message the author made in this book? Will it have a permanent or temporary effect on you? Why?

3. Based on the definition of micro aggression (unintentional prejudice insults to underrepresented populations through actions or statements), describe a few scenarios in the story that reflect micro aggression behaviors. How could those behaviors be avoided?

4. Another lesson throughout the novel is openness to other cultures. Describe scenes that appealed to you and the results of this openness.

5. Sandi and Denny had personal complications during their first year of marriage. Discuss which of those newlywed problems were innate to most marriages and which were not and why? Did the marriage seem realistic? How did they overcome these obstacles?

6. Sandi had trouble separating her expectations of her new career, marriage, and her reality. Did the plot help

you understand her reactions? Did the self-talk help you understand her character and expectations? Discuss a time when your own expectations caused you stress or misunderstanding.

7. How did this story affect your emotions? Did you become more aware of the sacrifices that Blacks make daily? Did scenes evoke sadness or empathy? Were you inspired to take actions today that could help alleviate unfair social justices? Discuss why or why not.

8. What passages impacted you the most? Discuss why these sections appealed to you.

9. Discuss the duality in the 1960s Blacks were forced to walk each day. How has duality stayed the same? How has their situation changed?

10. How did the death of Dr. Martin Luther King, Jr. change the destiny of Blacks? Has his dream been fulfilled?

# CITATIONS

**Lesson 8**

[1]Twain, Mark. *The Adventures of Huckleberry Finn*. United States: CreateSpace Independent Publishing Platform, 2015.

**Lesson 9**

[1]Twain, Mark. *The Adventures of Huckleberry Finn*. United States: CreateSpace Independent Publishing Platform, 2015.

[2]Ibid.

**Lesson 17**

[1]Twain, Mark. *The Adventures of Huckleberry Finn*. United States: CreateSpace Independent Publishing Platform, 2015.

**Lesson 48**

[1]Douglass, Frederick. "Frederick Douglass: The Hypocrisy of American Slavery." *The History Place - Great Speeches Collection: Frederick Douglass Speech - The Hypocrisy of American Slavery*, 1996. https://www.historyplace.com/speeches/douglass.htm.

[2]Burns, Stewart. *To the Mountaintop: Martin Luther King, Jr.'s Sacred Mission to Save America, 1955-1968*. San Francisco, CA: HarperSanFrancisco, 2005.

**Lesson 54**

[2]Burns, Stewart. *To the Mountaintop: Martin Luther King, Jr.'s Sacred Mission to Save America, 1955-1968*. San Francisco, CA: HarperSanFrancisco, 2005.

Made in the USA
Monee, IL
05 March 2023

29220429R00203